W9-DHM-409

Etherege and the Seventeenth-Century Comedy of Manners

By DALE UNDERWOOD

ARCHON BOOKS 1969

©Copyright, 1957, by Yale University Press
Reprinted 1969 with permission of Yale University Press
in an unaltered and unabridged edition

[*Yale Studies in English, Vol. 135*]

SBN: 208 00764 4
Library of Congress Catalog Card Number: 69-15693
Printed in the United States of America

TO CLARENCE ALONZO UNDERWOOD

Preface

I

FORMALLY, as the title indicates, the central concern of this volume is with the plays of Etherege. And in these terms the purpose of the study is threefold: to define a configuration of forces in seventeenth-century thought and society which helps us to understand more fully the nature of Etherege's plays (Chapter 2); in the light of these forces, to reinterpret the plays as literary and comic art (Chapters 3–6); to view the plays, thus interpreted, as continuing and modifying some of the principal traditions of pre-Restoration drama (Chapters 7–8). Informally the intention of the study is to suggest through Etherege's plays as a case in point a new or at least extended view of Restoration comedy of manners as a genre. In these terms the volume's formal limitation of scope requires a word of explanation.

The initial interests of which this study is a consequence began with the awareness that despite the excellent work of Nicoll, Krutch, Dobrée, Lynch, and others, a significant set of relations between Restoration comedy and its historical background had been insufficiently explored. My original intention, accordingly, was to re-examine in the light of these relations the plays of the best and most distinctive comic dramatists of the period—Etherege, Wycherley, Congreve, and Vanbrugh. But in the course of this undertaking, two emerging convictions prompted a change of plan. First, it became clear that, although the plays produced by these writers are by no means so homogeneous in character as they are commonly thought to be, their generic relationship to the intellectual and social traditions in which I was interested could be more fully demonstrated in a detailed study of a few plays than in a cursory study of many. Second, I became increasingly convinced that the configuration of historical forces with which I hoped to shed further light upon the Restoration comedy of manners could also be used to illuminate some essential but neglected relationships between that body of drama and other characteristic forms of Restoration literature, particularly the heroic drama and the verse satire. In the face of these two convictions, what had originally been planned as a single volume was divided into two. The present work has, it is hoped, adequate justification in itself. But it is also designed to provide detailed analyses upon which the subsequent and more general examination of Restoration comedy and its relations to other literature of the period will draw.

In this respect I have for a number of reasons chosen to begin with the plays of Etherege. As most scholars of Restoration drama have agreed, Etherege was the first to develop fully the distinctive type of comic drama which is further exemplified in the works of Wycherley, Congreve, and Vanbrugh. His plays seemed, therefore, the logical place to begin a re-examination of the genre. Further, as the following chapters will make clear, the sequence of his plays offers an especially full demonstration of the ways in which the traditions of pre-Restoration comedy were progressively molded into a distinctly Restoration form. Finally, among the major comic dramatists of the period, the plays of Etherege have received the least critical attention and have, I believe, been the least adequately understood.

II

This volume is a condensed version of a doctoral dissertation submitted to Yale University in the spring of 1952. Later in that year Professor Thomas H. Fujimura's *The Restoration Comedy of Wit* appeared in print. Portions of that study, particularly Chapter 3, "The Intellectual Background of Wit Comedy," explore some of the terms and traditions with which this volume is concerned. Most conspicuous in this regard is the interest of both works in seventeenth-century libertinism, Epicureanism, and naturalism. But the nature of these elements in the historical background of the time is interpreted rather differently by the two studies. And their relevance to Restoration comedy is viewed in markedly different ways.

In preparing this work, I have been especially indebted to Professor Maynard Mack, who supervised it as a dissertation and whose continued interest and encouragement have helped bring it to publication. I am also indebted to my friend and colleague, Charles Feidelson, Jr., whose criticisms, if they could all have been followed, would have resulted in a better book; to members of the committee for the Yale Studies in English who read the manuscript of the book; and to Benjamin C. Nangle for his help in seeing the work through the press. Finally, for her unstinting labors and good will, I owe more to my wife than I can well express.

D. U.

Branford College
Yale University
June 1, 1957

Contents

Part I

PRELIMINARIES

I

The Problem

"THE Restoration Comedy of Manners" is a phrase with which today's general reader or follower of the theater is likely to have a vague familiarity. He may never have heard of Etherege or *The Man of Mode* but he will probably know something of *The Country Wife* and *The Way of the World*. To the extent, however, that his understanding of these works reflects the prevailing convictions of either current theatrical revivals or professional critics, his attitude may justifiably be one not only of mild indifference but of puzzlement. He has probably been told on the one hand that the Restoration dramatists—the Renaissance alone perhaps excepted—represent the period of fullest flowering for English stage comedy. But he is likely to have been told also that these dramatists created a verbally brilliant yet essentially casual, topical, and uncomplicated body of plays; that they were concerned solely with the surface manners of a small and specialized segment of Restoration society; that the manners were characterized by witty cynicism and sexual promiscuity; that the plays, like the society, were largely divorced from the central problems and preoccupations of their age; and that they have little or nothing to say concerning the perennial problems of man.

How these characteristics constitute the flowering of English comedy is a question which the inquiring reader is too often left to answer for himself. But to the extent that he gains assistance on this point, he is likely to fall into further doubts regarding others. From Dennis, for example, to the present day, one persisting line of writers has felt that the dramatic intention and value of the best of Restoration comedy lie in the portrayal of manners—in the comic depiction of the social behavior which characterized a particular historical society. But an equally persistent contention has been that the real comic end, and the virtue if any, lie in the display of wit. Dr. Johnson's statement concerning Congreve may not be familiar to the general reader, but it succinctly summarizes this school of belief: "He formed a peculiar idea of comick excellence, which he supposed to consist in gay remarks and unexpected answers." [1] The same essential idea is less gently voiced by Granville-

1. Samuel Johnson, *Lives of the English Poets*, ed. George Birkbeck Hill (Clarendon Press, 1905), *2*, 228.

Barker: "For these gentlemen the stage and its actors are just a gaudy means to the exhibiting of their precious wit." [2] And a host of other critics both early and late have held opinions which, if less ingenuously expressed, do not differ in kind. One obvious basis of contention between these two schools of opinion is, or should be, whether the universally acknowledged wit in the plays is to be viewed as the author's or as expressive of the manners portrayed. The distinction, in other words, relates to "point of view" and raises the question as to what perspective if any the author has on the material he employs. This question has also been a subject of disagreement. But it involves other and to the general reader perhaps more familiar difficulties.

One of the commonest labels applied to the Restoration comedy of manners is the word "realistic." However slippery the term here as in most literary contexts, it suggests that the plays are distinguished by a circumstantial representation of at least a portion of their age. Yet at the same time that they have been thought realistic, they have with equal frequency been considered "artificial" in some special and distinctive sense beyond that in which all art must deserve the term. Lamb's thesis in this regard is too well known to require comment. [3] And while contemporary scholars are likely to feel that his attitude was naïve, their concern with the problem is no less great and their solutions often not strikingly different: "The term Artificial Comedy is properly attached to the works of the period, not because the life depicted did not exist, but because the actual circumstances and relations are suffused with an atmosphere of rosy unreality which makes endurable what would otherwise be quite intolerable." [4] Apart from some questioning of the word "rosy," one may want to know what in the actual make-up of the plays provides the "atmosphere" of unreality and how this consideration relates to the question of manners and wit. But on the basis of this formulation the comedy has been thought to be at once realistic *and* artificial. [5] A more common device for bringing these mutually repellent terms into some kind of counterpoise has been to assume that the representation is realistic so far as it goes but that, in the words of Hazlitt, "the springs of nature, passion, or imagination are but feebly touched" in the characters. [6] Whether this limitation is in the plays or in the society depicted is not, however, always made clear. And when it is,

2. H. G. Granville-Barker, *On Dramatic Method* (London, Sidgwick and Jackson, 1931), p. 130.

3. "On the Artificial Comedy of the Last Century," *The Works of Charles and Mary Lamb*, ed. E .V. Lucas (London, Methuen, 1903–05), *2*, 141–7.

4. Bartholow V. Crawford, "High Comedy in Terms of Restoration Practice," *Philological Quarterly, 8* (Oct. 1929), 346.

5. *Ibid.*, pp. 343–4.

6. "Lectures on the English Comic Writers," *The Collected Works of William Hazlitt*, ed. A. R. Waller and Arnold Glover (London, Dent, 1902–04), *8*, 73.

differing opinions again ensue.[7] The problem once more concerns the author's point of view—his perspective upon the comic world which he portrays. More fundamentally still, it concerns the grounds on which we must determine the nature, meaning, and value of the plays. Are we to approach them in terms of their realistic portrayal of manners or in terms of some special comic artifice which either transcends or violates the methods and values of realism?

These questions impinge upon still a further problem. A handbook of the drama by two contemporary scholars states "of the best of the Restoration dramatists" that "they consistently neglected the development of their characters and their plots in order to concentrate on the graceful turn of a phrase or the witty expression of a sarcastic speech." [8] The quotation leans, that is, to the wit and artificiality schools of opinion. At the same time it reminds us that the element of style itself has frequently been viewed as the real artistic end or at least the main virtue of the Restoration comedy of manners. We may recall Whibley's belief that "diction" for Congreve "was a chief end of comedy." [9] And this line of thought will lead us back once more to Hazlitt and his conviction that the works of Congreve are "a singular treat for those who have cultivated a taste for the niceties of English style." [1]

These several lines of persisting interest—in the manners and wit, in the realism, artificiality, and style—unquestionably correspond in some way to distinctive characteristics in the plays. And the many studies which those interests have produced have added much to our understanding of this body of drama. At the same time a preoccupation with these aspects of Restoration comedy has served to distract us from other lines of investigation which might best resolve the divergency of views. The concern with manners has focused our attention upon the society depicted, which we do well to understand as fully as we may. But an understanding of the society or of its manners does not constitute an understanding of the plays. The same is true of the wit, the realism, or the style. It is logically possible that any or all of these may be in fact the expressive end at which Restoration comedy aims. If so, we must call these works dramas in only a very special sense. But it is

7. See John Palmer, *Comedy* (London, M. Secker, 1914), pp. 32-3: "In the comedy of manners men and women are seen holding the reality of life away, or letting it appear only as an unruffled thing of attitudes. . . . This is the real justification of the term 'artificial comedy' as applied to the plays of Etherege and Congreve." But see Henry Ten Eyck Perry, *The Comic Spirit in Restoration Drama* (Yale Univ. Press, 1925), p. 140: "Etherege was not interested in what his lovers were really like, but only in what they did and how that might be made entertaining to his audiences."
8. Fred B. Millett and Gerald E. Bentley, *The Art of the Drama* (Appleton-Century, 1935), p. 106.
9. Charles Whibley, "The Restoration Drama, II," *Cambridge History of English Literature*, ed. A. W. Ward and A. R. Waller (Putnam, 1907-33), 8, 182.
1. *Works, 8, 71*.

also possible that these characteristics are aspects of more inclusive interests and of larger dramatic designs. If this is so, we shall discover the fact only by examining with some care the formal nature of the plays. And it is in this regard that the Restoration comedy of manners has been least carefully inspected.

It has not, of course, been in this regard ignored. From the work of Lynch and before her Palmer and earlier still from Hazlitt, we have been given useful observations concerning the characteristic make-up of Restoration comedy. For each of these writers the comic world of the plays falls into two essential parts—the people of "true wit and perfect fashion" and those who only ape "the smartness of the times." [2] For Lynch these two classes are to be judged by different comic standards. We laugh at the latter for the awkwardness of their aping. We laugh at the former both because of the affectation which their social mode demands and because of the conflict which a successful compliance with the mode sets up between true human impulses and the fashionable attitudes required.[3] The thesis is at the least suggestive; and whether or not one accepts it finally as an accurate statement of comic form and meaning, it provides a helpful point of departure for further investigation. At the same time, neither Lynch nor those who have explored the concept after her would presumably wish to maintain that it constitutes an adequate account of the formal character of Restoration comedy. Yet it would seem that only through some such account can we best decide what the nature of that comedy is and how, if at all, the several elements of manners, wit, realism, artificiality, and style constitute aspects of a unified comic expression.

In undertaking to give such account for the plays of Etherege as a significant case in point, the present study tries to avoid the methods and predilections of any special school of critical practice. Its approach, moreover, is not made in specifically dramatic or theatrical terms. It is merely mindful of the fact that, apart from its language, the chief materials of a play are characters, actions, and settings, and that if the play is a work of literary art, these materials will be arranged in some kind of expressive form. By inspecting that form in some detail it tries to contribute something to our understanding of Restoration comedy. It seeks to persuade the reader that neither wit nor, in the simply topical senses of the word, manners are the final concern of the chief comic drama in the period. It proposes instead that these elements contribute to a distinctive kind of comic expression whose nature and meaning transcend the questions of both realism and artificiality; that in these terms the comedy of the plays is neither casual nor superficial but a

2. John Palmer, *The Comedy of Manners* (London, Bell, 1913), p. 86.
3. Kathleen M. Lynch, *The Social Mode of Restoration Comedy* (Macmillan, 1926), pp. 7–8, 216–17.

thoughtful, carefully ordered, and pervasively ironic form of drama; that while the plays deal with a special society they project through it problems fundamental not only to the seventeenth century but to the nature of man.

That these convictions do not derive solely from a formal analysis of the plays will be apparent. The analyses themselves will suggest—if such a suggestion is necessary—that Restoration comedy can be adequately understood only when placed in its historical context. And it is with certain parts of this context that the present volume has its second major concern. The concern is again one which grows directly out of preceding investigations. In some respects the historical background of Restoration comedy has been thoughtfully examined. Lynch, among others, has believed seventeenth-century *préciosité* to be important in understanding the society and to some extent the formal character of Restoration comedy.[4] And Dobrée and Montgomery have seen reflected in the plays the skeptical, rationalistic, and experimental temper of the times.[5] Each of these studies has made useful contributions. But our growing knowledge of seventeenth-century intellectual and social history suggests that there are significant areas of relationship between the comedy and its age which have not yet been adequately explored.

The historical explanation for what is commonly called the cynicism and immorality of Restoration comedy has traditionally been that of Macaulay—a reaction to the moral repressions of the Interregnum, a swing of the pendulum, a letting off of steam.[6] And it was at this alleged cynicism and immorality that the eighteenth and nineteenth centuries, following Collier, leveled their attacks.[7] Current writers have from time to time advanced somewhat different or additional theories. But in an attempt to examine the plays as comedy rather than morality, modern criticism has tended either to ignore the immorality or to consider it as merely part of the "harmonious and just" laws of the imagination by which the historical society reflected is faithfully portrayed.[8] But such a disposition does not really settle the question. If the immorality is there, it must be expressive of something. And the question is whether it expresses merely immorality or something more specific.

---

4. *Ibid.*, ch. 5 and *passim.*

5. See n. 9 following.

6. Thomas Babington Macaulay, *Critical and Historical Essays*, ed. H. D. Sedgwick (Houghton, Mifflin, 1900), 5, 57–8. See also Joseph Wood Krutch, *Comedy and Conscience after the Restoration* (2d ed. Columbia Univ. Press, 1949), pp. 24–6.

7. The attacks had begun, of course, before Collier. See Krutch, *Comedy and Conscience*, pp. 92–103. Lamb, Hazlitt, and Hunt were among the few 19th-century critics who attempted to evaluate the comedy on different grounds.

8. Palmer, *Comedy of Manners*, p. 292.

Dobrée, like Montgomery, has been of the latter opinion. He has seen in the comedy the reflection of "a great curiosity and a desire to experiment." [9] This curiosity and desire are manifested chiefly in "the attempt to rationalize sexual relationships." "They [the society reflected in the comedy] found that, for them at least, affection and sexual desire were quite separate, and they tried to organize society on that basis. Love, in which the two feelings are imaginatively fused, scarcely existed for them. And since they accepted man as a licentious animal, it meant, of course, that if life was to be easy, the pursuit of a mistress must be an acknowledged amusement. . . . It [the comedy] said in effect, 'here is life lived upon certain assumptions; see what it becomes.' " It is in this attempt to rationalize sexual relations that Dobrée finds the characteristics which make the comedy "different from any other comedy that has ever been written." [1] This conviction approaches a point of central interest for the present study. But it provides an insight which is susceptible to considerable expansion and, I believe, qualification. If the convictions and temper of the society depicted in the Restoration comedy of manners were experimental, they were not primarily so in a positivistic sense—to be identified with the scientific "positivism" of the Royal Society. And they were chiefly, I think, something quite different. They were more nearly, for example, Pyrrhonistic. More precisely still, they were "libertine," a term which it will be a purpose of the next chapter to define.

But they were much more than this. They were also in certain ways *honnête homme* or "honest man." And the attempt to be both at once involved an intricate set of contradictions and inconsistencies from which to no small degree Restoration comedy derives its form and meaning. But there was more still. Libertinism and the honest-man tradition were only two of the forces which in the social and intellectual context of the time generated a host of disparities and conflicts wonderfully rife with comic potentialities. The society of the Restoration comedy of manners may be viewed as in large part the product of two broadly opposing sets of traditions: on the one hand Christianity and Christian humanism, the "heroic" tradition, the honest-man tradition, and the tradition of courtly love; on the other, philosophic and moral libertinism, Machiavellian and Hobbesian concepts as to the nature of man, and Machiavellian ethics. The form and meaning of the plays reflect the juxtaposition of these two sets of traditions and the oppositions and conflicts which ensue. It is consequently against the historical back-

9. Bonamy Dobrée, *Restoration Comedy 1660–1720* (Oxford Univ. Press, 1924), p. 20. See also Guy Montgomery, "The Challenge of Restoration Comedy," *University of California Publications in English, I* (1929), 131–51.

1. *Ibid.*, pp. 20–3. Elsewhere (p. 52) Dobrée believes that the prose style of Restoration comedy constitutes "the chief difference" from earlier English comedy.

ground involving these traditions that we can best understand not only the sources and nature of the problems with which this body of drama deals but the literary and dramatic character of the plays.

But there is still more involved. This configuration of intellectual and social forces provides in a sense the surface and topical experience with which the comic dramatists worked. Within this historical context were problems less specialized in time and place—of concern to the traditions mentioned and, therefore, to the seventeenth century, but broadly pervasive of the human predicament. At the heart of the conflict between the two broad sets of traditions was a basic disparity of belief concerning the nature of man. At one level of concern this disparity involved conflicting attitudes toward such ethical problems as the individual versus society, freedom versus restraint, self-interest versus obligation, and—in a special but no less crucial sense which we shall explore—the question of "pleasure" versus "virtue." At a slightly different level other issues were involved. Each of the traditions was in some integral way concerned with the relation of passion to reason, reason to nature, and appearance to reality. Finally, each was faced in its own particular way with a problem embracing all these—the relation of nature and art. Each of these concerns defines an important aspect of meaning in Restoration comedy of manners. We shall accordingly be better prepared to understand that comedy after some fuller inspection of the historical traditions at work.

2

The Fertile Ground

I

THE TERM "libertine" as indicating merely a person of loose morals has had a commonplace application to Restoration comedy. But as it is used in this study, its significance for that comedy has been little explored.[1] The word has not, in fact, been much employed in intellectual and social studies of seventeenth-century England.[2] To the extent that it has been used it has taken its definition largely from sixteenth- and seventeenth-century France. But the signification of the term in these periods and in subsequent histories of them has been protean. Careful and scholarly works such as Pintard's *Le Libertinage érudit* extend the term from the sober and circumspect Gassendi and Sorbière, the friend of Hobbes, to the far from circumspect Chapelle and Cyrano de Bergerac; from the rationalism of Naudé to the Pyrrhonism of La Mothe le Vayer.[3] It is clear, therefore, that the highest common denominator for the word as it has been applied to the seventeenth century is little more specific than a penchant for free thought and free inquiry—a general attitude of skepticism toward dogma as such.

1. Fujimura's *Restoration Comedy of Wit* is the most notable exception. See Preface above.
2. A few studies of the Restoration have employed the term in senses similar or related to those with which we shall be concerned. See especially Louis I. Bredvold, *The Intellectual Milieu of John Dryden* (Univ. of Michigan Press, 1934), chs. 1 and 2; and Clara Marburg, *Sir William Temple; A Seventeenth Century "Libertin,"* Yale Univ. Press, 1932. In the field of the Renaissance and early 17th century, several studies have dealt with traditions of "naturalism" which bear upon our concern with the libertine. Among these, Bredvold's "The Naturalism of Donne in Relation to Some Renaissance Traditions," *Journal of English and Germanic Philology, 22* (Oct. 1923), 471–502, is an early and particularly useful contribution. John F. Danby, *Shakespeare's Doctrine of Nature* (London, Faber & Faber, 1949), and R. C. Bald, "Edmund and Renaissance Free Thought." *Joseph Quincy Adams Memorial Studies,* ed. James G. McManaway and others (Folger Shakespeare Library, 1948), pp. 337–49, have contributed additional but more specialized information. Perhaps the work which has most fully stressed the general currency of naturalistic thought in England during the Renaissance and 17th century is Hiram Haydn's *The Counter-Renaissance* (Scribner's, 1950) ; but Haydn's investigation does not extend beyond the early 1700's.
3. René Pintard, *Le Libertinage érudit dans la première moitié du XVIIᵉ siècle,* 2 vols. Paris, Boivin, 1943.

As the Restoration characteristically used the word, it meant something a good deal more specific. Though its usage looked more toward predilections of temper and behavior than an intellectual system, it tended to reflect a rather persistent body of thought. And its doctrines were sufficiently familiar and widespread to be of concern to virtually every field of the period's literature. The fact is perhaps most readily evident from the number and variety of works having the word "libertine" in their titles. One thinks, for example, of Shadwell's drama, *The Libertine;* or "Ned" Ward's heavyhanded satire, "The Libertine's Choice"; or Etherege's lyric, "The Libertine." [4] A casual inspection of these works will indicate not only that the libertinism with which they deal involves a common set of ideas but that the ideas had become sufficiently commonplace to be formulated into clichés. Once familiar with the clichés, the reader may find them on every hand—in the comedy, the heroic drama, the verse satire, and perhaps most significantly as repeated objects of attack by the clergy and moral essayists. [5]

But he will find them outside the Restoration too. For the libertinism with which we are concerned belongs to what may safely be called a seventeenth-century tradition in England as well as in France. We shall later turn to this problem in detail. But both the fact and nature of the tradition may be broadly surmised if we compare, say, Garasse's *La Doctrine curieuse des beaux esprits de ce temps*, Rosimond's *Le Nouveau Festin de Pierre* (the principal source of *The Libertine*), and Rochester's "Satyr against Mankind." [6] Rather clearly the libertine doctrines set forth in these as in innumerable other works of the period had become thoroughly familiar in English as well as French literature long before the Restoration. In seventeenth-century drama the Don Juan legend, with which both Shadwell and Rosimond deal, had itself become a locus of libertinism as we shall understand the word, and had assimilated most of the libertine doctrines and practices reflected in the Restoration comedy of manners. This fact will be of particular in-

4. Ward's satire was published in 1709, a date which places the work just outside the chronological period with which this study deals. But its ideas were clearly a part of the Restoration concern, as the following pages will make clear.

5. The attacks of the moralists were commonly leveled at the "Epicurean"—a term virtually synonymous with "libertine" in the 17th century, as we shall presently note. For a representative list of such attacks see Marburg, *Temple*, pp. 23–4. But the list could be greatly augmented. Edward Reynell's *Advice against Libertinism* (London, 1659), for example, is of special interest both for the extended treatment of its subject and for its appearance on the eve of the Restoration. Meric Casaubon's *A Treatise concerning Enthusiasme* (London, 1655) is also of interest as one of the few essays before Charleton's to stress the distinction between classical Epicureanism and the debased popular views.

6. François Garasse, *La Doctrine curieuse des beaux esprits de ce temps* (Paris, 1624); Rosimond's play is most readily available in *Les Contemporains de Molière*, ed. Victor Fourmel (Paris, 1863), 3, 313–77. For Rochester's poem, see following citations.

terest for a later chapter. It serves here to emphasize that the libertinism in which we are interested was not a localized phenomenon but a prominent and pervasive concern of the seventeenth century.

We have suggested that this concern was less with a systematic body of thought than with attitudes and modes of behavior. Libertinism, in fact, could scarcely by its nature have become a philosophic system. One might rather call it, though perhaps with misleading gravity, a "way of life." Further, since it was much more conspicuous as a popular than as a learned tradition, its ideas have commonly the blurred and eclectic character of popular thought. As a result of all this, it is not readily susceptible to precise definition; and its full range of meaning for this study will emerge only in the successive chapters of the volume. For our purposes here, however, some provisional definition is essential. And since our first concern is with the Restoration, we may turn to some works of that period for the attitudes with which we shall need to deal.

In this respect Oldham's verse attack upon the libertine is especially useful. It is so hysterically exaggerated in its satiric inversion of tone that it is at times nearly incoherent. But its opening stanzas supply most of the essential terms.

> Now Curses on ye all ye vertuous Fools,
>   Who think to fetter free-born souls,
>   And tie 'um to dull morality and rules.
>   The Stagarite be damn'd, and all the Crew
>   Of Learned Ideots, who his steps pursue.
>
>   .   .   .   .   .
>
> But damn'd and more (if Hell can do't) be that [thrice]
>   cursed name,
>   Who e're the Rudiments of Law design'd;
> Who e're did the first model of Religion frame,
> [And by that double Vassalage enthrall'd Mankind;]
> By nought before but their own power or will confin'd:
> Now quite abridged of all their Primitive Liberty
> And slaves to each capricious Monarchs Tyranny.
> More happy Brutes who the great Rule of Sense observe,
>   And ne're from their first Charter swerve.
>   Happy whose lives are meerly to enjoy,
> And feel no sting of sin which may their bliss annoy.
> Still unconcern'd at Epithets of ill or good.
> Distinctions, unadulterate Nature never understood.
>
>   .   .   .   .   .

> Virtue, thou solemn grave impertinence,
> Abhorr'd by all the men of wit and sence,
>
> . . . . .
>
> That makest us prove to our own selves unkind,
> Whereby, we Coals and Dirt for diet chuse,
> And, pleasure, better food, refuse.[7]

The one essential point which is not explicit in these lines is the one with which an attempt at logical definition should begin. Philosophically the libertine was an antirationalist, denying the power of man through reason to conceive reality. And here Rochester's "Satyr" provides a characteristic statement:

> Reason, an *Ignis fatuus* of the Mind,
> Which leaves the light of Nature, Sense behind.[8]

Accordingly the libertine rejected the orthodox medieval and Renaissance concept of universal order and of man's place and purpose therein:

> And 'tis this very Reason I despise,
> This supernat'ral Gift, that makes a Mite
> Think he's the Image of the Infinite.
>
> ("Satyr against Mankind," p. 37.)

His ends were hedonistic, "Epicurean," and embraced the satisfaction of the senses in accordance with the "reasonable" dictates of Nature— that is, in this case, one's "natural" impulses and desires. On this point Rochester's lines may be compared with Oldham's:

> Thus whilst against false reas'ning I inveigh,
> I own right Reason, which I would obey;
> That Reason, which distinguishes by Sense,
> And gives us rules of good and ill from thence;
>
> . . . . .
>
> Your Reason hinders; mine helps to enjoy,
> Renewing Appetites, yours would destroy.[9]

7. John Oldham, *A Satyr against Vertue* (London, 1674), pp. 2–5.
8. *The Collected Works of John Wilmot, Earl of Rochester*, ed. John Hayward (London, Nonesuch Press, 1926), p. 36. All subsequent references are to this edition.
9. *Ibid.*, p. 38. On this point Shadwell's libertine, who in turn closely echoes Rosimond, indicates the "orthodoxy" of Rochester's lines:

> Nature gave us our Senses, which we please:
> Nor does our Reason war against our Sense.
> By Nature's order, Sense should guide our Reason,
> Since to the mind all objects Sense conveys.

The Complete Works of Thomas Shadwell, ed. Montague Summers (London, Fortune Press, 1927), *3*, 26.

Finally the libertine considered human laws and institutions as mere customs varying with the variations of societies and characteristically at odds with Nature as, of course, with "right reason." On this point Shadwell's libertine provides further confirmation:

> Of Nature's freedom we're beguil'd
> By laws which man imposes.   (p. 60)

Thus for the libertine the great watchwords became Nature and Reason. But Nature here, whatever else it signified, had as its supreme prerogatives and values "freedom" and "pleasure." And reason became a somewhat special kind of empirical common sense. Not only did it "distinguish by sense" but it was taken out of its metaphysically ratio-cinative or intuitive role and limited to the immediate and practical world of human behavior and institutions.[1] Lacking the conservatism of Montaigne and the Greek Skeptics but conforming to a naturalistic tradition which we shall need to explore, the libertine revolted in action as well as in thought against the customs of his society. Among these revolts was, on the basis of a naturalistic concept of love between the sexes as only physical appetite, the revolt against the custom of marriage as well as against the traditional conventions and attitudes of courtly love. To varying extents the institutions and concepts of family, church, and state were also objects of attack. All these characteristics—the antirationalism; the "Epicureanism"; the opposition of nature and custom; the revolt against the latter in the name of nature, freedom, pleasure; the naturalistic concept of love, with here an especial emphasis upon freedom; the particular and consequent revolt against marriage and the more conventional attitudes toward love in general—these constitute basic aspects of a form of libertinism reflected not only in the Restoration comedy of manners but in literature of the Restoration and seventeenth century at large.

It is apparent even from so brief and provisional a definition that at least three philosophic lines of thought are involved: Epicureanism, skepticism, and a type of primitivism or naturalism for which unfortunately there is no other received name but which will be readily recognized by students of both classical and modern thought.[2] It is apparent also that in a learned sense these lines of thought have become rather thoroughly blurred and intermingled. To understand the sig-

1. We should not overlook the significance of the libertine's stress on "right reason" when compared with the right reason of more orthodox traditions—of Richard Hooker, for example, or the Cambridge Platonists. The point will be of interest for a later section of this chapter.

2. The most useful and exhaustive reference here and for the following comments on classical primitivism is Arthur O. Lovejoy and George Boas, *Primitivism and Related Ideas in Antiquity,* Johns Hopkins Press, 1935.

nificance of libertinism for Restoration comedy we shall need to look briefly both at these individual sources and at their confluence within the tradition.

II

To the extent that the Restoration libertine has been noted by students of English literature, he has most commonly been labeled an "Epicurean." That the word is employed on some sufferance is indicated by the fact that it is usually put in quotation marks. Yet it is only partly a misnomer. It marks primarily a distinction between popular and learned thought. In the Restoration itself, "libertine" and "Epicure" were virtually interchangeable terms for the majority of writers who dealt with them. And though the words were often linked by little more than a broadly pejorative meaning, their relationship was usually more precise. "Ned" Ward's libertine exclaims,

> O Great Lucretius, thou shalt be my Guide,
> Like thee I'll live, and by thy Rule abide:
> Measure my Pleasures by my Appetites,
> And unconfined, pursue the World's Delights.[3]

The ignorance regarding Lucretius is profound. Yet the quotation reminds us that even at an informed level Epicurus and his famous disciple could be important sources of libertine thought.[4] The hedonistic ethics with pleasure as the summum bonum was, we have seen, a central doctrine for the libertine and provided a rallying point in his revolt against the prevailing ethics of "virtue." Beyond that the individualistic and egocentric aspects of Epicurean ethics were congenial to the libertine both in themselves and in their corollaries. There was, for example, the denial of an ordained and fixed order in nature and consequently of any absolute justice and law.[5] On these grounds among others the libertine could dismiss orthodox morality as mere custom. And here the Epicurean attack upon religious "superstition" in general could also be utilized. Again, the Epicurean withdrawal from the duties and activities of citizenship supported the libertine's similar withdrawal and his scorn of conventional values regarding public life and institutions.[6]

---

3. Edward Ward, *The Libertine's Choice* (London, 1709), pp. 7–8.
4. Robert Boyle is typical of the Restoration and of the 17th century at large in charging most libertine thought to Epicurean sources. See *Works* (London, 1772), 4, 152.
5. *Epicurus. The Extant Remains*, ed. Cyril Bailey (Clarendon Press, 1926), pp. 47–9, 103–5.
6. See "Principal Doctrines" VII and XIV, *ibid.*, pp. 97–9, and the famous dictum "Live unknown," p. 139.

Finally, the sensationalistic bent of Epicurean epistemology contributed
to a number of libertine attitudes, most of which are at least adumbrated
in the quotations from Shadwell, Rochester, Oldham, and Ward noted
above.[7] It could be used to support the philosophical antirationalism of
the libertine and could lead to the particular kind of empiricism reflected
in such clichés as "the Light of Nature, Sense." In turn, as the Rochester
and Shadwell quotations make clear, the stress upon the senses as a
source of knowledge could easily lead to the senses as a source of pleasure, and thence to an ethics of sensualism—an ethics which the libertine
could find already formulated in the teachings of the Cyrenaics and
which at the popular level of thought had for centuries been associated
with Epicurus himself.[8] While in these as in most other respects the
libertine's use of Epicurean thought involved obvious distortions, there
were numerous passages in the writings of Epicurus which the libertine,
by disregarding the context of the total system, could cite as authority
for his beliefs. Not the least of these concerned the dictum, "follow
Nature." [9] But it is here also that the libertine reveals most clearly his
awareness of other traditions in Western thought.

In its broadest terms the libertine's concern with the physical appetites and passions of man as a legitimate part of his nature bears a
pertinent relationship to much that has been considered typically hu-
manistic in both the Renaissance and seventeenth century. Whether one
views these periods through the eyes of Burckhardt or of Tillyard and
Bush, the characteristic concern of the humanist was with the "whole
man," and contrasted with the purely intellectual or spiritual preoccupations of the classical Stoic and the ascetic lines of medieval Christian
tradition. The libertine could thus, when he chose to do so—and with an
ironic consciousness and meaning to which we shall return—justify
his stress upon the physical desires in terms of the prevailing morality
against which he was for the most part in revolt. Rochester was in certain senses at least interested, like the orthodox Christian humanist, in
reuniting "nature" and "grace," the physical and the spiritual man,

7. For the Epicurean stress upon the senses as a source of knowledge and a criterion
of judgment, see especially the "Letter to Herodotus," *ibid.*, pp. 21 and 53.
8. The chief source of Cyrenaic thought for the 17th century was, of course,
Diogenes Laertes. But for the Restoration Sir Thomas Stanley's popular *History of
Philosophy* (London, 1656), though based in large part upon Diogenes, offered not
only an additional source of information but a careful distinction between Cyrenaic
and Epicurean doctrine.
9. See, for example, Fragment 21, *Epicurus,* p. 109: "We must not violate nature,
but obey her; and we shall obey her if we fulfil the necessary desires and also the
physical." Among other favorite citations for both the libertine and his attackers were
such familiar passages as Fragment 59, p. 135: "The beginning and root of all good
is the pleasure of the stomach; even wisdom and culture must be referred to this." Also
Fragment 23, p. 127: "But I summon you to continuous pleasures and not to vain
and empty virtues which have but disturbing hopes of results."

by the proper relation of reason and the passions.[1] It is more a point of interest than surprise, therefore, to find both the libertine and the Christian humanist citing the same classical authors and frequently identical passages as authority for the Nature which they espoused.[2]

But it is important to stress this broad similarity of concern between libertinism and the more received lines of thought only that we may in turn enlarge upon the differences. It is by now generally understood that the naturalism of the libertine stems chiefly from a specialized medieval and Renaissance tradition to which such figures as Jean de Meun, Rabelais, and Montaigne have been commonly linked. To some extent we have also been aware that this tradition finds expression, however fragmented or diluted, in later English writers such as Marlowe, Donne, Suckling, Randolph, and thence to the Restoration. Finally, the ways in which this naturalism stands apart from the more orthodox thought of the time has been at least broadly adumbrated. Bredvold has shown that in many of the early love poems of Donne, Nature as norm and guide stands in contradistinction and opposition to custom—that is, the authority of society and its accepted code of morality; that the laws of this Nature are viewed, therefore, as countering the traditional *Jus naturale* or universal "Law of Nature," the conventionally accepted basis of morality since classical times; that by the laws of this Nature, the physical appetites are given free reign; that love between the sexes is viewed as simply one of those physical appetites; that in this respect as in others, freedom, inconstancy, change are part of the laws of Nature; that in all these respects the nature of the beast is not essentially different from man, that it provides, indeed, a justification and pattern for man in his own attempt to follow Nature; that finally conventional man in his enslavement by custom has fallen from his initial bliss, innocence, and natural goodness in the Golden Age of antiquity, when under the "Golden Laws of Nature" man had complete liberty to indulge his natural appetites and when

> Women were then no sooner asked then won,
> And what they did was honest and well done.[3]

1. Thus "right reason" for Rochester is one

> That bounds Desires with a reforming Will,
> To keep them more in vigour, not to kill.
>
> ("Satyr against Mankind," Works, p. 38.)

2. Cicero was perhaps the most common meeting ground, particularly in Bks. III–V of *De finibus*, where his doctrine of following Nature is fully set forth. The doctrine is prevailingly Stoic and Peripatetic. But individual passages, particularly through the mediation of Montaigne and Gassendi, were nonetheless put to service by the libertines. Compare Gassendi's use of passages from *De finibus* and *De officiis* in his "De virtutibus," *Opera omnia* (Lugduin, 1658), 2, 748–9, and the excerpts from Théophile in the Notice of his *Oeuvres complètes*, ed. Alleaume (Paris, 1856), 1, lxvi.

3. See "Naturalism of Donne," *JEGP*, 22, 475.

Historians have long been aware that while this particular tradition of naturalism derived from "the confluence of many currents of thought, medieval and classical,"[4] one of its chief and ultimate sources was classical primitivism. What has been insufficiently stressed are the pertinent if at first glance paradoxical similarities which it bears specifically to the primitivistic teachings and practices of the Cynics. Certain aspects of Restoration comedy with which the subsequent chapters of this study will be concerned necessitate our glancing at this relationship.

If the general reader today is aware of the Greek Cynics at all, he is likely to think of them in terms of their contributions to Christian asceticism and to be understandably startled at any suggested relationship with the libertine. To an extent such a reaction is historically justified. In most respects the Cynics espoused what is commonly called the "hard" type of primitivism, whereas the "Golden Age" for which the libertine characteristically professed—with whatever degree of gravity—a nostalgia, belongs to the "soft" strains of primitivistic thought.[5] But what we tend especially to forget today is that the Greek Cynics generally and particularly such major figures as Diogenes had, as Lovejoy and Boas have noted, two sides to their coin.[6] If their rigoristic tendencies on one side could support Christian asceticism, their hedonistic tendencies could be used on the other to support the libertine.[7] For mortification of the flesh and the natural desires of the body was by no means a characteristic of Cynic teaching. On the contrary both Antisthenes and Diogenes professed in this respect to be the only intelligent voluptuaries.[8] Since the desires of the body were "natural," one could follow Nature in the Cynic's terms only by gratifying these desires freely though not, of course, excessively. And the pleasure derived from such gratification was natural and therefore legitimate. Since the desires of sex as part of the bodily appetites were also natural, they

4. *Ibid.*, p. 493.

5. Concerning these distinctions in classical primitivism, see Lovejoy and Boas, *Primitivism*, pp. 9–10.

6. See *ibid.*, pp. 120–1.

7. Milton, among many others, provides us with evidence regarding the ambivalent character of Cynic influence in the 17th century. (The ambivalence, as we shall presently note in part, is characteristic in Western thought at large.) In "Areopagitica," *The Works of John Milton*, gen. ed. Frank Patterson (Columbia Univ. Press, 1931–38), *4*, 299, Milton groups together Epicurus, "that libertine school of *Cyrene*," and "the *Cynick* impudence" as "sects and opinions . . . tending to voluptuousnesse, and the denying of divine providence." But Comus condemns "the Cynic Tub," together with "those budge doctors of the Stoic fur," for teaching "the lean and sallow Abstinence." See "Comus," lines 706–9, *Poems of John Milton*, ed. James Holly Hanford, 2d ed. New York, Ronald Press, 1953. The libertines themselves persistently manifest a similar doubleness of view. Like Comus, Rochester's "Satyr against Mankind," though clearly displaying the ultimate influence of Cynic naturalism, has its sneer for the Cynic "Tub." See *Works*, pp. 37–8.

8. The question debated by scholars as to whether Antisthenes was in fact a Cynic does not alter his usefulness for our purposes here.

too were to be gratified as promptly and easily as possible.[9] It is here that the Cynic's extreme practices and "freedom"—a favorite word for them as for the libertine—most clearly suggest those later practices by which the libertines so much dismayed their contemporaries and succeeding generations. The public "indecencies" of both were much of a kind.[1] For both, the behavior—at least in theory—was to be justified as a revolt from the artificial restrictions of custom, as an attempt to free the whole natural man. And for the Cynic no less than for the libertine, love as a physical appetite was logically a matter of variety, inconstancy, change.[2] Consequently for one as for the other, free love was an essential in following Nature, and the institutions of marriage and family artificial impediments thereto.[3] And here as in other respects the Cynic, like Oldham's libertine noted above, could cite the animal world as norm.[4]

These similarities are but details of a more fundamental and paradoxical relationship. The cornerstone of the libertine's revolt against his society was, we have said, the opposition of Nature to custom, with the latter embracing both conventional institutions and conventional morality. The concept of this opposition was, of course, of ancient lineage even in classical times. But it is in the fully developed and intransigent primitivism of the Cynics that the opposition as later propounded by the libertine is most categorically developed. For the Nature which the Cynics espoused was that of the "original" or primitive man, stripped of the institutions, laws, and technology which man's "art" or "civilization" had produced but which the Cynic viewed as corruptive or repressive. Such a concept of Nature negated not only the Jus naturale but the entire institutional, moral, and intellectual order based upon it. As a consequence, certain further details of Cynic doctrine—and of classical primitivism as a whole—look toward the later attitudes of the libertine. The general character of Cynic thought tended to reduce in effect if not in theory both reason and philosophy to a matter of "common sense" rather than learned and metaphysical speculation. It could lend support accordingly to the philosophical antirationalism of the

9. See Lovejoy and Boas, pp. 128–9.

1. Compare Diogenes Laertes, *Lives of the Eminent Philosophers*, Loeb Classical Library (Harvard Univ. Press, 1950), 2, 71, and John Harold Wilson, *The Court Wits of the Restoration* (Princeton Univ. Press, 1948), pp. 39–42.

2. For the 17th-century libertine, particularly as we shall find him in Restoration comedy, this attitude reflects also certain specialized lines of courtly love convention, as readers of Sidney's *Arcadia*, D'Urfé's *L'Astrée*, and the "Platonic" drama of the Cavalier courtiers are aware. The point is discussed in subsequent portions of this study.

3. Diogenes Laertes, 2, 75: "He [Diogenes] advocated community of wives, recognizing no other marriage than a union of the man who persuades with the woman who consents. And for this reason he thought sons too should be held in common."

4. *Ibid.*, p. 25. For the idea of the animal as norm in classical primitivism see Lovejoy and Boas, ch. 13. For the currency of the idea in 17th-century France, see George Boas, *The Happy Beast*, Johns Hopkins Press, 1933.

libertine.[5] Again, the Cynics' contempt for established public institutions and ambitions prompted a withdrawal much like the libertines' from conventional public activities and duties.[6] Further, since the natural desires which the Cynic, like the libertine, viewed as the only necessary and valid ones were few and easily gratified, his morality in certain directions tended like the libertine's to sanction a life of leisure if not indeed of laziness.[7]

In these respects as in others primitivistic teaching could be viewed by the libertine as coalescing with the doctrines of the Epicure. It seems clear, in fact, that at least by the Middle Ages certain aspects of the two traditions had at the popular level of thought become thoroughly merged. We learn from Guibert that Jean de Soissons, who devoted himself to licentiousness and a life of "pleasure," believed that wives should be common and that fornication as a natural activity was not a sin.[8] And to Glaber the Catharists who practiced a form of erotic primitivism and held that the pleasures of sex were not sinful were "Epicurean heretics."[9] By 1433, living "according to Nature" was for Valla the distinguishing characteristic of the Epicurean. But the Nature which his Becadelli espouses is a distorted and popular combination of Epicurean and primitivistic thought.[1] We are prepared to find, accordingly, that in Jean de Meun, Rabelais, Montaigne—those writers whom scholars have viewed as principal sources of influence for libertinism—there exists a blend of both Epicureanism and naturalism.[2] The Epicurean and naturalistic propensities of the seventeenth-century libertine with whom we shall be concerned must be viewed in the light of a long and developing tradition.

But there remains the third principal aspect of that tradition, of which we must take some account if we are to see the Restoration libertine in reasonably full intellectual perspective. That he was in some sense a skeptic has been generally allowed. The increasingly skeptical climate in which he flourished and the radical temper of his revolt from orthodoxy prepare us to find some element of skepticism in his beliefs. But concerning its precise nature or its significance within the libertine

---

5. Diogenes Laertes, 2, 55: "As Plato was conversing about Ideas and using the nouns 'tablehood' and 'cuphood,' he [Diogenes] said, 'Table and cup I see; but your tablehood and cuphood, Plato, I can nowise see.'" See also *ibid.*, p. 107.

6. For the Cynic's view, see Lovejoy and Boas, p. 121.

7. Concerning the conflict in Cynic teaching between this tendency and their "gospel of work," see *ibid.*, p. 122.

8. Guibert de Nogent, *De vita sua*, iii.16, in Migne's *Patrologia latina, 156, 950*.

9. Rudolph Glaber, *Historia sui temporis*, iii.8, in *Patrologia latina, 142, 659–63*.

1. Laurentius Valla, *De voluptate ac vero bono libri III*, Basle, 1519.

2. The precise character of the blend is a vexed question for each of these writers, but it is one which need not detain us here. For an excellent brief discussion of the problem with regard to Rabelais and Montaigne see ch. 9, "Follow Nature," of Arthur Tilley's *Studies in the French Renaissance*, Cambridge Univ. Press, 1922.

tradition there has been much less agreement and only limited investigation. Our immediate interest in these questions will not require us to invade in any detail the broad field of skepticism as a historical movement. Some generalizations in this regard will help, however, to focus the problems at hand.

We may begin by noting that both the libertine and his age talked of skepticism in at least two fundamentally different senses even though they themselves were frequently unmindful of the distinction. The one involved skepticism in the true philosophic sense, that is a belief that all knowledge is uncertain. And here the libertine's antirationalism— his denial of reason as an instrument of philosophic speculation and consequently his distrust of philosophic speculation itself—is concerned. But in another sense the libertine viewed himself as a skeptic simply by virtue of doubting the orthodox dogma of his times, by engaging in what is usually called free thought. To an extent these two kinds of skepticism might resolve into one. A distrust of dogmatizing must necessarily involve a distrust of dogma. But the inverse need not be true. We have already seen that in some respects the libertine merely replaced one set of dogmas with another. And we shall later see that much which lay behind his rejection of traditional orthodoxy was scarcely conducive to skepticism in the strict philosophic sense. Yet it is not easy either in the libertine's temper and pronouncements or in those of his age to divorce the two tendencies. When James Buerdsell wrote that "the prevailing Humour of Scepticism [has become] so extreamly Modish that no Person can be that self-admir'd thing, a Wit, without it," or when Charles Blount asserted that "all Philosophy, excepting Sceptism, is little more than Dotage," there are good reasons for doubting that the skepticism involved was philosophically pure.[3] The wits whom Buerdsell had in mind must certainly have included many a libertine like Rochester. And Rochester's "Light of Nature, Sense" was hardly compatible with the skeptical doctrine of either Pyrrho or the New Academy.

The difficulty here is symptomatic of a central inconsistency which characterized both the Restoration libertine and his predecessors and which resulted in part from the eclectic nature of their thought. When Shadwell's libertine exclaims that "Sense should guide our Reason"[4] he is, like Rochester, asserting the empirical nature of knowledge. The empiricism is scarcely that of the Royal Society. It represents a dogmatic sensationalism at which the libertines arrived chiefly through a distorted use of Epicurean thought.[5] But they were here on dangerous

---

3. James Buerdsell, *Discourses and Essays on Several Subjects* (Oxford, 1700), p. 205; *The Miscellaneous Works of Charles Blount* (London, 1695), p. 157.
4. See p. 13, n. 9, above.
5. These distinctions, like most others involving problems of intellectual history, are

ground which few of them managed with impunity. For while they persistently relied upon "common sense" or simply "sense"—implying, of course, the evidence of the senses—to deride the "whimsies" of philosophical rationalism, they frequently employed for the same purpose the dialectics of Greek skepticism, which invalidated the senses as a reliable source of knowledge. For most of them the inconsistency could be resolved at least on the surface by the distinction between what was "good" and therefore "right" ("There is no right or wrong, but what conduces to, or hinders pleasure") and what was "true" in any absolute sense.[6] This distinction also can be related to certain tendencies broadly characteristic of the periods in which the libertine flourished— the concern, for example, of both the Renaissance and seventeenth century with morals to the relative neglect of metaphysics, and the related and increasing tendency to separate in use as well as method the supernatural and the natural. In these respects the libertine reflected with his age the expanding influences of philosophic skepticism. But the essential inconsistency of his doctrine was not thereby corrected, nor was the underlying failure to distinguish always between his two kinds of skepticism.

This is another way of saying that the libertine did not always keep clearly in mind the relationship between his rejection of orthodoxy and the bases for doing so. But apart from certain special considerations which we shall explore, the confusion was a natural one in the context of the times, particularly at the more popular levels of thought. Most of the disruptive forces to which the libertine was exposed attacked the traditional set of dogmas by proposing others. At the same time most of the proposed dogmas themselves assailed in one way or another the orthodox concept of reason and its place in man's nature and world. That this was true of both Epicurean and primitivistic thinking we have seen. But it was no less true of the mechanism of the "new science," the rationalism of the Averroists, the pragmatism of Machiavelli, the faith of Luther and Calvin.[7] Inevitably, therefore, these various movements tended as disruptive forces to join hands with philosophical skepticism. Yet in the welter of conflicting systems and tendencies which

---

not absolute. The skepticism reflected in Restoration comedy was part of the general skepticism of the time. So, too, was the experimentalism of the Royal Society. Some degree of interaction must, therefore, be taken for granted. And evidence of such interaction will be subsequently pointed out. The need for distinctions is nonetheless important. The typical Restoration libertine had as little real interest and faith in the activities of the Royal Society as he did in the rationalistic philosophers who were rejected by both.

6. See Shadwell, "The Libertine," *Works, 3,* 28.

7. Thus Luther: "We know that reason is the devil's harlot. . . . It is Satan's wisdom to tell what God is, and by doing so he will draw you into the abyss. Therefore keep to revelation and do not try to understand." Quoted by Preserved Smith, *Age of the Reformation* (Henry Holt, 1920), pp. 625–6.

characterized both the Renaissance and seventeenth century, the precise ways in which these alliances could be logically justified did not always receive scrupulous attention. The bases, consequently, on which both the libertine and his age challenged traditional dogma were likely to be blurred.

Notwithstanding, neither the special nature of philosophical skepticism as a disruptive force nor its particular contribution to his revolt was for the libertine entirely obscured. But here again some distinctions are in order, even though they must be made at a peril which is perhaps too obvious to require comment. There were at least three broad types or perhaps one should say areas of skepticism to which the libertine was exposed and which in one way or another help us to understand him. To speak of these influences in categorical terms of traditions or "schools" is to distort the facts. The history of thought in general and of skepticism in particular cannot readily be reduced to schemes and classes. And yet a degree of classification is necessary. It will be particularly helpful to us here.

The system of Greek thought which is commonly known as Pyrrhonism was transmitted to the sixteenth and seventeenth centuries chiefly through the writings of Sextus Empiricus.[8] It asserted that all knowledge is questionable, that both the senses and reason are in this respect unreliable, and that the only logical attitude, therefore, is one of suspended judgment in all matters of speculation. Only through such an attitude might one attain that peace of mind, the ataraxia, which was the goal of the skeptic as well as the Epicurean and Stoic. It questioned the absolute reality of the orthodox Law of Nature and Law of Nations, stressed the relativity of justice, and viewed all laws and institutions as only custom. Notwithstanding, the Pyrrhonist in terms of action was a conservative and conformist. Since all knowledge is doubtful and a true science of ethics therefore impossible, one should adhere to the established customs and institutions of his country as the simplest and sanest course of action.

The libertine could draw upon this thinking as he found it in the writings of Sextus Empiricus himself, of such figures as Montaigne and Charron, or of fellow libertines or quasi-libertines like La Mothe le Vayer.[9] That not all of it would be congenial is evident. What he took was in part determined by the interplay between these ideas and other

8. For the following summary I have drawn chiefly upon Vol. *1, Outlines of Pyrrhonism,* of *Sextus Empiricus,* trans. by the Reverend R. G. Bury, Loeb Classical Library, 3 vols. London, William Heinemann, 1933. Among the many studies of Greek skepticism, I have found Victor Brochard, *Les Sceptiques grecs* (2d ed. Paris, J. Vrin, 1932), the most useful.

9. Montaigne's *Apology for Raymond Sebond* and Charron's *De la sagesse* were especial sources of influence for the libertines. See Pintard, *Libertinage érudit, 1,* 65ff. and *passim.*

converging traditions of thought, especially the Epicurean and primitivistic. In some ways Pyrrhonistic skepticism could coalesce with
these other influences beyond the broad and common attack on the
orthodox concept of universal order. In other respects the several traditions were as clearly in conflict. We have noted that while the
Pyrrhonist questioned the evidence of the senses, the Epicurean relied
upon it. And while both the skeptic and the primitivist viewed conventional institutions and morals as custom, the one sanctioned conformity and the other revolt. We shall find increasing evidence that
what the libertine, particularly in the Restoration, selected from these
sources was determined chiefly by the extent to which the ideas negated
conventional thought and values. The irrational element in such a controlling impulse toward negation suggests not merely a disenchantment with but a psychological and spiritual privation of what it seeks
to destroy. The impulse must finally, therefore, be self-defeating; and
we are accordingly prepared for one of the central ironies upon which
the Restoration comic dramatists dwelt.

Meanwhile a second line or mode of skeptical thought was available
to the libertine. Its historical movement is usually traced from Socrates
through the New Academy to Cicero, and particularly from thence to
the Renaissance. In terms of a "school" the characteristics of this movement are more elusive and equivocal than is the case with Pyrrhonism.
It was charged by the Pyrrhonists with being dogmatic instead of
genuinely skeptical because it denied the possibility of absolute truth.
But it was also charged with dogmatism for asserting that some
kinds of knowledge are more probable or more nearly certain than
others.[1] And while modern scholarship has questioned the justness
of both these criticisms, they help us to understand how this particular
line of thought could mean rather different things to different people. To a few in the seventeenth century the nescience of the New
Academy was as unqualified as that of the Pyrrhonist.[2] But for most
it represented a milder if less determinate mode of skepticism and one
more nearly congenial to developing tendencies of the time. A familiar
passage from Dryden is here to the point: "My whole discourse was
sceptical, according to that way of reasoning which was used by
Socrates, Plato, and all the Academics of old, which Tully and the
best of the Ancients followed, and which is imitated by the modest
inquisitions of the Royal Society. That it is so, not only the name
will show, which is *an Essay,* but the frame and composition of the
work. You see it is a dialogue sustained by persons of several opinions,

1. See *Sextus Empiricus, I,* 139.
2. See Thomas Fitzherbert, *Treatise concerning Policy and Religion* (London,
1615), pp. 4–5.

all of them left doubtful, to be determined by the readers in general." [3] Apparently what skepticism here at least meant to Dryden—if it meant anything beyond a literary method—was an awareness of the vanity of dogmatizing without at the same time dismissing the possibility of knowledge. If this was true of Dryden, it tended also to be true of his age. A belief in total nescience seems not to have been widespread in either the Renaissance or seventeenth century. What this tradition of skepticism could contribute most fully to these periods was a creative rather than a destructive use of doubt, a caution and openness of mind in the pursuit of truth, rather than its dismissal. More easily than Pyrrhonism it could become a part of the "scientific method," a guide rather than opponent in the modest inquisitions of the Royal Society. [4]

The character of this skepticism for the libertine must necessarily have been ambivalent. Since its attack upon the senses was in certain ways less devastating than that of Pyrrho, it could spare the libertine some of the inconsistencies which a strict Pyrrhonism would enforce. There is even in the probability doctrine of Carneades a kind of empirical and practical "common sense" which the libertine no less than his age could find congenial. [5] At the same time the method and temper of this skepticism helps to define what the libertine was not. Caution and openness of mind, we have seen with sufficient clarity, were not among his distinguishing characteristics. And his contempt in the seventeenth century for the aims and activities of the Royal Society cannot be accounted for merely as traditional satire against the "projector" or "virtuoso." Genuine experimentalism and suspended judgment were almost as inimical to the psychological need lying behind his revolt from conventional society as was that society itself. Only a belligerent and destructive dogmatism could satisfy that need. Consequently any true skepticism was for him out of the question. Since the bulwark of traditional thought was rationalism, he could attack that thought by employing the arguments of the skeptic. But since a part of that bulwark was also a careful control of the physical and appetitive man, he attacked it also by a glorification of the senses. If, in the process, his empiricism looked at times toward some of the more respectably skeptical movements of his age, it was not because the disinterested pursuit of truth was his primary motivation.

This prepares us to understand the libertine's position regarding a third area of skepticism in his time. The relation of Christian skepticism

3. "Defense of an Essay of Dramatic Poesy," *Essays of John Dryden*, ed. W. P. Ker (Clarendon Press, 1900), *1*, 124.
4. That Pyrrhonism itself was not unimportant in the development of scientific method has been frequently proposed. See Brochard, *Sceptiques grecs*, pp. 375ff.
5. For a brief and lucid statement of this doctrine see Norman Maccoll, *The Greek Sceptics* (London, 1869), pp. 59–61.

—whether medieval, Renaissance, or seventeenth century—to traditions of classical thought need not concern us. Nor need we pause over the divorce between theology and philosophy which characterized aspects of that skepticism. The libertine was as antitheological as he was antiphilosophical; and the relative claims of one field or the other had little significance for him. What we need to note is that here again, as with all the traditions of thought to which he was exposed, the libertine could find both something to his liking and something which he was obliged to reject, and that the consequences of his choice added further paradox and inconsistency to his body of beliefs.

In itself the antirationalism of the Christian skeptic had for the libertine an obvious importance. It presented one more source of attack upon the traditional structure of orthodox thought. Together with the pietism of Augustine, it helped to promote a distrust of reason which the libertine could join to the influences of skepticism in general. But the specifically Christian context of this distrust had a special meaning. If reason was inadequate as a source of knowledge, man could know his divine relationship to God only or primarily through faith. But the impeachment of reason for most Christian skeptics was based upon the natural depravity of man.[6] To the empirically minded libertine this placed the Christian's assumption of man's divine potentialities upon particularly untenable grounds. If one admitted man's depravity and that neither rational nor empirical knowledge could, therefore, justify Christian belief, then the assertions of faith became even more whimsical and unfounded than those of rationalism. They required a willing suspension of disbelief which defied the libertine's common sense.

If one rejected faith, however, he might still accept the assertion of man's depravity. This is precisely what the libertine, especially in the Restoration, did—and with peculiar consequences. Stripped both of his godlike reason and the divine grace which comes through faith, depraved man is reduced to the level of an animal. This is essentially where the primitivistic naturalism of the libertine had already placed him, but with a difference. In the first case man is alleged to be naturally corrupt not only in his reason but in his instincts, senses, and desires. In the second man is naturally good, with his senses and instincts providing the surest guide to action. The discrepancy brings us to a crux in libertine belief arising from the influence of contradictory traditions. For if the naturalism of the libertine looked one way toward the primitivist's Golden Laws of Nature, it looked another way toward the naturalism of Machiavelli and later of Hobbes, whose con-

6. The Augustinian doctrine of grace was here, of course, a central source of influence.

ception of the natural man in moral terms was not greatly different from that of Augustine and the Christian skeptics.[7]

There is at least an implied recognition by most seventeenth-century libertines that the stress upon freedom of indulgence led in actuality to a state of "war" much like that which characterized the natural man for Machiavelli and Hobbes. The more idealistically minded might tend to skirt this consequence of "liberty." But the Restoration libertine, particularly as we shall find him in the comedy of manners, is always fully and ironically aware of this reality. He insists, in fact, upon man as naturally self-seeking in motivation and ruthless in his means. And while he accepts this as part of a Machiavellian and Hobbesian nature, it is a nature that is never free from the overtones of Christian sin. That subscribing to such a nature placed him in a highly anomalous position Rochester can again bear witness. Of the rightness of instinct and the senses there is no doubt. It is only for that "vain Animal" who follows "false reason" that

> The Senses are too gross; and he'll contrive
> A sixth, to contradict the other five:
> And before certain Instinct, will preferr
> Reason, which fifty times for one does err.
>
> ("Satyr against Mankind," *Works*, p. 36)

The rightness of liberty based upon instinct and the senses is equally clear.

> My Reason is my Friend, yours is a Cheat:
> Hunger calls out, my Reason bids me eat. (p. 38)

Thus this Reason, too, is "righted." But the consequences are not explicitly acknowledged. They must be inferred from the section of the poem immediately following in which the warfare among beasts, based on natural necessities and desires, is "in Justice . . . wiser found" than conventional man's warfare as it in actuality exists.

> With Teeth, and Claws, by Nature arm'd, *They* hunt
> Nature's allowance, to supply their want. (p. 39)

Darwin and Tennyson's "Nature red in tooth and claw" come hauntingly to mind. And we are prepared for the ethics of expediency which must logically follow:

---

7. For the question as to whether Hobbes did in fact posit the natural depravity of man and for his relation in this respect to St. Augustine, see *Leviathan*, ed. Michael Oakeshott (Oxford, Basil Blackwell, 1946), pp. liv–lv. For our purposes here, however, these questions are largely academic. Ch. 13 of *Leviathan*, "Of the Natural Condition of Mankind as concerning Their Felicity and Misery," will serve sufficiently to establish the points with which we are concerned.

> Those Creatures are the wisest, who attain
> By surest means, the ends at which they aim.   (p. 38)

There is here, certainly, little of the "Golden Age" primitivist's optimism. Whatever the libertine took from this naturalism would require a radical reorientation if it was to be allied with the naturalism of Machiavelli and Hobbes. Yet with conscious irony the two were combined into a nature whose inconsistencies were sufficiently submerged to avoid practical embarrassment. The one proposed freedom, indulgence, pleasure; the other, self-interest, aggression, conquest. Together they produced an egocentrically oriented concept of nature in which indulgence was purchased through aggression, and pleasure through conquest, and in which by definition individual fulfillment and social order were in perpetual opposition.

There could be no question in any orthodox context that this was indeed the nature of the beast. The libertine accepted himself as such and so did the conventional society from which he revolted. For the latter his beastliness had three central terms: atheist, sensualist, and naturalist. They were terms which society had applied to him—characteristically as "Epicure"—since at least the Middle Ages. And what he added to his doctrine and practice in later periods was not designed in the eyes of conventional society to improve the nomenclature or the evaluation. He combined the three major traditions of heterodoxy in Western thought—Epicureanism, skepticism, and naturalism. And he consistently took from each those features diametrically opposed to conventional beliefs. That historically his own tradition should therefore stand especially apart as the precise antithesis to the developing lines of orthodoxy is to be taken for granted. What remains to be noted is that this antithesis became itself, particularly in popular thought, a kind of tradition. As heterodoxy came increasingly to flourish from the late Middle Ages into the Renaissance and thence to the seventeenth century, the antithesis acquired additional points of reference which made it still more dramatic and historically significant.

III

In the concluding chapters of this study we shall find that the opposition of what was sometimes called in popular thought the "epicure" and the "stoic" became near the beginning of the seventeenth century a prominent concern of dramatic comedy, that the concern increased as the century progressed, and that the ideas and dramatic practices involved provide a principal antecedent for the Restoration comedy of manners. The precise nature and meaning of this opposition will be an interest of the later chapters. We should note here that the "epicure" is in general the libertine whom we have at hand and that the "stoic" who opposes him embodies broadly the moral and social orthodoxy of his time. The epicure represents the beast in man, the stoic, man's conventionally alleged moral possibilities. While the epicure glorifies the senses, the stoic glorifies reason; while the epicure follows "pleasure," the stoic follows "virtue." Consequently, to the epicure's "freedom," the stoic opposes restraint; to his individualism, conformity; to his self-interest, obligation and duty; and so on through a list which will by now be largely self-evident.

From one view these oppositions readily suggest two broadly conflicting aspects of man's nature. And it is to their point in the drama that they do so. From another view they present what have always been two possible answers to the fundamental problem of the individual in society. And this also is to their purpose in the plays. At the same time they present, on the one hand, that blend of Academic, Peripatetic, Stoic, and Christian thought which from the Middle Ages had constituted the accepted moral code, and, opposing it on the other, the combination of Epicurean, skeptical, and naturalistic ideas with which we have been concerned. That this opposition had become a traditional interest in drama long before the Restoration will be evident in the final chapters of this study. But there is ample evidence for the tradition outside the drama too.

Guillaume du Vair's statement that one must choose between two opposing philosophies, Nature and Stoicism, looks in a general way toward the opposition of "epicure" and "stoic" in seventeenth-century drama.[8] Though du Vair's use of terms may seem at first glance curious, it was not peculiar to him or his time. We have previously referred to Valla's *De voluptate,* one chapter of which has the heading "Antonius pro Epicuréis, & pro natura contra Stoicos." The two antagonists in Valla's works are scarcely pure Epicurean and Stoic in the strict philosophic sense. Nor do they reflect in specific detail the full range of opposing traditions which we have here subsumed under the terms. But they move within much the same broad areas of concern. The central issue "aut voluptatem, aut honestatem bonum esse," states in the learned as well as the popular sense the basic point of opposition. But "voluptatem" has become both sensualistic and naturalistic, and "honestatem" has become in many respects a statement of the moral position which we shall find opposing the "epicure" of English drama.[9]

The distinctive association of Nature with Epicurus had been made,

8. *Les Oeuvres politiques et morales* (Geneva, 1621), p. 899.
9. That the moral positions are not identical is indicated by the fact that in Valla's work a third speaker argues the superiority of the Christian to both the Epicurean and Stoic.

however, long before Valla. Lactantius' condemnation of the Greek philosopher for "following Nature" caused a later disciple, Gassendi, no little dismay.[1] But for patristic thought, whatever the influences upon it of classical philosophy, the fundamental fact of Nature and particularly of human nature was, of course, the Fall. To follow Nature would be, therefore, to yield to the debased senses and desires of post-lapsarian man.[2] This, we have seen, was what the Epicurean was characteristically charged with doing. And the Nature involved was not essentially different from that defended by Valla's Epicurean and con-demned by his Stoic. The popular opposition of "epicure" and "stoic" thus becomes even more extreme, absolute, and archetypally meaning-ful than the learned opposition between Epicurean and Stoic philosophy.

Yet that the two philosophical schools of thought should lend their names to the popular tradition was almost inevitable. At either level "pleasure" and "virtue" constitute the crux of the opposition. And the terms in themselves suggest a fundamental point of divergence in the moral problem of man—the egocentric interests of the individual versus his commitments to the group.[3] It was perhaps also inevitable, then, that with the advent of Epicurean and Stoic philosophy, the opposi-tion of pleasure and virtue became a central point of departure in ethi-cal thinking and remained as such from the Hellenistic period to the seventeenth century. For Cicero, like others before him, all moral philosophies were reducible to this distinction. And it became for him the chief basis on which Epicurean thought was extruded from fellowship with the other principal traditions of Greek ethics—all of which had as their central concern virtue or "moral goodness."[4] This division continued to prevail from the Middle Ages to the seventeenth century. With the advent of Christianity it became a distinction not merely between unacceptable and acceptable traditions, but between impious and respectable thought. It was assuredly not pleasure alone which set Epicurean thinking apart from respectability and the con-vergence of Academic, Peripatetic, and Stoic philosophy into Christian and Christian humanist orthodoxy. Nor was it on this basis only, we

1. Gassendi, *Opera, 2,* 749.

2. St. Ambrose is of special interest here since his writings reveal an unusual degree of influence by the pagan philosophers regarding the "law of nature." While he is not always clear or consistent about the status of this law in postlapsarian man, he is repeatedly explicit concerning its corruption by the Fall and the consequent need of the written law to take its place. See Epistolarum classis II. lxxiii, in *Patrologia latina, 16,* 1251ff.

3. See Cicero, *De officiis,* i.ii. A line of classical writers from Aristotle to Cicero himself (*De finibus,* v.x–xiii) had, of course, established in Western thought the con-cept that "self-love" was the foundation of virtue. But the concept as commonly un-derstood—at least until the 18th century—did not alter the essential moral problem in the opposition of pleasure and virtue or the persistent charge that the followers of pleasure were reprehensibly individualistic and self-interested.

4. *De finibus,* ii.xiii–xiv, v.viii; *De officiis,* i.ii.

have seen, that it became itself the center of converging heterodox traditions which make up the "epicure." But pleasure, together with "atheism," constituted its chief impiety in the eyes of the devout.

Indeed, at both the learned and popular levels and from the Middle Ages to the seventeenth century, pleasure became not only the schematic opposite of virtue in ethical and moral thought but its common seducer. One of the more interesting expressions of this opposition was the widespread interpretation of Hercules at the fork in the road as representing the choice between Pleasure and Virtue.[5] But the opposition is a commonplace in the literature and ethical writings of the times. For Alain of Lille the "daughters of the old Idololatria" lure men from virtue into intemperance because "they sweetly bear on their lips the melody of pleasure."[6] The idea is much the same as that expressed by Reason in the *Roman de la rose*.[7] But it is much the same, too, as the assumption which runs through English literature from the Renaissance to the Restoration. One thinks at once of Spenser's Bower of Bliss and Milton's *Comus*, but the same essential view is found in a varied host of less important works ranging from Daniel's "Complaint of Rosamond" to the Cavalier drama which constitutes one of the chief antecedents for Restoration comedy and which is the subject of a later portion of this study.[8] Among the philosophic writers of the Renaissance and seventeenth century, the especially persistent attack upon the Epicureans by the Platonists and Neo-Platonists from Ficino to John Smith helped to fix the opposition of pleasure and virtue in the public mind.[9] But it had been further fixed by the fact that since the patristic period pleasure, like pride, had been a commonly ascribed cause of the Fall.[1] Of all this the libertine was fully aware. And it brings us not only to an especially significant crux in the relation of the libertine to orthodoxy at large but also to a point of central importance for Restoration comedy.

5. For a brief but relevant discussion of this story in medieval and Renaissance literature, see Hallett Smith, *Elizabethan Poetry* (Harvard Univ. Press, 1952), pp. 293ff.

6. *The Complaint of Nature*, trans. by Douglas M. Moffat (Holt, 1908), p. 60.

7. Guillaume de Lorris and Jean de Meun, *Le Roman de la rose*, ed. Ernest Langlois (Paris, Firmin-Didot, 1914-24), *2*, lines 4463ff. The opposition between pleasure ("Deliz") and virtue is here part of Reason's extended distinction between youth and old age.

8. Cf. "The Complaint of Rosamond," *Samuel Daniel*, ed. Arthur Colby Sprague (Harvard Univ. Press, 1930), lines 267, 362, and *passim*.

9. Thus Palingenius' *Zodiack of Life* opens with the opposition between the gardens of Pleasure and of Virtue. The rejection of the first and acceptance of the second are preparatory steps in the approach to the Neo-Platonic gardens of creation.

1. The idea of pleasure as causing the "fall" of man existed also in classical primitivism (see Lovejoy and Boas, p. 149). This fact, together with the general contempt of the Cynics in particular for "pleasure" and their corresponding stress on "virtue," heightens the paradoxical relation of the libertine's "naturalism" to its classical sources. The point is of special interest for the discussion which follows.

IV

In our investigation of the libertine thus far we have chiefly stressed his opposition to received lines of thought. We have noted, however, that in certain ways he could be said to share rather than reject some of the accepted attitudes of his time. There was, as a case in point, his professed concern with the whole man, the desire to reconcile reason to passion, grace to nature. As a result the libertine—with whatever gravity—was almost as preoccupied with the Fall of Man as was the orthodox Christian. There was, to be sure, a difference. "Mother Nature" was his "goddess," from whose providence man had fallen and through whose kindness and favor he might yet be reclaimed.[2] But this difference was not the easy one which it might at first appear to be. "Mother Nature" even before the Stoics had been a commonplace metaphor of frequently indeterminate meaning. And the phrase, whether or not used by a libertine, could not be counted upon to indicate any real deification of nature. Apart from that, Nature had been a goddess to Matheolus and Spenser as well as Théophile. Further, the libertine commonly discarded the use of "Mother" altogether. This left merely the command to "follow Nature"—a motto for redemption which in itself could have been worn by many a Christian of the seventeenth century.

The point, then, was not that the libertine followed Nature in attempting to regain his "state of grace." It might rather seem to be that his nature was that of the beast, not man. But to this the libertine would reply that his nature was, notwithstanding, the real one and that the supposed nature of the Christian humanist was merely the result of "false reason"—that *Ignus fatuus* of the mind. This, however, extends rather than solves the difficulty. The libertine was philosophically an antirationalist. But some degree of antirationalism was, of course, at the heart of Christian orthodoxy. Even Aquinas had allowed that there were limits to what man's reason was either permitted or able to know. And the Christian as well as the libertine commonly allowed that man had fallen through intellectual pride, through attempting to exceed those limits. The difference of opinion was a matter of degree. For the libertine was not totally antirationalistic. He, like the Christian humanist, followed "right reason," and the similarity often produced interesting results. Rochester believed of right reason that

2. This, of course, is the central idea in Oldham's satire noted above. See also Shadwell, *Works, 3,* 25–6; and *Le Procès du poète Théophile de Viaux,* ed. F. Lachèvre (Paris, H. Champion, 1909), *1,* 382. The ultimate influence of classical primitivism and its concept of the Golden Age is in each of these cases apparent.

>   . . . Thoughts were giv'n for Actions Government;
> Where Action ceases, Thought's impertinent.
> Our Sphere of Action is Lifes happiness,
> And he that thinks beyond, thinks like an Ass.
>
> ("Satyr against Mankind," *Works*, p. 38)

Of "false reason" and of man's fall through his pride in it, he draws this picture:

> Pathless, and dangerous, wand'ring ways, it takes,
> Through Error's fenny Bogs, and thorny Brakes:
> Whilst the misguided Follower climbs with pain,
> Mountains of Whimseys, heapt in his own Brain,
> Stumbling from thought to thought, falls headlong down
> Into Doubt's boundless Sea, where like to drown,
> Books bear him up awhile, and makes him try
> To swim with Bladders of Philosophy,
>
>   .   .   .   .   .
>
> Huddled in Dirt, [the] reas'ning Engine lies,
> Who was so proud, so witty, and so wise:
> Pride drew him in, as Cheats their Bubbles catch,
> And made him venture to be made a wretch:
> His Wisdom did his Happiness destroy,
> Aiming to know the World he should enjoy.   (p. 36)

It is impossible here not to think of a contemporary of Rochester who was hardly a libertine and who, through the mouth of Raphael, counseled our first father (the immediate subject, of course, is astronomy and the "new science"):

> Solicit not thy thoughts with matters hid:
>
>   .   .   .   .   .
>
> Think only what concerns thee and thy being.

Thus Adam, as yet unfallen, is

>   . . . taught to live
> The easiest way, nor with perplexing thoughts
> To interrupt the sweet of life, from which
> God hath bid dwell far off all anxious cares.
>
>   .   .   .   .   .
>
> But apt the Mind or Fancy is to rove
> Uncheckt, and of her roving is no end;

> Till warn'd, or by experience taught she learns
> That not to know at large of things remote
> From use, obscure and subtle, but to know
> That which before us lies in daily life,
> Is the prime wisdom; what is more, is fume . . .[3]

Nor can we fail to realize that Rochester's description of man's fall is also the fall of Satan, concerning whose attempt to "swim with Bladders of Philosophy" Milton wrote, "Vain wisdom all, and false Philosophie."[4] That the libertine can sometimes sound curiously like the Christian is not due merely to the fact that the libertine is Rochester. It looks toward a basic concern and a major ambiguity which we shall find in Restoration comedy. But there is more to the situation. For Rochester was not only an "epicure" but a "naturalist." And if Adam's living the "easiest way" and enjoying the "sweet of life" suggests the "natural bliss" which both the Epicurean and the primitivists professed to seek, that is also to our point. But there is more.

Rochester's attack in the same poem upon man's "boasted Honour," his "dear bought Fame," his "laws" and "arts" and "policies" reminds us again that the naturalistic tradition from which the libertine in part derives was also to a degree antirationalistic. It, too, viewed man's fall in terms of intellectual pride. A passage from Montaigne may, accordingly, be compared with Rochester's and Milton's: "The care to increase in wisdome and knowledge was the first overthrow of man kinde: it is the way whereby man hath headlong cast himselfe downe into eternall damnation. Pride is his losse and corruption."[5] The pride of intellect here involved not only philosophic speculation but, in the broad and classical sense of the word, man's "art"—both his laws and institutions (that is, "customs") and his technology. In other words, man had fallen from his original and primitive state of bliss by following the Ignis fatuus of what the orthodox called "civilization." If the libertine were to redeem his fall by following Nature in this frame of reference, he could do so only by freedom from the artificial and corruptive restrictions of custom. This we know the libertine proposed to do—which meant avoiding among other things the custom of marriage. And his own fall from this state of naturalistic bliss would come through a relapse or surrender to the "unnatural" world of law and order. Thus those who attempted to make the libertine conform to conventional morality and institutions could be viewed as "Satan." We are prepared, then, for the libertines in Ward's satire who were persuaded "T'abridge their Pleasure, and conform to Rules":

---

3. *Paradise Lost*, ed. Merritt Y. Hughes (Odyssey Press, 1935), Bk. 8, lines 167–94.
4. *Ibid.*, Bk. 2, line 565.
5. *Essayes*, trans. John Florio, World's Classics (Oxford Univ. Press, 1924–29), 2, 222–3.

> But when the cunning Fiend had made them eat,
> They found the Lushious Promise but a Cheat.[6]

This seems certainly a volte-face for the libertine after rubbing elbows with orthodoxy in the Rochester poem. But again the case is not so simple. Much that had always been involved in man's art or civilization—and therefore his "customs" or "rules"—was inimical to Christian values in its concern with this-worldliness. And primitivism either directly or through other traditions such as Stoicism helped to focus Christian conscience upon the vanity of seeking after "the goods of Fortune." In his disdain of "the great business" of the world, the libertine could, and we shall see that he did, add this quiver to his bow. But lying outside the main traditions of Christian thought were sectarian strains of more fully developed Christian primitivism which challenged the whole orthodox structure of man's art. Like Ward's libertines they viewed society's customs as the "cunning Fiend." The institution of marriage itself was thus sometimes called into question. The libertine's frequent assertion that God made women "free" and that the introduction of marriage constituted a fall of man usually involved an ironic awareness of some Christian authority.[7] Marriage accordingly became a "sin." The irony was not mitigated by the traditionally touchy position of marriage even within the central Christian dogma.[8]

The sense in which the libertine could here be said to rub elbows with the devout becomes especially involved, as we shall see in the following chapters. If at first glance the involvement seems more a matter of wit than of consequence, it looks nevertheless toward central prob-

---

6. *Libertine's Choice*, pp. 3–5. Compare again the opening lines of Oldham's poem quoted above. The beginning of Dryden's "Absalom and Achitophel" is also of interest in this context:

> In pious times, ere priestcraft did begin,
> Before polygamy was made a sin;
> When man on many multiplied his kind,
> Ere one to one was cursedly confin'd;
> When nature prompted, and no law denied
> Promiscuous use of concubine and bride . . .

The Poetical Works of John Dryden, ed. George R. Noyes (Houghton Mifflin, 1909), p. 109.

7. The Carpocratians were probably the most widely known of the early heretical sects who preached and apparently practiced a "community of wives." But the 17th-century libertine was more likely to be familiar with the heresy through the *Roman de la rose* or the alleged doctrine and practices of such contemporary sects as the Familists. See Ch. 4, p. 67, following.

8. Much of the libertine's satire on marriage had been thoroughly traditional since at least the Middle Ages, as a comparison of Restoration comedy with Chaucer's Wife of Bath and the *Roman de la rose* will make clear. But the fact that monastic and other clerical influences had contributed to that tradition obviously added to its ironical attraction for the libertine.

lems concerning the libertine or "epicure," his relation to the "stoic,"
and the importance of this opposition for Restoration comedy. That
the libertine kept before him two opposing frames of meaning for the
Fall of Man will in itself prove significant. That he consistently and
ironically juxtaposed them tells us something of his motives. But that
the terms of the opposing views tend at certain levels to coalesce suggests his awareness of an essential ambiguity either in the problem
involved or in the nature of the opposition or both. Two further traditions with which we must be concerned add to the complexity of the
situation and to its potential for comic drama.

V

The entire range of Renaissance courtly love attitudes and practices
was, of course, directly available to the Restoration through both native
and Continental literature. Their presence in the Restoration and its
comic drama was in many ways conditioned by the court milieu of Henrietta Maria and by French préciosité in the last half of the seventeenth
century. But apart from these specialized influences, the general tradition
of courtly love contributes to the role of the libertine. Particularly in
their more idealized versions, the assumptions of courtly love and the
naturalism of the libertine could scarcely be compatible bedfellows.
They offered instead opposite extremes regarding the nature of love
and the relationship of the lovers. But they did more. They complicated still further the already complicated relationship of the libertine
to the society of his times. For in his attempt to attain his naturalistic
state of grace in a society of unnatural and restrictive customs, the
professed values of courtly love within that society presented still
another and more specialized set of customs as obstacles. His characteristic solution to this problem was to seek his libertine ends by
assuming the guise of the courtly lover. His own Machiavellian
postulates concerning the nature of man were thus wonderfully con-
firmed. Yet at the same time he coalesced by this stratagem with an
old and familiar problem within the traditions of courtly love itself.
The promiscuous sensualist mouthing protestations of eternal devotion had been a stock figure in both the literature and practice of courtly
love long before the Restoration. In this respect, then, as in others the
problems which the libertine posed for Restoration comedy concerning
the nature of love and its operation within the established institutions
of society were an inherent part of the whole courtly tradition.

As a result, the libertine's opposition to the "stoic" took on additional significance. Dressed as "passion" his libertine appetite could
plead, when it served his purpose, the far more respectable sanctions
of courtly love for behavior which in many respects was as disruptive

of established institutions as was his open libertinism.[9] The stoic is of special interest because he adapts or attempts to adapt courtly attitudes to the requirements of the established moral and social order. He attempts among other things to serve both passion and reason.[1] And in this attempt he inevitably raises questions which counterpoint those raised by the libertine. For the stoic of seventeenth-century comedy also proposes to accommodate the whole man. His watchword in doing so, however, is virtue, not pleasure; and the end he characteristically seeks for his love or passion is marriage. He subscribes, in a word, to the orthodox institutions and concepts of "civilization." This brings us to the final paradox and most pervasive irony in the make-up of the libertine: He too subscribes to "civilization" at the same time that he subscribes to naturalism. For the Restoration libertine this aspect of his ethos is indicated by the phrase "honest man."

Honnête homme or honest man has been historically a term even more protean in meaning than libertine. For the Restoration we know that its primary source of reference was the contemporary court society of France. And the chief significance of this historical and social context is that it emphasizes a divorce between the manners and the morals which in preceding periods had traditionally been implicated in the term. Concerning the distinction between its "sens aristocratique et mondain" and its "sens bourgeois et moral," Magendie reminds us that "Dans la belle société, l'acception mondaine est définitivement établie, et les traites vertueux de la génération précédente n'ont eu aucune influence. L'honnête homme est celui qui manifeste dans le monde, avec ce minimum de vertu indispensable aux relations sociales, les qualités de politesse, d'esprit, de conversation, de grâce, qui, comme dit Mme de Motteville, observe 'cette civilité apparent qui se pratique dans le monde, au milieu de la haine et de l'envie.' "[2] The words of Mme de Motteville are suggestive, as our investigation has already led us to expect, of much that engaged the interest of the Restoration comic dramatists. We shall want presently to turn to that point. The quotation will serve here to establish one aspect of meaning for the phrase "honest man" as it is used in this study: the stress upon "les qualités de politesse, d'esprit, de conversation, de grâce"—a concern, in other words, with the surface mode and manners of social behavior,

9. Such courtly assumptions, for example, as that love as a matter of "Fate" is an overwhelming passion which renders resistance to its impulses impossible, and that as such it is a law unto itself.

1. The absurdity in any learned sense of calling a devotee of passion a "Stoic" is, of course, apparent even when, as in the drama which we shall inspect, he controls or at least reconciles his passion with his reason. The absurdity, however, is somewhat mitigated by the tendency of Stoicism in the Renaissance and 17th century to be less condemnatory of the passions than in its classical periods.

2. Maurice Magendie, *La Politesse mondaine et les théories de l'honnêteté en France au XVIIe siècle* (Paris, F. Alcan, 1925), 2, 892.

but a rejection of the moral values upon which those manners had traditionally been based.[3]

Some of the immediate and practical consequences of this rejection are clear. With the Nature of Hobbes and Machiavelli dressed in the clothes of the honest man, life became a ruthless and self-seeking battle for survival, conquest, power, conducted beneath an urbane veneer of "politesse." And this situation merges with that of the libertine posing as courtly lover. But there were less obvious and more profound disparities involved. The libertine of the Restoration was in many ways an honest man in temper as well as external manners. The full quality of this temper is evasive of definition, and we must wait for further evidence to supply it. But its traditional characteristics are generally understood. They suggest such words as restraint, moderation, imperturbability—a reasonable control and skeptical detachment which are diametrically opposed to the aggression of the Machiavel, the indulgence of the "epicure," the rampant freedom of the "naturalist." Yet, however paradoxical, these oppositions assume an archetypal character. They point to the distinction between what may be viewed on the one hand as innate, spontaneous, instinctive, and on the other as consciously self-imposed and designed—the distinction, that is, between nature and art. And with these terms we come to the paradox which lies at the heart of the Restoration libertine as we shall find him in the society of the comedy of manners.

The elegance, the refinement, the politesse of that society bespoke an obvious consciousness of art. And here, at least by implication, art and nature were viewed as one. That refinement was to be "easy and natural" was no less a commonplace in manners than in literature. But from another view, the case was dramatically altered. *Homo lupus* concealed beneath a veneer of politesse could provide the dramatist with the incongruity of the Machiavel masquerading as the honest man. It could thus remind him of the discrepancy between appearance and reality. But it could also persuade him of the profound and ironic opposition of nature and art. The situation was much the same for libertine appetite calculatingly dressed in the sighs and protestations of courtly passion. Encompassing all this was the paradox of a society whose tone and temper could accommodate on the one hand unrestricted liberty, indulgence, self-assertion, and on the other conformity, restraint, and studied detachment. At the heart of these incongruities and of the whole pervasive complex of oppositions which we have re-

3. This divorce of manners and morals did not, of course, originate in the Restoration or the contemporary court society of France, as the reader of Jacobean comedy is aware and as will be sufficiently clear in the final chapters of this study. But that politesse was to be justified in terms of orthodox morality had been the assumption inherited from the tradition of the "Renaissance gentleman." See Castiglione, *The Book of the Courtier,* trans. Thomas Hoby, anno 1561 (London, D. Nutt, 1900), p. 111.

viewed was the espousal and assimilation by the society in Restoration comedy of two antithetical concepts of nature and, therefore, of art.

For the libertine-Machiavel art must mediate, as it had from Plato to the Renaissance, between the individual *qua* individual and the individual as a member of society, but with a profound difference. To the Restoration comic "hero" who followed nature in the libertine-Machiavel sense, art and nature were at opposite poles. The function of art was to pander to nature by concealing it, and art thus became primarily an instrument of deception, aggression, and power. Viewed from this angle restraint was merely calculation; and politesse, refinement, and good breeding, far from being "natural," were only nature's bawds, springes to catch woodcocks. We shall find accordingly that in the game of survival which is a central part of Restoration comedy, it is of the utmost importance not to mistake art for nature.

But the age's insistence upon refinement as "natural" was not primarily an artful deceit. Nor was it in itself a paradox. It was paradoxical only as it revealed a concept of nature which in implications and values was fundamentally antithetical to the naturalistic individualism of the libertine Machiavel. For nature in this second sense was oriented beyond the individual to the group. It subordinated instinct to education, impulse to discipline, the part to the whole, the individual to society. Art thus became one with nature; it was nature to advantage dressed. It revealed rather than concealed her; and its end was not aggression and conquest but the maintenance of order, balance, harmony. It therefore served individual fulfillment by the keeping of degree and measure, by conformity and restraint.

These two divergent concepts of nature and art answer roughly to the two most fundamental and divergent impulses and values of Etherege's society: the pursuit of pleasure and at the same time the pursuit of what Palmer calls "form," but which we may better call order. The pervasive concern with affectation, the insistence upon "good form" as opposed to "bad form," was not an idle enforcement of conformity for its own sake or for the sake of "fashion." Nor was it merely a kind of aesthetic fastidiousness in which "life was . . . stuff for a finished epigram." [4] It was part of the admonition to follow nature. But within the single admonition the dual demands of pleasure and order were constantly at strife. "A pox on 'em [i.e. fops]," cries Wycherley's Horner, "and all that force nature, and would be still what she forbids 'em! Affectation is her greatest monster." The passage then expands into the characteristic theme of appearance versus reality: "Most men are the contraries to what they would seem." The bully is a coward, the trustee a cheat, the churchman an atheist, and so on. "And we they call spendthrifts, are only wealthy, who lay out his

4. Palmer, *Comedy of Manners,* p. 91.

money upon daily new purchases of pleasure." [5] The passage presents
a curious but typical non sequitur. The concern with affectation, the
deriding of the fop and all who "force nature," has little direct bearing upon the "purchase of pleasure." The fop, indeed, is busily attempting himself to purchase pleasure. But for him the attempt is seen as a
violation of Nature. And Nature here is not the individualistic and
unbridled nature of the libertine, but the nature of gradation and of
order through restraint, the nature for which affectation is the "greatest monster." It is also rather clearly a nature belonging to the Christian-classical traditions against which the libertine-Machiavel was in
revolt. We have thus come full circle in our preliminary inspection of
that revolt. We may consider now its significance for Restoration
comedy.

5. *William Wycherley,* The Mermaid Series, ed. W. C. Ward (Scribner's, n.d.),
p. 257.

Part II

ETHEREGE'S PLAYS

3

The Comic View—*The Comical Revenge*

THE first play of Etherege, *The Comical Revenge, or Love in a Tub,* was produced in March 1664, about four years after the official resumption of theatrical activity in the Restoration. Its place in the history of English drama has been the subject of wide disagreement. And while this is formally a problem for the concluding portion of this study, we may profitably approach the critical concerns of the present chapter by noting some of the current views regarding the play's historical significance. For Harbage as for many others the significance is considerable since the play is believed to mark "a divisional point in the evolution of comedy of manners"—a point, that is, between pre-Restoration comic practice and the works of the major Restoration writers, from which the subsequent lines of development for comedy of manners extend.[1] Palmer, of a similar but more extreme opinion, believes that the English stage "had not yet seen a comedy . . . in the least resembling *Love in a Tub.*" [2] But for Lynch the work is merely a "fusion of certain familiar plot conventions of English comedy." It "did not define, to any appreciable degree, the spirit of Restoration comedy." [3] And for Krutch, "It might have been written before the civil war." [4] For all these writers, however, the play's claim to importance has been thought to rest essentially on only one part of the work—the prose or "comic" portion of it. And those who have upheld the claim have based their case on one or more of three elements involved: the wit and style, the principal character, Sir Frederick Frollick, and the *recherche de la femme* in which he is chiefly engaged. The work as a whole, it has been commonly agreed, is a dramatic hodgepodge, a confused mixture either of old and new elements or of elements entirely traditional.[5]

1. Alfred Harbage, *Cavalier Drama* (New York, Modern Language Ass'n of America, 1936), p. 86.
2. *Comedy of Manners,* p. 64.
3. *The Social Mode of Restoration Comedy,* p. 144.
4. *Comedy and Conscience after the Restoration,* p. 18.
5. Ashley H. Thorndike, *English Comedy* (Macmillan, 1929), p. 294, considers the play merely a "confusion of heroics, humours and intrigues." William Archer, *The Old Drama and the New* (Dodd, Mead, 1929), p. 189: "There is, in short, no trace of anything that can be called artistry either in the invention or in the ordering of the incidents."

Careful examination will reveal that the play is in fact a blend of elements old and new. But Restoration comedy is itself such a blend. Its basic materials, forms, and themes are in many important respects as old as Lyly, though they come to the Restoration with the marks of all the intervening periods of English comedy upon them. They become peculiarly Restoration by a process of rejection, addition, and refinement. *The Comical Revenge* stands at the beginning of this process. It is in large part a reworking of traditional materials which are not yet fully conscious of their Restoration destiny. The essential outlines are there, but they are in some respects still faintly perceived and projected. As a result there is much which in terms of later practice is irrelevant and intrusive. Nevertheless, in being dismissed as merely traditional, certain aspects of the play have had their significance for that practice and for the work itself obscured. Moreover, while the elements of wit and style, the character of Sir Frederick Frollick, and the action in which he is mainly involved have a special importance for the comedy of manners, that importance can be adequately defined only in terms of the total play. Finally, the work as a whole expresses a view and purpose which can be shown, I believe, to anticipate more precisely than any play before it the comedy found in the later and major works of the period.

The Comical Revenge has four plots and groups of characters largely, in terms of action, independent of each other. They concern the "widow wooing" of Sir Frederick; the attempted gulling of a country knight, Sir Nicholas Cully, by two city rogues, Wheedle and Palmer; the slightly sketched adventures into gallantry of Sir Frederick's valet, Dufoy; and in the Fletcherian sense of the word a "tragi-comic" action revolving about the household of Lord Bevill.[6] The first three of these plots are in prose and obviously comic in treatment and tone. The fourth is in heroic couplets and is "heroic" in tone. The largely independent development of these several actions and the marked distinction in tone have made it easy to assume that the work is without a unity of concern. An inspection of its structure will suggest the contrary.

The first two scenes establish with clearness and precision the major lines of interest for the play. We are first introduced in considerable detail to the character and modus vivendi of Sir Frederick, who then provides us with the essential facts concerning Sir Nicholas. He is "a fellow as poor in experience as in parts, and one that has a vainglorious humour to gain a reputation amongst the gentry, by feigning good

---

6. "A tragi-comedy is not so called in respect of mirth and killing, but in respect it wants deaths, which is enough to make it no tragedy, yet brings some near it, which is enough to make it no comedy." Preface ("To the Reader") of "The Faithful Shepherdess," *The Works of Francis Beaumont and John Fletcher,* gen. ed. A. H. Bullen (London, George Bell, 1908), *3, 18.*

nature and an affection to the king and his party." [7] That Sir Frederick is himself a member of the "king's party" is apparent. That he is the epitome of "good nature" and that, unlike Sir Nicholas, he seems eminently qualified by experience and parts for his chosen mode of living have already been made clear by the preceding portion of the play. When Sir Nicholas attempts a literal and ludicrously unsuccessful impersonation of Sir Frederick's role, what has been an implied relationship becomes explicit. Sir Nicholas as an unqualified aspirant to Sir Frederick's mode of life is the latter's foil, with a set of comic relations which we shall presently explore.

With Cully introduced, Sir Frederick turns to the second line of action involving the love of Beaufort for one of Lord Bevill's daughters:

SIR FRED. But, pray, my lord, how thrive you in your more honourable
    adventures? Is harvest near? When is the sickle to be put i' th'
    corn?
BEAUF. I have been hitherto so prosperous,
    My happiness has still outflown my faith.
    Nothing remains but ceremonial charms,
    Graciana's fix'd i' th' circle of my arms.
SIR FRED. Then you're a happy man for a season.
BEAUF. For ever.
SIR FRED. I mistrust your mistress's divinity; you'll find her attributes
    but mortal. Women, like jugglers' tricks, appear miracles to the
    ignorant; but in themselves they're mere cheats.   (7)

This juxtaposition of Beaufort's romantic attitude and Sir Frederick's disenchantment takes form as plot with the introduction of the third action. Sir Frederick learns that the Widow Rich desires to meet him. He greets the intelligence with, "What? the widow has some kind thoughts of my body?" (8). And when informed that she "loves" him, he replies, "Well, since 'tis my fortune, I'll about it. Widow, thy ruin lie on thy own head. Faith, my lord, you can witness 'twas none of my seeking" (8). Sir Frederick's intentions are obviously not the honorable ones of Beaufort, as the earlier sections of the exposition have prepared us to expect. The distinction completes the expository pattern by which we understand the play's intent: A central set of attitudes and mode of behavior are to be contrasted with, on the one hand, an attempted imitation and, on the other, attitudes and behavior diametrically opposed. And the play's serio-comic division in tone and treatment reduces

---

7. *The Works of Sir George Etherege*, ed. H. F. B. Brett-Smith, the Percy Reprints No. 6 (Oxford Univ. Press, 1927), p. 7. All subsequent references to the texts of Etherege's plays are to this edition; but I have used the modernized spelling and punctuation of the edition by A. Wilson Verity, *The Works of Sir George Etherege*, London, John C. Nimmo, 1928. When only page references are necessary, the number of the page is parenthesized and inserted in the text.

this tripartite interest to the still more fundamental opposition of two contrasting worlds of values, attitudes, and action.[8]

The "heroic" plot of *The Comical Revenge* is an elaborate love-versus-honor imbroglio which has affinities with both Cavalier drama and Corneille and which looks in many ways to the heroic play of its time. In every dramatically important point this group of characters and actions is antithetical to the prose portion of the work. There is first of all the code of honor which regulates the actions and attitudes of all the characters and in the love-honor conflict invariably triumphs over love. Further, and of special interest, the pursuit of this honor as well as love is treated by the play as a "passion"; and thus the confusion into which that pursuit throws all the characters is viewed as a triumph of passion over reason.[9] Again, we see this code of conduct as the dictates of custom, running counter to the reasonable dictates of Nature.[1] Finally, the love in this portion of the play contrasts point by point with the attitudes toward love in the prose portion. Not only is it "honorable" and a passion, rather than merely a physical appetite, but it possesses most of the other characteristics and employs most of the jargon of the more idealistic varieties of seventeenth-century courtly love convention. Beauty is the source of love; constancy is a sine qua non; the love is a dart inflicting fatal wounds; it is a pure and virtuous flame free of the taints of lust; it makes its entry through the eyes, and so on. The end which it unquestioningly seeks, however, is marriage.[2]

Each of the three plots in the prose portion of the play supplies its own opposition to this heroic-courtly world. But the contrast is most sharply focused, as we expect from the exposition, in the central character, Sir Frederick, who becomes thereby the play's comic "hero." And the crux of the contrast lies in his libertinism which, though less conscious and articulate in specific terms of "doctrine" than that of his successors in Restoration comedy, does not differ in its essential characteristics. Among them are his dedication to pleasure, particularly of the flesh; his naturalistic attitudes toward woman and love; his disdain of "honor" and "virtue," especially as these words regulate the conduct and values in the "heroic" world of the play; his revolt from conventional morality at large. Further, though this point too is less conspicuously

---

8. The centrality of Sir Frederick and his action has not always been recognized by commentators on the play. See John Wilcox, *The Relation of Molière to Restoration Comedy* (Columbia Univ. Press, 1938), p. 73, n. 10, for some of the structural devices by which that centrality is established and maintained.

9. *Passim,* but see especially pp. 40, 42, 44, and 46.

1. P. 20:

> But we by custom, not by nature led,
> Must in the beaten paths of honour tread.

2. This is, of course, no novel situation in 17th-century courtly love. The matter is discussed in Ch. 7.

stressed than in the later plays, it is clear that in some sense Nature and Reason constitute the norms for the behavior and attitudes involved.

But it is here that Sir Frederick's role, like that of his successors, acquires an added dimension. He is also in certain senses of the phrase the honnête homme of the seventeenth century : in his carefully detached and disenchanted lack of enthusiasm, his ironic contemplation of a world which is not what it seems, his equally ironic acknowledgment of his own frailties, the polish and restraint with which he expresses all this, his imperturbable "good nature," the "freeness of humour" and "carelessness of carriage" which mark his revolt from the ceremony and formalities of conventional society (8). The results of these two sets of characteristics are suggested in his opening speech. "I am of opinion that drunkenness is not so damnable a sin to me as 'tis to many ; sorrow and repentance are sure to be my first work the next morning. 'Slid, I have known some so lucky at this recreation, that, whereas 'tis familiar to forget what we do in drink, have even lost the memory, after sleep, of being drunk. Now do I feel more qualms than a young woman in breeding" (3).

It is characteristic of Sir Frederick as "honest man" that his wit here and throughout the play seems very casual and is in fact very studied. And it is characteristic of his role as comic hero that we can more easily relish the wit than formulate the precise attitudes at work. Though Sir Frederick talks of sin, he wishes, of course, to make clear that in one sense he is not really concerned with his moral state of health at all. He is only distressed by the physical discomforts of a "hangover." And his real desideratum, accordingly, is merely a stronger physical constitution. He also makes clear, however, that he may justify this desire in terms of libertine pleasure or "recreation." He may well, in fact, be implicating in the latter term, as the libertine commonly did, the Dionysian sanctions by which drunkenness, like other "Nature" and anti-Christian practices, became "re-creation" in a very literal sense. Yet he confronts the libertine sanction with the Christian deprecation, since, as he puts the case, the less the physical suffering the greater the Christian sin. And while he makes this statement chiefly to depreciate it, he depreciates the libertine values on their own terms too. The pleasure in his case leads to pain ; and the "lucky" consequence of the recreation for those more happily endowed by nature is to lose all memory of it.

As a consequence of all this, we are engaged by the comic hero's urbane self-deprecation, his clear awareness of opposing views, his refusal to take either them or himself quite seriously. Yet we are also engaged to ask on what grounds he subscribes to his nonetheless categorical libertinism. The answer to the question will seem in part apparent. In broad terms Sir Frederick is merely having fun turning the

moral order upside down—on the one hand by pricking the bubble of
our common pretensions, on the other by declaring for the rights to
forbidden fruits while at the same time acknowledging the tartness of
the taste. And his good-humored pleasure in doing so reminds us in
certain ways more of the merry scapegraces of Fletcher's comedies than
of Sir Frederick's successors in the Restoration. Among other things,
the comic hero is not yet overcast with that genuine and corrosive sense
of human debasement which characterizes the later plays. Yet his ironic
self-awareness and studied restraint of expression clearly distinguish
him from his predecessors. More specifically and precisely, the role which
he assumes, whatever as yet its degree of conviction, has an involvement of attitudes and values which is both generic to the Restoration
plays and distinctive of them. To resort to logical analysis in such a
matter is inevitably to destroy the immediate comic impact of the role.
But we shall gain a clearer sense of the comic meanings which lie within
the ambivalence and equivocality of the comic hero. We shall also see
more fully some of the archetypal elements in his role which relate him
to such varied characters as the comic Vice of the medieval morality play,
the Falstaff of *Henry IV*, and a long line of "Satanic heroes" in both
English and Continental literature. Finally, we shall have a firmer
awareness of the ways in which the historical traditions of thought and
behavior reviewed in the preceding chapter contribute to the Restoration
comedy of manners.

The key to each of these considerations is the hero's insistent equating,
as in Sir Frederick's speech, of sin and pleasure or "recreation." [3] This
reminds us that the Nature which the libertine followed was in most
respects the fallen Nature of traditional Christian thought. The comic
hero's acknowledgment of this fact is a requisite of his role, since it
principally determines the character of his revolt from conventional
morality and his status as comic hero. On the one hand that revolt is to
free the natural man. And here Nature as moral norm is good because
it validates the appetites and desires which conventional moral law
prohibits or restricts. To this extent the hero claims our sanction as
emancipator. On the other hand he justifies his revolt by the assertion
that man is naturally depraved. He is, in fact, the hero partly because
he exposes or claims to expose the debased reality which lies beneath
the false appearance of conventional moral pretensions. But he is partly
the hero, too, because he acknowledges and accepts this debasement in
himself. Here Nature as moral norm is good because it is the real and
the true. The hero can claim sanction, accordingly, as the "realist" and
truly honest man in accepting the existential facts of human nature. As

---

3. For this point and for the comments which follow, see again the works discussed
in the preceding chapter—the satires of Oldham and Ward and Shadwell's *The
Libertine*.

a consequence of these two norms, however, Nature becomes morally ambivalent. And the case for Christian sin must, therefore, be weighed against the case for libertine virtue. In acknowledging this fact the comic hero lays claim, in turn, to the sanctions and wisdom of the skeptic. He holds in counterpoise, as does Sir Frederick, the opposing claims to truth. But he is finally the hero as comic "Satanist." In discounting both his Christian sin and his libertine virtue, he accentuates his waywardness. And here Nature as norm is good only because it is bad—because it intransigently defies conventional morality on its own terms.

The circularity and inconsistency of these several positions become to an extent a further source of the comic hero's strength. By recognizing them he asks our increased sanction for his many-sided awareness and self-knowledge. Yet his comic strengths are also, of course, his comic weaknesses, as he again tacitly acknowledges, since in claiming such manifestly disparate sanctions he invites us to question them all. This is, in fact, his *raison d'être* in the Restoration comedy of manners. The several mutations of his role which we have here reviewed vary in their emphasis and meaning from author to author and from play to play. At their beginnings in *The Comical Revenge* they are little more than a lighthearted *jeu d'esprit*—a nimble dialectic of wit which explores the range of comic inversions and ambiguities to which they are susceptible. In Wycherley they are largely employed in an exacerbation of moral decay. In *The Man of Mode* they modulate toward a study in the Hobbesian and Machiavellian man; in *The Relapse* they approach the "thesis play"; in *The Way of the World* they become central terms in the hero's—and heroine's—explicit quest for reality. But each of these elements is to some extent in all the plays. And the quest for reality is for all of them—though it may not be for their characters—the controlling concern. The concern is ideally vested in the comic hero because the circularity of his assumptions is without a center. Or to put the matter more accurately and perhaps more meaningfully, his comic strengths lie in his negations, but his negations cancel each other out. Sir Frederick on the topic of marriage will provide a further illustration of the point.

SIR FRED. After I have had a little more experience of the vanity of this world, in a melancholy humour I may be careless of myself.
WID. And marry some distressed lady that has had no less experience of that vanity.
SIR FRED. Widow, I profess the contrary; I would not have the sin to answer for of debauching any from such worthy principles.   (83)

As in his opening speech, Sir Frederick successively assumes opposing positions. In the first, libertine values are expressed as conventional vanities; in the second they are the "worthy principles" of libertine doctrine. In either position marriage remains a trap; but in both, the op-

posing frames of value negate each other. In this respect too the central
character and action of *The Comical Revenge* stand at the opposite pole
from the heroic-courtly world of the play. Despite the staunchly "heroic"
tone of the latter, its condition in the play as a whole is fundamentally
comic. And it is in a sense quite basic to the play and to the Restoration
comedy of manners a comedy of "affirmations." A totally virtuous love
and a totally virtuous honor project the conflicts of their conventional
affirmations very much as the unconventional world of Sir Frederick
projects the conflicts of its libertine negations. In the total meaning of
the play each of these comedies qualifies the other. And the result is
once again chiefly vested in the comic hero, who arrives in the denouement of the work at a position midway between the two extremes. This
brings us to the central action of the play.

Sir Frederick's undertaking to seduce the Widow Rich shows many
lines of pre-Restoration descent which have not yet been fully shaped
to the Restoration mold. The Widow herself, for reasons to be discussed, must hereafter give way to the heroine as virgin. And with this
change go others in the hero, the wit, and the milieu. Sir Frederick's
drunkenness, his clamorous "alarms" to the ladies' "quarters" (5), his
"bloody war with the constable," his "general massacre on the glass-
windows" (6) will be replaced by the more "polite" and less lusty activities of playhouse, park, and drawing room.[4] With this change, in
turn, the comic wit will become less broad and frankly physical. Finally,
and perhaps most important, the hero's undertaking will not henceforth
have the genuine rather than feigned "good nature" which marks Sir
Frederick's enterprise and which makes it a "game" in some very
different senses from those which characterize the word in the later
plays of the period. Notwithstanding these distinctions, the central
action of *The Comical Revenge* represents in the essentials of its form
and meaning the "chase" or "love game" or "battle of the sexes" which
has long been recognized as a distinctive feature of the Restoration
comedy of manners. Some of the issues which it involves will by now be
self-evident. It is first of all the expression par excellence of the libertine's
"state of nature." For *The Comical Revenge* its values in this regard are
expressed rather more by the allegations of its wit than by the facts of
its action. But by allegation at least, it presents the egocentric and
appetitive man in the full assertion of his "freedom" and "pleasure"
—the sexual promiscuity, the aggression, the lack of honor, the per-

4. As everyone knows who has read the memoirs of the period, the playhouse, park,
and drawing room did not in the Restoration itself replace battles with the watch
and massacres of windows. They were only different aspects of the social scene. All
of which must qualify the concern with circumstantial "realism" in an approach to the
plays. If much of Sir Frederick's behavior does not belong in the fully realized world
of Restoration comedy of manners, it is not because the behavior was not part of the
historical society which the plays in part "reflect."

sistent inversion, in sum, of conventional moral values which these key terms of doctrine imply.

All these characteristics are at once enhanced and challenged by a further consideration which supplies the basic complication of action for virtually all Restoration comedy of manners. The comic world of the plays exists always within the larger world of conventionality. One of the many consequences is the imposition upon it by that world of a double standard of sexual behavior. For the object of the hero's quest, therefore, marriage becomes a necessity for two reasons: Without it the double standard enforces, as Sir Frederick puts it, her "ruin"; and further, since she is not permitted the freedom of her adversary, she must try to hold by the bonds of matrimony what will not hold itself. When Sir Frederick attempts to "creep into" the Widow's "favour" by reminding her that he would not be the first, she counters with the essential point that the first one "had a commission for what he did. I'm afraid, should it once become your duty, you would soon grow weary of the employment" (31). Thus confronted with the unnatural and restrictive custom of matrimony, the hero's recourse to seduction is not only a pleasure but a necessity no less categorical than is marriage for his opponent. But seduction is also, then, a symbol of his survival, his prowess, and, in a word, his status as hero. Sir Frederick's undertaking is accordingly "heroic" in a sense very different from that which characterizes the passionate quest for wedlock in the heroic-courtly world of *The Comical Revenge*.[5] Increasingly attracted by his adversary, he must try to gain his ends short of marriage. She, equally attracted, must gain her ends within it. Around this conflict develops the central action of all Etherege's plays. And the questions of reality and value which it involves are the fundamental concern of all Restoration comedy of manners.

Within this conflict are certain general and readily perceived sources of the comic. There is first the incongruity of the situation itself—a double standard of conduct within a frame of libertine belief. There is also the comedy of what we may call the discipline of feeling. In pursuit of their conflicting ends, the contestants must conceal and otherwise control their mutual feelings of attraction.[6] There is further the comedy

5. In this sense the "heroic" nature of Sir Frederick's role is stressed throughout the play. See as examples I.2, p. 6, and II.1, p. 16.

6. Numerous writers on Restoration comedy have dwelt upon this matter of "concealed feelings." Among them, Henry Ten Eyck Perry, *The Comic Spirit of Restoration Comedy* (Yale Univ. Press, 1925), p. 32, believes the concealment is prompted merely by "self-consciousness and pride." Lynch, as we have previously seen, believes it is only compliance with a fashion or "social mode." There are times and senses in which each of these explanations has validity, but each of them seems partial and in itself misleading. The concealment is always considered by the characters to be a matter of "reason" or "common sense" and becomes, in fact, a criterion for it. And while in these terms it involves a complex of values and convictions which are to be

of intrigue where, since neither honor nor virtue controls the action,
intellectual resourcefulness and self-control are the means and test of
survival. There is finally the comedy of wit in which the attitudes expressed have a level of comic appeal not dependent upon the circumstances of character or action. All these sources of comedy, however,
derive fuller and more precise meaning from the specific issues vested
in the convictions and attitudes of the comic hero. They are further
conditioned by a final aspect of his role.

In the opening scenes of the play the assurance and superiority of
Sir Frederick's wit increasingly converge upon the topics of love and
women. He insists upon the casualness and transiency of love as physical
appetite. He is equally confident in his understanding of women: "Some
women, like fishes, despise the bait, or else suspect it, whilst still it's
bobbing at their mouths; but subtilely waved by the angler's hand,
greedily hang themselves upon the hook. There are many so critically
wise, they'll suffer none to deceive them but themselves" (8). And
finally there is the confident statement of success as he sallies forth to
encounter the enemy: "Widow, thy ruin lie on thy own head." These
remarks prepare for some of the important if more obvious comedy of
the play, since in the undertaking which ensues they all redound upon
the hero's head. In his eventual surrender to his adversary he discovers
that though love may still be only an appetite and transient, it is far
from casual when aroused and unsatisfied. It is the Widow's subtlely
waved bait which is grabbed, rather than Sir Frederick's; and it is he
who is proved so critically wise that he'll suffer none to deceive him
but himself. Consequently it is his ruin which is most obviously brought
about rather than the Widow's. And though it is necessary to note that
his awareness includes all this, thus further complicating the comedy
of his role and of the play, his reversal is the pivotal event of *The
Comical Revenge*.

The central action of the play, then, is a movement projecting not only
the special comedy of a libertine caught in the snares of custom but a
host of universal significances in the experience of man: the strong
man proved weak; the defeat of reason by passion, the ideal by the real,
the individual by society; the fatal discrepancies between appearance
and reality, especially for one who had here been so critically wise; and,
embracing all these, the fall of man from a state of grace through the
defects of his nature. The comedy in all these respects, however, is com-
pounded by the libertine context which inverts their customary meaning.
By conventional standards Sir Frederick at the beginning of the play
is morally weak, not strong, a victim of his passions, not master of

discussed, it operates in the "battle of the sexes" first of all as an instrument of attack
and defense. This is made clear in *The Comical Revenge* (see IV.7, p. 62), where admission of love is viewed as a "weakness" in the war of conflicting aims.

them, and his fall is, therefore, his regeneration. To this extent the comedy of man is viewed, as it were, in conventional form and inverted content. More accurately, it is viewed simultaneously in the counterterms of libertine and orthodox belief. And here the view has a further complication. In the comic wit of the play, the relation between form and content is in a persistent state of flux. Since Sir Frederick himself, as we have seen, assumes alternate poses of Christian sinner and libertine hero, the course of his action involves a constantly shifting ambiguity concerning fall and regeneration. But the ambiguity involves, in turn, a comic paradox. Since Sir Frederick accentuates his heroic depravity by negating both his Christian sin and his libertine virtue, his fall in libertine terms becomes a kind of double negative. In the imagery of the play, depravity is "bound." More precisely and in the doctrinal terms of the libertines whom we have noted in the preceding chapter, Sir Frederick "falls" into "virtue." The questions which remain then as the central concern of the play are to what extent conventional virtue is "real" and to what extent it is "good."

In *The Comical Revenge* all these aspects of meaning are expressed chiefly through the wit. They have yet to be clearly articulated in the development of the action itself. Nevertheless Sir Frederick's shift of undertaking from seduction to marriage assumes at the denouement a form which raises the final comic questions very much as they will be raised in virtually all the later plays. The hero undergoes that "conversion" which will henceforth be his characteristic lot in the Restoration comedy of manners: "Widow, resolving to lead a virtuous life, and keep house altogether with thee, I have disposed of my own household stuff, my dear Mrs. Lucy, to this gentleman." [7] Sir Frederick clearly means not only that he intends to be virtuous in the orthodox sense but willingly so. And the ritualistic quality of the celebration at the close, with its music and dance, seems to lend sanction to his declaration. At its conclusion, in other words, the play seems to be repudiating the libertine postulates regarding love and resolving the comic oppositions and equivocalities of its structure into a statement of regeneration rather than fall. But the ritualism itself and the entire context of the close are, we shall find, rife with comic qualifications. And beyond that, the play as a whole and particularly the wit of the hero himself have rendered the word "virtuous" unstable. They have asked not only what true virtue is but what likelihood Sir Frederick has of fulfilling his promise in any conventional sense.

These uncertainties, in turn, envelop and qualify the apparent victory of the heroine. Like the hero, she too is conscious of the comedy in her position. Her closing "proviso," however brief here, has a significance

7. P. 84. He has, in fact, married Mrs. Lucy, his wench, to the unwitting Sir Nicholas by a trick or "intrigue."

which will expand this device in each of Etherege's plays and carry it throughout the comedy of the period to its final perfection in *The Way of the World*.[8] "Now I have received you into my family, I hope you will let my maids go quietly about their business, sir" (83). The statement has, of course, the honest-man wit and restraint. But the restraint is not mere fashion. It takes full account of the uncertainty in Sir Frederick's future actions. Hence the equivocality of the title itself. Who is revenged on whom and precisely how and to what extent? The nature of love and the problems of its fulfillment in the actual world of human institutions are left suspended in a condition of comic doubt. The range of doubt clearly does not include the love-and-honor values of the heroic-courtly world which, though not explicitly condemned by the play, are consistently qualified both by the nature of their own involvements and by the role and actions of the comic hero. If Sir Frederick's love proves to be virtuous, its nature will lie somewhere between the two extremes of the libertine and courtly worlds which constitute the play. And in this too Etherege's first comedy is prophetic of the plays to follow. The serio-comic duality of structure in *The Comical Revenge* will hereafter be abandoned. And the courtly love and honor values will not be projected in a distinct world of their own. But they will continue under various modifications to be an essential point of reference in the language, values, and meaning of the comedy of manners. They will continue also to represent the opposing extreme to the libertine world projected. And the comic hero's invariable course will be to end on a middle if still equivocal ground between the two.[9]

It is here that a final point in his fate becomes significant. If marriage constitutes his fall, the fall is not unqualified. Mrs. Rich has the three invariable attributes of the comedy of manners heroine—wit, beauty, and wealth—and they cover for the world of that comedy the full range of demandable virtues. By wit is meant always not merely "wittiness" but true understanding and intellectual resourcefulness.[1] If, therefore, a woman had wit, she understood her position in a world with a double standard of conduct. If she possessed sufficient self-control to act accordingly, she had an efficient virtue. The world of Restoration comedy dared ask for no more. But it is enough to make clear that if the hero

8. The famous "proviso" scene of Congreve's play is, of course, IV.5. But the entire course of the action between Millamant and Mirabell is itself an extended proviso. This is one of the many indications that Congreve's hero and heroine begin their relationship in the play where all of Etherege's couples end.

9. Wycherley's two mature works are here as in other ways exceptional in the Restoration comedy of manners canon. In *The Country Wife* the marriage resolution normally given to the comic hero is given instead to a secondary "hero," Harcourt. And though Manly in *The Plain Dealer* ends in wedlock, his role in other respects is divergent.

1. The meaning of "wit" in Restoration comedy of manners is more fully discussed in succeeding chapters.

was reduced to matrimony, his conditions were exacting. Wit satisfied the mind or reason; beauty, the senses or passion; and wealth, those practical aspects of living which no comedy of manners hero is ever "so foppishly in love" as to ignore.[2] His marriage, then, whatever the eventual realities of its nature, is not abandon. At its worst it is a compromise with the ineluctable desires of natural man in an unnatural society. At its best it possesses the essential foundations for fulfillment at a level above the libertine but below the romantic reaches of courtly assumptions. In this respect too the resolution of *The Comical Revenge* is on middle ground which, if less clearly defined than in the later plays, is still prophetic of them. And if in accepting this position with the imperturbable "good nature" and "common sense" of the honest man, Sir Frederick is no longer the comic hero in his original sense, neither is he quite the comic dupe. By inspecting now the man who is, we shall see some of the basic distinctions in these terms for the Restoration comedy of manners.

No other portion of Etherege's play is so fully derivative from pre-Restoration practice as the plot in which the country knight, Sir Nicholas Cully, comes to London to live the life of the beau monde and is fleeced in his attempt by a pair of city sharpers. Further, no other portion has so much that in terms of Restoration comedy of manners is irrelevant and intrusive. The Jacobean rookers, Wheedle and Palmer, clearly have no place on the later scene. Nor, in fact, are they an integral concern of the play itself. They lend ample support to the libertine attitudes and tone of the central action.[3] But the principal business of their intrigue is Jonsonian knavery, and their comic "fall" derives in the main from this concern. On the other hand, the victim of their endeavors, while scarcely less derivative, is far more to the point of the play and of the plays to follow. His specific milieu and behavior will, like those of the comic hero, undergo subsequent and basic alterations. But the lines of relationship between hero and dupe which are most essential to Etherege's play are equally essential for the later comedy of the period. And in part the relationship is both comic and essential because it is in part ambiguous.

Sir Frederick falls from a "state of grace" in which by the nature of things he seemed ideally to belong. Sir Nicholas falls by aspiring to a state in which by the nature of things he obviously did not belong. The comic hero and dupe thus define two distinct and fundamental

2. The phrase is taken from *The Man of Mode* where it is used in a different but related context. See Ch. 5 following.

3. They have, that is, not only the comic hero's attitude toward love, honor, and morality at large but also something of the libertine–honest-man involvement in their wit. See pp. 49 and 80 and the tavern episode in II.3.

patterns in the life of man. But the distinctions at once involve qualifications and similarities. Both, for example, aspire to the same libertine
state of nature; and both end up in wedlock. The hero, like the dupe,
has in some sense and degree aspired beyond the facts and limitations
of his nature. And the question of degree becomes immediately important. Sir Frederick in the last act of the play is the direct agent of
chastisement for Sir Nicholas' pretensions. He thereby consciously
maintains that sense of stratification—between hero and dupe, wit and
fool, gentleman and fop—which is the essence of Nature's "degree" in
the world of Restoration comedy.[4] But since at the same time the
cozener is himself conceivably cozened, the assumptions concerning
degree are subject to consideration. Whether, like the hero, man tries
to stay in what appears to him his natural realm or, like the dupe,
foolishly aspires beyond it, he is the victim of the comical revenge
which society and the inconsistencies of his nature heap upon him. But
within this fact lies the question as to what man's natural realm is. The
superior "experience and parts" which distinguish the libertine hero
from the dupe at the beginning of the play are no longer quite the same
as those which distinguish him at the end.

They are not, of course, unrelated. Sir Frederick marries wit, beauty,
and wealth. Sir Nicholas is unwittingly yoked by the hero to a whore.
The significance of the distinction looks to a further term of comic
involvement. The dupe has violated Nature through that unnatural
"monster" of the age, affectation. He has, as stated by the hero,
"feigned" the characteristics of the role to which he aspires. The hero
himself has been guilty in some sense of a similar violation; but the
similarities have again important differences. Whatever the status of
Sir Nicholas' libertine appetites and desires in themselves, his affectation of them is prompted, we have seen, more by fashion than conviction.
Its concern has accordingly been more with conformity than emancipation. He has, that is, been ruled by "custom"—of however new a
coinage—rather than Nature. And his affectation in all these terms
remains throughout the play the badge of his ignorance rather than
his understanding. The hero's affectation is less static and less simple.
It begins at the opposite pole. His initial pose is the consciously comic
projection of his understanding—his convictions, his emancipation, his
nature, his full awareness of the inconsistencies and discrepancies which
all these involve. As he engages in battle with his adversary, his posing
acquires additional meaning. It is in part his weapon of warfare, and
thus the continued mark of his understanding. Yet its denial of his

4. So far as I am aware the term "degree" is never employed in Restoration comedy
of manners to express the concept which is here discussed. I use the term, first, because
the comedy of the period does not provide another which is as nearly adequate, and
second, because it relates this aspect of the Restoration ethos to the medieval and
Renaissance sources from which it is rather clearly derivative.

emotions in love becomes at the same time a violation of Nature. This violation also relates him to the dupe; but it provides the final distinction. It involves the comic hero's recognition of the crucial fact that if Nature is to be followed in one sense, it cannot be followed in another. It is, in other words, his confrontation of the conflict between Nature and Art. The precise character and adjustment of this conflict will depend, of course, upon which Nature the hero proves finally to have—the Nature of libertine appetite and freedom or of marriage and virtue. And upon this question must depend the final relation of hero to dupe and the ultimate status of degree.

The fourth and very slight action of the play—the "fall" of Dufoy, Sir Frederick's valet, in his attempt to play the libertine gallant with the Widow's maid, Betty—supports and expands the central interests of the play. It first of all extends the libertine order to the third and lowest stratum of society and thus serves to universalize the comic world projected. From servant to country knight to aristocratic hero, this world asserts its libertine predilections and suffers a comical revenge for its aspirations. But within this extended order the action of Dufoy provides its own special comment.

Like Sir Nicholas, Dufoy in his attempted amour serves in part to sustain the libertine tone and values of the play in their opposition to the courtly love-and-honor values of the "heroic" action. The counterpoint is here especially sharp, since Dufoy employs the courtly forms and protestations for libertine ends.[5] His paleness and general debility come not from "love," however, as he protests (58), but from the "foul disease." And the comedy works many ways—not only across the courtly values of the "heroic" lovers, but across the values of the libertine hero. Contemporary audiences are likely to view with distaste the comic exploitation of venereal infection. But for the Restoration libertine with his honest-man self-awareness this aspect of reality had its peculiarly grim humor.[6] Following Nature brought sometimes less than bliss, and love could become in more than a figurative sense a disease. If then, like Sir Nicholas, Dufoy by his ineptness enhances the hero's finesse, he also, like Sir Nicholas, modifies the hero's values.

One further point remains. Dufoy, in imitating his master by pursuing his libertine designs upon the Widow's maid, is locked by the latter in a tub and banteringly twitted for his attempt. The episode enlarges not only upon the fate of Sir Nicholas, who for his aspirations has been "yoked" to a whore, but upon the possible fate of Sir Frederick himself.[7] The comedy of love and the comedy of man are expressed in

5. See p. 15. This device will hereafter be employed by the comic hero himself. Sir Frederick's sporadic use of courtly jargon is only for open derision.
6. Cf. Rochester's "The Maim'd Debauchee."
7. Dufoy is locked in an inverted tub through which his head protrudes. In other words he is "bound" or "yoked." The episode occurs in iv.6—after Sir Frederick has

the farcical image of Dufoy locked in a tub. And if the image is more jocular and less subtly defined than those in Etherege's later plays, it does not differ essentially in its implications.

---

begun to "fall" but before his final and overt capitulation in Act v. It therefore looks both backward and forward to the actions of the comic hero. And the twittings of the Widow's maid bear upon the comic issues of the play: "Now, if you please to make your little *adresse* and your *amour,* you will not find me so coy." "Why do you not keep your head within doors, monsieur?" (The pun, of course, is phallic.) "You begin to sweat, monsieur; the tub is proper for you." "How prettily the snail carries his tenement on his back! I'm sorry I am but his mistress: if I had been your wife, monsieur, I had made you a complete snail; your horns should have appeared" (59–60).

4

The Comic Form—*She Would If She Could*

ETHEREGE'S second play, *She Would If She Could*, was produced four years after *The Comical Revenge*—in February 1668. Most contemporary scholars, though differing as to what the distinction involves, have considered it the first fully developed comedy of manners within the Restoration.[1] In this respect we may view the play as a kind of primer for the later and major comedies of the period. In material, structure, and aim, Etherege has, as it were, stripped his play of all but the essential framework upon which the later works will make their own particular elaborations. At the same time he has in many important ways patterned his second comedy upon his first. In its characters the play provides the basic requisites for the Restoration comedy of manners. But with one exception the roles are continued from *The Comical Revenge*, though they now exist in pairs. For Sir Frederick there are two comic heroes, Courtal and Freeman; for the Widow a pair of heroines, Ariana and Gatty; and for the aspiring dupe, a pair of country knights, Sir Oliver Cockwood and Sir Joslin Jolly. To this group Etherege now makes the addition indispensable for the later comedy—a female dupe, Sir Oliver's wife. These characters constitute substantially the dramatis personae of the play. And the diagrammatic balance of the scheme is both pronounced and pertinent.

While the comic interrelations of this group also look to subsequent Restoration practice, they as fully look back to *The Comical Revenge*. The libertine character of the heroes is announced, of course, in their names. It is also announced in the opening lines of the play.

COURT. Well, Frank, what is to be done to-day?

FREE. Faith, I think we must e'en follow the old trade; eat well, and
  prepare ourselves with a bottle or two of good Burgundy, that our
  old acquaintance may look lovely in our eyes.   (91)

1. See Lynch, *Social Mode*, p. 149; Palmer, *Comedy of Manners*, p. 75. What has usually been thought the indispensable virtue of the play in this connection is that its comic world has now, as *The Comical Revenge* did not have, a homogeneous "social mode." But while the society of Etherege's second play is more nearly homogeneous in attitudes and values than that of any major work which follows in the period, this fact can hardly constitute its claim to distinction in the comedy of manners tradition. That tradition we shall find is based upon conflicting rather than homogeneous values and behavior.

Their attitude toward love as physical appetite is equally apparent; and their dedication to "freedom" and "variety" is a logical consequence. Taking one's freedom in the face of restrictive "custom" becomes, in fact, the chief and explicit concern of all the principal characters. At the same time the heroes are by their own assertions "honest men." And the expressions "honest man," "man of honor," and the equivalent "gentleman" become now central thematic terms in the language of the play. For the heroes and heroines with deliberate irony and for the others with varying degrees of awareness, the terms become standard designations for one who combines the temper and manners of the traditional honnête homme with libertine convictions and practice. In this specialized sense—which designedly calls attention to the discrepancy between surface manners and morals—the "honest man" becomes the "ideal" of the comic world in the play. As in *The Comical Revenge,* the chief vitality of this asserted ideal lies in its conscious negations. Its emphasis is more upon the orthodox ideals violated than upon the positive values affirmed, though the relation between the two constitutes the comic interest of the work.

As in *The Comical Revenge* again, the opening scenes establish all this. They establish, too, the essential conditions for the comic fall. Like Sir Frederick, Courtal and Freeman make clear by their wit their confident understanding of themselves, of the conventional world with its snares and pretensions, and of the character of their revolt from it. As much is true for the heroines. Their first brief but portentous appearance (101–4) announces their pursuit of "liberty" in the name of pleasure. They acknowledge the libertine premises concerning love, and they are in revolt against the conventional values and practices concerning matrimony (103). But they do not, of course, propose to take their "pleasure" outside it. Their understanding of the double standard and the position in which it places them is both clear and crucial. It reveals the principal basis for the sex antagonism—or in terms of the play's imagery, the sex warfare—in the world of the play.

> GATTY. . . . how I envy that sex! Well, we cannot plague 'em enough when we have it in our power for those privileges which custom has allowed 'em above us. . . .
>
> ARIA. But whatsoever we do, prithee now let us resolve to be mighty honest.
>
> GATTY. There I agree with thee. . . .
>
> ARIA. Upon these conditions I am contented to trail a pike under thee— March along, girl.   (103–4)

These closing lines of Act I complete the preparations for the central action. The heroines will "plague" the heroes for their greater liberty

but at the same time the heroes must be ensnared if the heroines are to
have their pleasure. The situation is by now familiar. Like Sir Frederick, the heroes at the end of the opening scene have prepared for their
"business" of seducing the heroines. And the comic pattern of cross
purposes in the earlier play is repeated. Through a series of encounters
the heroines hold out and the heroes eventually submit. All the sources
of comedy employed in *The Comical Revenge* are reutilized: the basic
comedy of situation, the comedy of disciplined feeling, of wit, of intrigue,
and the comic curve of the fall with its attendant implications. But again
the fall is not unqualified. These heroines too have wit, beauty, and
wealth. The heroes have made a reasonable compromise between passion and reason, between their imperfect nature and the imperfect world
of custom.

The nature of the compromise, however, is once more equivocal, not
only in its language but as that equivocality looks back to and is supported by the general structure of the play. The earlier reticences of
Sir Frederick and the Widow are now in a sense reversed. There is no
explicit promise or demand of reform and virtue. Instead open skepticism is expressed on every hand. And Freeman's "I hope we shall not
repent before marriage, whate'er we do after" (176) states the issue
in the resolution. The statement has, of course, its qualifications. The
heroes are to an extent only saving face for their fall by libertine standards. And both heroes and heroines are playing safe on an experience
that seems to counter previous convictions. The men have not, as they
claim, fallen through financial need (174). They have instead followed
the typical curve of the comic hero—from conviction to experience to
doubt. To Sir Joslin's question, "Is it a match, boys?" Courtal replies,
"If the heart of man be not very deceitful, 'tis very likely it may be so"
(176). "Heart" is characteristically in the libertine's vocabulary only
as a point of irony. It does not consort with "appetite." Courtal's use of
it here substantially innocent of irony betrays the curve of his experience. And again the ritualistic celebration with song and dance suggests
in its surface optimism not only "feasting" but fulfillment.

The nature of fulfillment, however, opens out into divergent possibilities after the manner of *The Comical Revenge*. The heroines accept
the heroes with this proviso: "And if, after a month's experience of your
good behaviour, upon serious thoughts, you have courage enough to
engage further, we will accept of the challenge and believe you men of
honour" (176). In the language and structure of the play, the chief
terms of the proviso—courage, challenge, men of honor—have all
become unstable in meaning. And "honor" has been the chief thematic
source of comic ambiguity. All the characters gravitate around it in
their respective orbits of perverted meaning. For Lady Cockwood the

word means chiefly "reputation"—a surface essential to be preserved while she takes or attempts to take her freedom outside matrimony.[2] It thus becomes synonymous with hypocrisy, with appearance which conceals reality. It is this honor which the heroes so sardonically expose, not only in the marriage hypocrisies of the Cockwoods but in the world at large. It represents for them the "honor" of the conventional world, which professes orthodox values and in reality violates them. The heroes might then accept the challenge of the heroines by becoming in marriage men of honor in this conventional sense—in which case they would continue to pursue their libertine pleasures, but beneath the cover of orthodox virtue. On the other hand they might accept the challenge as the men of honor they have openly professed to be throughout the play— that is, libertine "honest men" and, therefore, in the orthodox sense men of no honor at all. But finally in a third meaning "honor" suggests that reality and appearance might become one in a sense more nearly corresponding to conventional assumptions; that the "heart of man" might be capable not only of a love that is more than appetite but of good will and fidelity to commitment.

The male dupes of the play make their contributions to this problem much after the manner of Sir Nicholas in *The Comical Revenge*. To the heroes their status is clear: "Nature has so tuned 'em, as if she intended they should always play the fool in consort" (104). But they play Nature's fools most spectacularly in aspiring to play her heroes. And in doing so they at once enhance and question the role of those they imitate. Sir Oliver's first appearance in the play (his initial entry into the realm of the heroes) establishes this double function:[3]

> Methinks, indeed, I have been an age absent, but I intend to redeem the time; and how, and how stand affairs, prithee now? is the wine good? are the women kind? Well, faith, a man had better be a vagabond in this town than a justice of peace in the country. I was e'en grown a sot for want of gentlemanlike recreations; if a man do but rap out an oath, the people start as if a gun went off; and if one chance but to couple himself with his neighbour's daughter, without the help of the parson of the parish, and leave a little testimony of his kindness behind him, there is presently such an uproar that a poor man is fain to fly his country. As for drunkenness, 'tis

2. For Lady Cockwood as for all the other characters, the word is constantly being recouched in its precise implications. The following comments consider only the more persistent meanings.

3. The following discussion of the comic dupe is confined largely to Sir Oliver. His place in the marriage theme of the play gives him an importance greater than Sir Joslin's. In other respects the two have much the same characteristics and meaning.

true, it may be used without scandal, but the drink is so abominable, that a man would forbear it, for fear of being made out of love with the vice. (93)

In many respects Sir Oliver has learned the heroic manner rather well. "Redeem the time," "gentlemanlike recreations," and "[in] love with the vice" support the libertine tone and attitudes of Courtal and Freeman.[4] Yet from the heroes' point of view he is still demonstrably the dupe. Like Sir Nicholas, his first concern is social status. But he has in ways which distinguish him from his predecessor misjudged the role to which he aspires. The swearing, drunkenness, and generally clamorous character of his asserted exploits misinterpret what are by now the values of the libertine "honest man."[5] His status as dupe, however, is based upon more cardinal violations of Nature and Reason. Not only is he married, but he further succumbs to convention and custom by hypocritically concealing from his wife his libertine aspirations. Moreover he lacks in an especially crucial respect the natural endowment necessary for heroic grace: "Ay, ay, Sentry, I know he'll talk of strange matters behind my back; but if he be not an abominable hypocrite at home—and I am not a woman easily to be deceived—he is not able to play the spark abroad thus, I assure you" (100). And finally he displays an equally crucial deficiency in heroic wit: He is duped by his wife's hypocrisies into believing her a woman of "unblemished" virtue (94). As comic dupe, then, Sir Oliver is at once the victim and the embodiment of appearance opposed to reality—and at two contrasting levels. While he attempts to play the conventional hypocrite to his wife,

4. They do, in fact, a good deal more. Sir Oliver's "redeem the time," as one of the play's numerous verbal reminiscences of *Henry IV*, seems rather clearly to draw upon its biblical reference via Shakespeare's play. But even if here and elsewhere—for example, Lady Cockwood's "Peace, he may yet redeem his honour," when she thinks Courtal has at last arrived to cuckold his professed friend, her husband (110)— Etherege's play does not have in mind Prince Hal's own "redeeming time" and his and Hotspur's involvements in redeeming honor, the consequence of the association is precise and relevant. It involves contrasting ideals which provide points of opposition for both Etherege's plays and Shakespeare's. Falstaff, of course, would have relished the remarks of both Sir Oliver and Lady Cockwood. And it is not an incidental fact that Shakespeare's "fat knight" became the "hero" of Restoration courtiers such as Rochester. His "epicureanism," "individualism," and general witty disdain for conventional values and order place him in the libertine tradition—a tradition which he shares in part with many of the "Machiavellian villains" of Renaissance and 17th-century drama. Few historical lines of development for 17th-century comedy of manners are clearer in fact than the one by which the Renaissance "villain" and his "world" ("Thou, Nature, art my goddess") became the Restoration comedy of manners "hero" and his "world." We shall return to this point in subsequent chapters. The point is noted here because it indicates that the dupes of Restoration comedy, as well as the heroes, call conventional moral assumptions into question after a fashion rendered thoroughly familiar by a long line of antecedent drama.

5. He is really describing, as he will later attempt to enact, the "roarer" or "tearer" of 17th-century comedy. The heroes themselves refer to him as a "tearing blade" (96).

he is duped by her own conventional hypocrisy. And while he attempts to play the libertine hero, he is duped by those whose understanding of the role is more astute.

In all these respects he enhances the superiority of the heroes and helps to define their values. And the undertaking in which he is chiefly engaged continues in part this function. The heroes' design upon the heroines is ludicrously paralleled by the dupe's attempt to "engage" a town whore. But it is here at his most absurd that his role is most obviously double edged. His undertaking is frustrated by his wife, and he is "reconverted" to the joys of matrimony. His libertine aspirations lead to the same inexorable end as do those of the heroes. The heroes have, like the dupe, in some sense played the fool—but whether in their libertinage or in their marriage is, of course, the comic question.

The role of the female dupe, Lady Cockwood, is similarly double edged, but it makes its own distinct contribution to the meaning of the play. Like her husband's, Lady Cockwood's physical equipment is not of the best. But like her long line of successors in Restoration drama her chief comic inadequacy lies another way. It lies in her particular misunderstanding of the libertine–honest-man world to which she aspires and in her temperamental incompatibility with it. Having "interpreted after the manner of the most obliging women" Courtal's simple civility (98), she prepares like the heroes and her husband to take her pleasure outside matrimony. But to Courtal the quality of Lady Cockwood's pleasure is inimical to his own: "She would by her goodwill give her lover no more rest than a young squire that has newly set up a coach does his only pair of horses" (98). He must therefore appear to pursue her while in reality he flees.[6]

This relation of hero and dupe has several points of interest for the play and for Restoration comedy of manners. The libertine's casualness and variety of appetite fronted by Lady Cockwood's "enthusiasm" and "passion" have an obvious if specialized comic force. But there is less special comedy involved: the reversed order of pursuit, the libidinous male in flight before the libidinous female. Much of Lady Cockwood's comedy of character rests, in fact, upon very conventional attitudes toward the libidinous woman. The world of the play thus betrays once more the comic qualifications in its libertine ideals. That the male is naturally libidinous was taken for granted. That woman is the same, as "naturalism" would presuppose, seemed equally inescapable but much less palatable. A similarly unnaturalistic bias lies in a further double-standard attitude of the heroes. Lady Cockwood is old not so much in

6. The two heroines are lodged in Lady Cockwood's house. Therefore, as Courtal states the situation, "'twill be very necessary to carry on my business with the old one that we [the heroes] may the better have an opportunity of being acquainted with them" (98).

years as in use.[7] Although libertine literature professed to find the sex life of birds a commendable model, the preference of the comedy of manners heroes for virgins betrays their lack of ease with the "Golden Laws of Nature," and provides a further point of interest in the plays' concern.[8]

Courtal's flight from the passion and enthusiasm of Lady Cockwood has, however, further significance. Like her successors in Restoration comedy, the female dupe of the play embodies an anachronism. She is still in some respects of a "former age." She has not learned that courtly protestations are not "real." Her expectations imply all the courtly assumptions that run counter not only to libertine but in certain respects to traditional honest-man values: love as a passion; the lover as passionate, as indeed surrendered to the sway of passion; as constant, devoted, self-sacrificing, perpetually grateful for the "favor" of his mistress, and so on. Part of the comedy here, of course, as again with her successors, is that Lady Cockwood's professed passion so far as love is concerned is in fact only unselective concupiscence. But of her confusion in this as in most other respects she is largely unaware. She has, that is, lost her way among the conflicting sets of values in her society; and she cannot keep them straight even for purposes of appearance. As a result her unconscious confusions in such key words as "honor" have a particularly rich comic irony.

But the hero's distrust of "passionate lovers" goes beyond his revolt from courtly love. It is part of the general distrust—of the play, of its comic world, and of the age—of passion in all its manifestations. Lady Cockwood's enthusiasm leads her into precisely those social excesses which are cardinal offenses for the honest man with his detachment and restraint: "She is the very spirit of impertinence, so foolishly fond and troublesome" (98). But beyond that her passionate nature ill equips her for that reasonable imperturbability and self-control which is the test of the honest man in the face of a world habitually deceptive and out of joint. She, like her successors, is in frequent and comic fits of rage or despair or apprehension. In this respect as in others she is a foil for the central characters and a means of defining central values for the play.

Beneath Courtal's surface fastidiousness, then, is a more profound purpose and a more profound comedy: He avoids the entangling passions of Lady Cockwood only to become entangled in his own as he and Freeman pursue the heroines. As always there is a difference within

---

7. "An old puss that has been coursed by most of the young fellows of her country" (151).

8. The preference, of course, works more than one way and reminds us of the disparate views and values involved in the comic hero's role. In terms of Hobbesian and Machiavellian "Nature," the hero as aggressive "conqueror" would obviously find the resisting virgin bigger game than the eager female dupe.

the similarities. The hero compromises with his passion, the dupe is controlled by hers. But the comment of her role upon his is nonetheless telling, and it operates through virtually every aspect of her function in the play. As with the heroes—and her husband—the comic action in which Lady Cockwood undertakes to have her freedom and pleasure fails; and at the end of the play she, like them, is confined in the bonds of matrimony.

The concerns of the play as defined thus far in terms of character and action are given further expression by the structuring of scene. Here also the pattern has two essential parts—the realm of the dupes and the realm of the heroes. The division is so precise and so significant that we may tabulate it here for clarity of reference:

I,i	[Courtal's quarters]
	ii	Sir Oliver Cockwood's Lodging
II,i	The Mulberry Garden [a park]
	ii	Sir Oliver's Lodgings
III,i	The New Exchange
	ii	[Sir Oliver's Lodging]
	iii	The Bear [a tavern]
IV,i	[Sir Oliver's Lodging]
	ii	New Spring Garden [a park]
V,i	[Sir Oliver's Lodging]

Again like the patterns of character and action, the implications of this bipartite division in the physical world of the play work diverse ways. The two scenes of the first act have an expository significance which we shall presently inspect. But there and throughout the play the home of the Cockwoods alternates with settings which represent the libertine or "honest-man" values espoused by the heroes and aspired to by the dupes. The Cockwoods' home, on the other hand, represents in numerous ways a violation of those values. It becomes indeed the antithesis and finally the nemesis of them. The setting of the play has accordingly its own polarity. And as the heroes and, on either side of them, the dupes pursue their several actions through the comic curve which moves from undertaking to fall, they do so by shuttling alternately between the two poles, whose values stand as thesis and antithesis. The process begins in the heroes' quarters and ends in the home of the dupes. It has developed from what seemed an initial point of stability—the heroes' libertine "state of grace"—through a state of instability between the two poles to what might seem a point of new stability at the opposite pole, marriage. But since the resolution of the play opens out into divergent possibilities for the future, the poles of setting may, like the other polarities of the play, again assume their opposition. They suggest, then, like the total structure of the play, an opposition possibly basic to man's nature and life: the life of marriage, of family and home, in opposition to the life of "liberty," successive aspects of which are emphasized by the settings of park, "exchange," and tavern.

This interlocking movement of character, action, and setting establishes the general outline of the play's comic form. At every basic point of structure there exists a fundamental opposition: In character, man versus woman and hero and heroine versus dupes; in action, the "heroic" undertaking versus farcically false imitations; in setting, the opposition just described; in being, appearance versus reality; in values, orthodoxy versus heterodoxy. To an extent these polarities make certain unambiguous assertions concerning the nature of man. They define, that is, real oppositions and distinctions in his nature. At the same time the comic movement of the play suggests innumerable ways in which these apparently absolute polarities may in reality be reversed or resolved in coalescence. And underlying them all as at once the final and only absolute standard and yet the central and most pervasive source of doubt is the question of Nature and Reason. These ambiguities in meaning correspond to what may be called the ambiguity in aesthetic form: on one hand the diagrammatic simplicity, precision, balance, and logical order; on the other, the tacit or alogical counterforces by which these aspects of structure are persistently modified. Some further details of this situation will help us more fully to understand both the character of the play and its place in Restoration comedy of manners.

As exposition the two scenes of the opening act establish the essential form and issues of the play in a fashion broadly typical of subsequent practice. In outline they present a structure of obvious balance and symmetry. The first scene, we have noted, is set in the realm of the heroes, the second in the home of the dupes. The first scene gives us the men of the play; the second the women—a division which stipulates the opposition or warfare of the sexes. The first scene opens with the heroes and progresses to the dupes. The second scene opens with the dupes and progresses to the heroines. Yet in each of these cases, while the obvious distinctions involved are being insisted upon, they are also by implication being potentially qualified. In both scenes, for example, the dupes in part define the nature of their role through the facts of their marriage. But in the first scene Sir Oliver's discourse on marriage works another way as he correctly describes what would be the restrictiveness of any marriage for "natural," or as Courtal puts it, "Christian liberty." [9] The fact is given immediate though still implied pertinency by

9. P. 95. Courtal's witticism is here as elsewhere only in part an inversion of values. It is in part the libertines' awareness, discussed in Ch. 2, of the primitivism involved in certain sectarian strains of Christian doctrine. But this in turn connects with the

Sir Oliver's progressing at once to the topic of the two heroines. As a result the libertine undertaking of the heroes is launched within the foreboding shadow of the dupe's marriage. In the second scene, in turn, the two heroines are lodged in Lady Cockwood's house because they are "kinswomen." But they are lodged there too because they are akin in other ways which modify the distinctions between heroines and dupe so assertively maintained by the surface movement of the scene. Since both heroines and dupe are women in a world of libertine belief and a double standard of conduct, they are equally committed to the necessity of marriage. To what extent, then, are they similarly committed to the hypocrisies which, as part of the scene, Sir Oliver and his wife enact? The heroines at the end of the scene embark upon their undertaking with the same shadow as lies upon the heroes at the end of the scene preceding. Both are at once potentially comic doom and doomed.

Act II, which begins the "development" of the play or the process of uniting the opposing forces of Act I, continues the overt balance and symmetry of structure as the several classes of character are recombined in the successive confrontations of the act—hero versus heroine, hero versus female dupe, male dupe versus female dupe. The first scene, with its initial encounter of heroes and heroines, takes place in a park and is a model of "correctness" for the warfare of the sexes which contrasts with the succeeding scene in which hero encounters female dupe. As a pure battle of wit and therefore a test of survival, its general nature has been noted in *The Comical Revenge* and will be further considered in the following chapters. Our interest here is with the ways in which the details of setting lend implicit support to the form and meaning of the play.

As a central aspect of scene in Restoration comedy of manners, the park reflects in itself much that is characteristic of the honest-man world of the plays. It involves, indeed, the most inclusive and essential terms of value—art and nature, order and pleasure. But when filled with the characters and actions typical of the scene, the park becomes an almost definitive expression of that world. It is the ideal arena not only for the game of love but for the game of life. Further, as invariably played in the park, the game embodies those disparities which give the comic view of the plays much of its power and meaning. The formal character of the park, which bespeaks its state of art, contributes its own irony to the state of nature for which it is the setting—the amoral appetitiveness, warfare, and general self-seeking. But finally the careful order of the park, with its walks, arbors, and shrubbery, repeatedly becomes in effect a maze in which endless contretemps and

whole vast controversy of the 17th century over "Christian liberty." Dryden's "Absalom and Achitophel" is here again a point of interest.

mésalliances occur; in which, that is, the comic world becomes lost among what seemed the precisely ordered surfaces of life.[1] The mise en scène thus proposes with particular clarity the comedy of art and nature which is a principal concern of the Restoration comedy of manners. It suggests that the disparate values of its comic world may at best offer a way of confronting with skill and poise the uncertainties and inconsistencies of life. But it suggests also that at worst those values may represent a fruitless entanglement in conflicting aims and beliefs.

As denouement the final act, consisting of a single scene, brings these as well as the other issues of the play to their comic resolution. In doing so it employs its own distinctive balance and symmetry which in terms of both form and meaning will also prove characteristic of later practice. It has three well defined phases which recapitulate the themes and structure of the play as a whole. It threatens first to convert the heroes to dupes; it then re-establishes their superiority as heroes; and finally it suspends their status on a middle ground of equivocality. The immediate significance of this movement derives from the developments in Act IV. At the end of that act the initial undertakings of heroes and dupes have all been leveled to a condition of mutual exposure and stalemate. This development in a world of egoistic quests and "Machiavellian" intrigues makes its obvious comment upon the values and assumptions involved. But it has also generated a punitive counterplot against the heroes by the female dupe which further challenges their status.

Act V opens with the heroes' attempt to undermine the plot, thus reasserting control of their world and re-establishing their status. But in a mode of high farce which is itself a kind of reductio ad absurdum of their roles, their initial attempt is frustrated; and they are tripped up in the realm of the dupes precisely as in the opening scene of the play the dupes were tripped up in the realm of the heroes.[2] In the middle phase of the act, however, they regain their control and status by the superiority of their wit. They re-establish Sir Oliver as dupe by persuading him of his wife's "unblemished virtue." They re-establish Lady Cockwood as dupe by permitting her to save her "honour" (that is, her "reputation") but at the price of surrendering both her libertine undertaking and her Machiavellian attempt to match her wit with theirs. The only remaining question in their status is their relations with the

1. Further characteristic details of scene support this view. As in the scene of Etherege's play, for example, the women frequently wear masks, thus adding to the metaphorical masking of character and action which is a chief source of comic involvement. Further, such scenes commonly occur at night so that the involvement becomes quite literally a case of "man in the dark."

2. In their successive calls at the home of the dupes, one of the heroes is forced to take perilous refuge in a closet, the other under a table. The farcical situation is an obvious reversal of the opening scene in which the two dupes (in Lady Cockwood's case, through the agency of her maid) successively call at the home of Courtal.

heroines. The denouement moves accordingly to its third and concluding phase where, as we have in part seen, the positions of heroes
and heroines alike are left in a state of doubt.

This last stage of resolution has in itself a balance of form, movement, and meaning which deserves some final notice. It is a comic
counterpoint consisting of three voices—the heroes and heroines, the
Cockwoods, and the "choral" voice of Sir Joslin Jolly. As the heroes
make their first step toward an agreement on marriage, Sir Joslin enters
with a song:

> A catch and a glass
> A fiddle and a lass,
> What more would an honest man have:
> Hang your temperate sot,
> Who would seem what he's not;
> 'Tis I am wise, he's but grave. (175)

This, of course, is the libertine or "honest-man" doctrine of the heroes
at the beginning of the play, and seems accordingly to accentuate the
bondage for which now at its close they have begun negotiations. On
the other hand it is now asserted by Sir Joslin, the comic fool, and in a
context so absurd as to qualify its values.[3] Moreover both heroes and
heroines are at the moment disguising their feelings by libertine rather
than conventional posturings and thus "seeming what they're not" in
ways that suggest their real desires are nearer those of the "temperate
sot" than the libertine.

As they move, however, into their closing proviso concerning "challenge" and "honor," the terms of their agreement are dubiously extended to the resolution of the Cockwoods. Sir Oliver endorses the
joys of marriage with "Never man was so happy in a virtuous and a
loving lady" (176)! And Lady Cockwood resigns herself to wedlock
with "Certainly fortune was never before so unkind to the ambition of
a lady" (178). Sir Joslin then gives the final word for the libertine:

> I gave my love a green gown
> I' th' merry month of May,
> And down she fell as wantonly
> As a tumbler does at play. (179)

And Sir Oliver balances this by a final tribute to marriage:

3. Sir Joslin's "humour" whenever he became drunk was to bring a pair of "servants"
to visit his nieces, the heroines. This was the means originally employed by the heroes
to gain access to the heroines. Sir Joslin now brings a pimp and a whore dressed as a
man. The parallel comments, of course, upon more than the ridiculous "libertinism"
of Sir Joslin.

> Give me thy hand, my virtuous, my dear:
> Henceforwards may our mutual loves increase,
> And when we are a-bed, we'll sign the peace.   (179)

The two dupes have the two final speeches of the play and they now stand at two opposite extremes of value. The heroes and heroines stand at the moment somewhere between the two, and thus themselves in a state of ambiguous balance in their wit, awareness, and restraint. The superior art by which they have throughout their conflict controlled their natural desires may henceforth become the art by which those desires are nurtured. That, however, is but one of the many questions posed in the final comic balance of the play. Like all the others, the question of art and nature has moved through one stage of its comic issue in the life of man. But the resolution of that stage reposes the question for the stage to come.

5

The Comic Values—*The Man of Mode*

ETHEREGE'S third and last play, *The Man of Mode, or Sir Fopling Flutter,* is one of the acknowledged masterpieces of Restoration drama. Properly understood it is also, I believe, one of the masterpieces of English comedy. In both contexts it gives a certain definitive and final form to lines of interest which had gathered through the course of seventeenth-century dramatic practice and which in eighteenth-century drama were either abandoned or transformed into new values and assumptions.[1] At the same time, though it was produced eight years after Etherege's second comedy, its immediate lines of development stem from his previous works.[2] The outlines of *She Would If She Could* are clearly discernible in it; but they have been enlarged and realigned in comic meaning. And in this process the third comedy looks back in some significant ways to the first. While our interest, then, in moving from the first to the second play was to see how a given set of concerns developed into a more fully integrated and distinctive expression, we shall want now to see how aspects of both works become part of an enlarged and modified comic view. We shall want also to see how this development gives a more comprehensive and, from its particular point of view, a consummate definition to those questions of reality and value which constitute the essential interest of Restoration comedy of manners.

For each of these considerations we may best begin once more with the "hero." By the end of the expository first act we have learned that Dorimant—who "has more mistresses now depending than the most eminent lawyer in England has causes" (208)—has before the play

---

1. The practice of grouping Restoration drama with that of the 18th century is open, I believe, to question. The last part of the 17th century is in many profound respects a period of transition. But its drama, and particularly its comedy of manners, is in more ways the end of an era than the beginning of a new one. The principal traditions which produced Restoration comedy have their final voice in Pope, Swift, and Gay. Goldsmith and Sheridan, for all their alleged revolt from "sentimental" comedy, are essentially of a different world, and one much closer to Steele and Cumberland than to Etherege, Wycherley, and Congreve.

2. *The Man of Mode* was first produced in March 1676, after all but one (*The Plain Dealer*) of Wycherley's plays had appeared. But it does not seem likely that the changes which we are about to note in Etherege's final comedy can be attributed to direct influence from the preceding works of his contemporary.

seduced one member of its comic world, is about to succeed in seducing another, has laid plans for the immediate seduction of a third, has encouraged the marriage of a friend in the hope that he may thereafter more easily seduce the wife, and, finally, has been the dubious "ruin" of one who is dismissed as merely a "true-bred whore." [3] While there is much in this notable activity which is characteristic of the earlier comedies, there are also fundamental shifts in emphasis. The markedly more numerous and involved undertakings of the hero are no longer primarily the expression of libertine freedom, variety, and "epicurean" pleasure. These are allegedly doctrinal terms of value for him still. But his activities are now explicitly and predominantly the expression of what in the earlier plays was largely implied and secondary—a Hobbesian aggressiveness, competitiveness, and drive for power and "glory"; a Machiavellian dissembling and cunning; a satanic pride, vanity, and malice; and, drawing upon each of these frames of meaning, an egoistic assertion of self through the control of others.[4]

These shifts of emphasis in the hero correspond to further changes of form and meaning in the play. The use of a double plot shows lines of relationship with *The Comical Revenge*. Yet the total action of the play is now "heroically" single after the fashion of *She Would If She Could*. It is still concerned with the comedy of the fall. But it is preeminently a comedy of power in a wider and more sobering sense than in either of the earlier works. Specifically it involves the hero's conflict with and ultimate conquest of several contrasting "worlds" within the total world of the play. This comedy of power and conquest remains in part one of appearance versus reality, though its implications in these latter terms also acquire new meaning. The hero is now acclaimed at the end of the play as a very "civil" gentleman although he has behaved throughout very much like a villain. But this development, in turn, is part of the larger comedy of values. While the hero is repeatedly viewed by the various worlds of the play as "devil," he also "has something of the angel yet undefaced in him" (210). The vitality and meaning of the play derive primarily from the problems which this duality creates not only for those conquered by the hero but possibly by the end of the play for the hero himself. And the issues at stake include further terms of value. They reflect, for example, a corresponding duality in Art and

3. The "whore's" illiterate "billet-doux" at the end of the act (204) provides a significant climax to the "undertakings" of the hero which have been the major concern of the exposition.

4. See *Leviathan,* p. 35: "Joy, arising from imagination of a man's own power and ability, is that exultation of the mind which is called *Glorying.*" Also p. 64: "So that in the first place, I put for a general inclination of all mankind, a perpetual and restless desire of power after power, that closeth only in death. . . . Competition of riches, honour, command, or other power, inclineth to contention, enmity, and war: because the way of one competitor, to the attaining his desire, is to kill, subdue, supplant, or repel the other."

Nature. If by nature the hero seems in some respects a devil, he is one with superior intelligence and great physical attraction. And these gifts of Nature are further enhanced by his art—his impeccable dress, the consummate "good breeding" of his manners (when, of course, he wishes to have them such), the skill and polish of his wit, the restraint, self-control, and order which all these accomplishments require. Yet if his art serves thus to enhance his nature, it also serves to conceal it. In the language of the play, the hero is the supreme "dissembler" of his comic world. He is at the same time the full embodiment of those inter-related but disparate assumptions and values which we have reviewed in the second chapter of this study. And while in all these respects he is the Restoration "man of mode," he is also the embodiment of archetypal problems and values in the life of man.[5]

Here again the characteristics of the hero's role are broadly generic for Etheregean comedy. What distinguishes them from the earlier works is not only the shifts in emphasis among them but the wider, more varied, and more fully defined context in which they operate. Each of the several worlds conquered by the hero has its particular set of values which in some way qualifies his. But he, in turn, in some way qualifies theirs. The relationships involved, however, are not static. They have their own distinctively comic development through the action of the play. By inspecting that development we derive an account of the play's own values, including a final definition for Etheregean comedy of Nature and Reason. And here, though the carefully guarded surfaces of *The Man of Mode* continue to reflect the pervasive ambiguity of the earlier plays, they are more committed in their treatment of the liber-tine-Machiavel "honest man." With this commitment go further changes in concern. The question remains as to what Nature in reality is. But the several discrete worlds stress more fully now the fact of Nature's diversity. The question accordingly is not only what apparent aspects of Nature are real but which of them in terms of value are to be most approved. Dorimant wins, if not like Edmund in *King Lear* his "land," then at least his supremacy in the worlds he conquers by his gifts from Nature and his exercise of an amoral wit, passion, and art. Yet while

---

5. In this regard the similarities between Dorimant and the Don Juan of 17th-century drama seem especially noteworthy. The libertinism, the seeming rationality, the wit and general polish of manner, the physical attractiveness, the "Machiavellianism," the Satanic egoism, pride, and malice are among the specific characteristics which they share. The similarity is especially apparent in the Don Juans of Molière, Rosimond, and Shadwell—the versions with which Etherege and the Restoration were most familiar. (Shadwell's *The Libertine* was produced in June 1675, nine months before Etherege's play.) At the same time it seems apparent that the 17th-century concerns reflected in Dorimant and Don Juan are to be related to those which produced the "Machiavellian villain" of pre-Restoration English drama. The Jacobean and Caroline comedy discussed in the final portion of this study shows further aspects of this rela-tionship.

he is thus the comic conqueror, he is also in less ambiguous and qualified senses than his predecessors the comic villain. In this respect, indeed, *The Man of Mode* presents a special problem in the Restoration
comedy of manners and an exception to its general practice. Its treatment of the problem, however, reflects those values which are typical
of its genre.[6]

The two interlocking plots of *The Man of Mode* mark the division
of the play into two basic though again interlocking worlds of value.
Each has further divisions or "worlds" within it. But the characters of
the minor plot are distinguished from those in the major, which centers
upon the hero, by being neither libertine nor Machiavellian. Their values
may for the moment be labeled merely "traditional" or "conventional,"
and include concepts of genuine honor which contrast with the libertine-
Machiavel "mode" exemplified by the hero. This bipartite division in
the play is thus reminiscent of the similar division in *The Comical Revenge*. Meanwhile the major plot provides in its totality much the same
general pattern of action for the hero as in each of the earlier plays.
Though he now engages simultaneously in three principal "intrigues"
as compared with two in the second play and one in the first, the total
course of his action ostensibly moves in much the same fashion from
undertaking to fall. Here too, however, there are fundamental modifications.[7]

The lines of both continuity and change are especially evident and
meaningful in Dorimant's undertaking with the first of his female
dupes, Loveit. Though she has been seduced by the hero before the
action of the play, Loveit continues in many ways the role of Lady
Cockwood. She too is the embodiment of "passion," and she has many
of the courtly assumptions concerning love which characterize her predecessor. As a result she seems initially to stand at the opposite extreme
from the libertine appetite and values of her seducer. And his alleged
desire to escape from her passion seems again to prepare for the comedy
of his being caught in his own as he engages in subsequent battle with
the heroine. Yet like Lady Cockwood, Loveit seems in other ways to
maintain the distinction in "degree" between dupe and hero: She is unwittingly used in the latter's further undertakings; and she fails in her

6. Critics have frequently likened Dorimant to Horner in Wycherley's *The Country
Wife*. But apart from their busy sex lives, the two characters are fundamentally different. Horner is the sheer sensualist whom Dorimant has too often been thought to
represent. He has little concern with power and self-assertion as such. In the Machiavellian aspects of his role, Dorimant is more fully related to Congreve's villains, Maskwell
in *The Double-Dealer* and Fainall in *The Way of the World*. Congreve's comic heroes,
to the extent that they play the Machiavel, do so primarily as a necessity for survival
in their world.

7. This progression in the number of the hero's intrigues or undertakings is not an
incidental one. It corresponds to the increasing complexity and articulation of the
successive plays.

counterintrigue against him. Here her role as dupe seems chiefly defined by the inferiority of her "wit" and by her lack of self-control.

Despite these similarities, the role of Loveit has essential differences from that of Lady Cockwood. She has none of the grossly ridiculous excesses and incongruities of the earlier dupe and her more characteristic descendants in Restoration comedy. Her passionate love is simply that, not concupiscence in courtly disguise.[8] It is her seducer who now assumes this mode of hypocrisy in the comic world of the play. Nor does the dupe now expect honor from others while practicing dishonor herself. She is no longer, in other words, the embodiment of that extreme discrepancy between appearance and reality which Lady Cockwood represented in the earlier work and which is now vested primarily in the hero. She is instead chiefly the dupe because she is helplessly the victim of a passionate love and nature which prevent dissembling in a world where the nature and art of the hero make dissembling a requisite for survival. What principally distinguishes Loveit, then, from the non-libertine world in the minor plot is her excessive and uncontrollable passion. She has been drawn into the orbit of the hero by that passion, but within the major plot she represents a variant world of her own. And if as such she continues in some respects the role of Lady Cockwood, she continues in others the values of the courtly world in *The Comical Revenge*.[9] The three plays of Etherege thus treat in three different but related ways and contexts what may be called the "problem of passion" in Restoration comedy of manners.

The problem has further ramifications in the Dorimant-Loveit relationship. Though the hero's sexual appetite stands initially at the farthest remove from Loveit's courtly passion, it is the dupe's uncontrolled passion of love which is the fullest object of torment by Dorimant's superficially controlled but in reality equally unbounded passion for conquest, power, and the exercise of malice.[1] As this conflict pro-

8. Loveit's name, particularly in the general context of Restoration practice, is, in fact, misleading. In her passion Loveit as comic dupe is more like Mrs. Marwood in *The Way of the World* than she is like Lady Fidget in *The Country Wife* or Lady Wishfort in *The Way of the World*, who are more fully in the line of descent from Lady Cockwood. Unlike Mrs. Marwood, however, Loveit's passion does not involve her in playing the "Machiavel." These distinctions, like those noted above in the "heroes" and "villains," suggest the variety of mutations by which the characteristic concerns of Restoration comedy of manners are expressed.

9. The specialized involvements in "honor" which distinguish the heroic-courtly world of *The Comical Revenge* have in Loveit, as in the minor plot of *The Man of Mode,* been largely normalized. Consequently Loveit's courtly assumptions concerning honor merge in most respects with those of the traditional honest man and of Christian-classical orthodoxy. But in seeking fulfillment outside marriage, Loveit's passion invokes also the courtly honor of secrecy and thus merges with the code of expedient "honor" which operates in the world of the libertine hero.

1. See Loveit's awareness: "You, who have more pleasure in the ruin of a woman's reputation than in the endearments of her love" (270). Compare Belinda's similar understanding that "he is never well but when he triumphs, nay, glories to a woman's

gresses, the dupe's open passion increasingly reflects those emotions which covertly characterize the hero's—"jealousy, indignation, spite, and thirst of revenge" (213)—while in Dorimant's conflict with the heroine, his passion and his appetite may possibly be converted to love. These developments in passion merge with a similar comedy in wit. Loveit's original belief in honor, faith, constancy, devotion are clearly not the beliefs of the libertine-Machiavel, as the initial encounter of hero and dupe makes clear.

DOR. Love gilds us over and makes us show fine things to one another for a time, but soon the gold wears off, and then again the native brass appears.

LOV. Think on your oaths, your vows and protestations, perjured man.

DOR. I made 'em when I was in love.

LOV. And therefore ought they not to bind? Oh, impious!

DOR. What we swear at such a time may be a certain proof of a present passion; but, to say truth, in love there is no security to be given for the future.   (216)

The question of "binding," of course, goes back to the provisos concerning "honor" and "virtue" in the resolution of the previous plays. But at the moment the hero's wit seems to establish the superiority of his views despite the fact that his art, even in such apparent candor, still conceals his real nature and convictions. His "oaths," as the play has already made clear and will presently make clearer in the seduction of Belinda, are not at all a "certain proof of a present passion" so far as love is concerned. They are instead part of the hero's disguise for his libertine appetite.[2] But in either case the assumptions involved are antithetical to those of the dupe. And they prepare for the questions to be raised in the play's denouement, when the hero's oaths will again be sworn to the heroine.

But by the time of the denouement, the dupe's belief reveals a change of view: "There's nothing but falsehood and impertinence in the world, all men are villains or fools" (286). Her conviction now echoes the disenchanted assumptions of the libertine-Machiavel, while the hero in

---

face in his villainies" (273). Compare also Dorimant's "He guesses the secret of my heart!" (242), when Medley reminds him that some men "fall into dangerous relapses when they have found a woman inclining to another" (242). The "secret" of Dorimant's "heart" becomes at the end of the play the principal comic question, as we shall see in more detail.

2. Thus, following his seduction of Belinda:

MED. You have had an irregular fit, Dorimant?

DOR. I have.

Y. BELL. And is it off already?

DOR. Nature has done her part, gentlemen; when she falls kindly to work, great cures are effected in little time, you know.   (260)

the act of his "conversion" may possibly be approaching the initial position of the dupe. At beginning and end, however, the professed convictions of both call each other into question. In the total structure of the play they are mutually suspect because they are mutually oversimple. Neither of them gives an adequate account of Nature—either in its diversity as demonstrated by the differing worlds of the play or in its paradoxical potentials as demonstrated by the developments within those worlds. Yet the precise extent of falseness in the wit of either hero or dupe is part of the ambiguity in the resolution of the play. Loveit's concluding conviction that all men are villains or fools has as its immediate provocation the two "men of mode," Dorimant and Sir Fopling. She has just suffered the final "villainy" of the one in being exposed to the "impertinence" of the other. To this extent her conviction seems justified. Beyond that she has just witnessed the general acceptance of the hero as a very "civil" gentleman though he has in many and perhaps in all ways continued to the last to play the villain. In this respect her statement is justified by the total world of the play. Concerning the hero they have all—with the possible exception of the heroine—played the fool.

Nevertheless it is Loveit who does so last and most spectacularly. In calling Fopling a fool she has unwittingly fulfilled the intrigue of the hero against her and thus added the final stroke to the triumph of the "villain." Her wit has been at once wiser and more foolish than she knew, at once true and false. And its final if still equivocal obliquity derives chiefly from the fact that she remains to the last too passionate still. In this respect she assumes her closing relationship to the hero. Her conviction is juxtaposed with his avowal to the heroine: "But now my passion knows no bounds" (279). Whether this unbounded passion is in reality one still of conquest and power or now of love is, however, part of the concluding question.

The question has meanwhile been enlarged and more precisely defined by the further intrigues of the hero. His seduction of Belinda, as the second line of action in the major plot, establishes her as a second comic dupe. In doing so it enlarges the comedy of values. Unlike Loveit, Belinda is not the embodiment of passion or of courtly assumptions. Essentially she belongs to what we shall presently see is the traditional honest-man group of the minor plot. Her seduction becomes one aspect of Dorimant's power over and control of that world. But unlike the other members of it, she is drawn into the libertine-Machiavel orbit of the hero by her love. Knowing the folly of her actions, she not only succumbs to the hero but joins him in playing the Machiavel, thereby further contributing to her own undoing.[3] Her comedy in both respects

3. For the comedy of power between the hero and his dupe, see III.2, p. 227. For the comedy of the dupe as Machiavel, see II.2, particularly Belinda's closing lines in the

lies in the triumph of her passion over her reason. Her principal weakness in terms of value, however, is not the excess of passion but the capacity of her love to corrupt her understanding. While in these terms she has still a relationship to Loveit, she also prepares for the hero's third intrigue, his undertaking to seduce the heroine, Harriet.

In the hands of the heroine, Dorimant too undergoes the conflict between passion and reason which has been the characteristic lot of the comic hero—though the reason here, of course, is that of the libertine-Machiavel. But he is here again to be distinguished from his predecessors and from the customary Restoration practice. He has not, as we have seen, played the Machiavel primarily at the prompting of his reason—as a deliberate badge of his revolt from conventional morality or as a necessity for survival or even as a calculated device for libertine appetite. He has, like his dupe, Belinda, played the role chiefly at the prompting of his passion, though in his case the passion has been one less of "love" than of self-love. While his attraction to the heroine, then, involves a conflict between passion and reason, it is more fundamentally a conflict in passions—of love on one hand and power and control on the other.[4] Consequently the most immediate question at the end of *The Man of Mode* is not, as in the previous comedies, whether the hero's love will eventually prove to be only libertine appetite or something more. The question is still present, but it depends on the precedent consideration as to whether in his professed passion of love Dorimant is still playing the Machiavel. This, of course, is to ask whether his desire for conquest is still stronger than his desire for love. But it is also to ask what, for the hero, the nature of love itself involves—how much of its passion is assertion of self and how much is self-submission. As a result, while the course of his final intrigue calls into doubt the value of his previous convictions, it also questions the nature and value of his passion. In these terms the play, despite the special aspects of its treatment, continues a central interest in the Restoration comedy of manners.[5] And to this interest the heroine makes a significant contribution.

In itself the role of the heroine in *The Man of Mode* shows the least change from preceding practice of any character in the work, though it acquires fuller meaning through its expanded context. Like her predecessors, Harriet is the heroine chiefly because she has sufficient wit and self-control to withstand the assaults of the hero and to hold out, at least through the end of the play, for marriage. In contrast to the dupes, she has kept her virtue by refusing to be drawn into either the libertine

---

scene (218) and her earlier aside: "Now to carry on my plot; nothing but love could make me capable of so much falsehood" (212).

4. See his asides after each of his first two encounters with her—III.3, p. 237, and IV.1, p. 249.

5. For this interest, as for most of the others which characterize the genre, *The Way of the World* provides a culminating perfection of expression.

or Machiavellian elements of Dorimant's world. In these respects and in others she belongs to the traditional honest-man group of the minor plot. She thereby not only remains the final and crucial point of resistance in the hero's conquests but threatens to draw him into the world of honor from which he has seduced the dupes. Yet she is not herself entirely a member of the traditional honest-man world. She has much of the combativeness which characterizes the hero; she is almost as fond of and quite as skilled at dissembling as he; and she is far from immune to the pleasure of conquest and power. She has, that is, some of the nature and most of the art of the hero. And she shares in the "problem of passion" that runs through the characters and actions of the major plot. She has something of Loveit's intensity but with a greater self-control. And she has something of the dupe's courtly desires but with sufficient wit to understand their necessary limitations given the problematic nature of man and particularly the hero.[6] Finally, while she has something of Dorimant's pride and self-assertion, she has a greater willingness to submit herself to the "bonds" of love. She combines, in sum, distinctive attributes from the two basic worlds or plots of the play. At the close of the comedy, therefore, one possibility for hero and heroine is that they may combine the best of the two contrasting worlds —the passionate vitality of one and the stability, order, and honor of the other. But there is also the possibility, as further inspection will reveal more clearly, either of stalemate arising from a deadlock of opposing powers or of a continued war of conflicting aims in which one of the adversaries will finally become the conquered "victim" of the other. The element of passion involved in each of these eventualities remains for *The Man of Mode* as for Restoration comedy of manners at large the most pervasive source of doubt. Meanwhile its place in the play's scheme of values is further defined by the characters and actions of the minor plot.

The minor plot of *The Man of Mode* is divided into two groups of characters. In one is what we have called the traditional honest-man world—Young Bellair, Emilia, whom he unqualifiedly wishes to marry, and Lady Townley, whose house becomes the principal setting in which the several worlds of the play commingle. In the other are the two parents, Old Bellair and Lady Woodvil. As members of an older generation, and one should perhaps add of the landed gentry, the parents are opposed by all the other worlds of the play not only because they represent the "former age" but because they also represent the broadly prevailing world of established institutions and customs which has not

6. Thus in answer to Dorimant's vows of reform: "In men who have been long hardened in sin we have reason to mistrust the first signs of repentance" (278). And again, "Though I wish you devout I would not have you turn fanatic" (278-9).

heretofore been projected in the dramatis personae of Etherege's comedies but against which the world of the hero has from the first been in
revolt. As members of this older world the parents are further distinguished by lacking the temper, understanding, and manners of the
honest man. Yet they possess a set of moral attitudes which puts them
in a world of genuine honor. And in this respect they are like the honest-
man group of the minor plot but strikingly unlike the libertine-Machiavel world of the hero. In the play's comedy of values the parents represent one extreme for which the "mode" of the hero provides the
opposite. The traditional honest-man group stands between the two as
a mean and, in terms of the play's own values, the nearest approach to
an ideal. Consequently, while the deficiencies of the parents are to be
measured chiefly by their lack of true honest-man attributes, they serve
also to qualify the characteristics of the hero.

In the parents there is no discrepancy between appearance and reality.
Yet their inability to distinguish between the two and between art and
nature in the worlds about them consistently makes them the comic
dupes. They readily mistake the outward forms for the reality of love
in the mock courtship of their children (222–4). And Lady Woodvil
is as readily fooled by the dissembling of Dorimant in his assumed role,
calculated to win her favor, of "Mr. Courtage," a professed admirer of
"the forms and civility of the last age" (193). But while the parents
are here the dupes through the deficiencies of their particular world,
they emphasize the fact that the more fashionable worlds which reject
them are also fooled by appearance and art through a concern with
different values. In their disregard for the manners of the honest man,
the parents are the only ones not taken in by the modish surfaces of the
hero. This situation of give-and-take between the old world and the
new works, however, in different ways. One aspect of the elder Bellair's
attitude toward love and marriage is summed up in his request, "Please
you, sir, to commission a young couple to go to bed together a God's
name?" (280) "A God's name" sufficiently distinguishes the world of
the parents from that of the hero. But the assumptions involved concerning the desires of love are not very different from the appetitive
convictions of the libertine. For the problems posed by *The Man of
Mode,* both are inadequate.

Again the play gives an easy sanction to the revolt of its "young
couples" against the custom of parentally arranged and economically
motivated marriage. Old Bellair's "The rogues ha' got an ill habit of
preferring beauty" (223) states one aspect of the revolt. And he himself comically exposes the inconsistency in his world between custom
and nature as he also prefers beauty in becoming enamoured of Emilia.
At the same time his "undertaking" with her, a parallel to the activities
of the hero, is pointedly honorable. He not only wishes to marry her

but, for all his farcical lack of honest-man polish and restraint, possesses a genuine good will and good nature which contrasts with the very different character of the hero's undertakings.

Nevertheless the lack of the honest man's restraint and balance of temper remains a major deficiency in the parents' world of values. Old Bellair's ebullient good nature, in itself an essential requisite for the honest man, is entirely without the equally requisite self-control. It converts in an instant into impetuous fits of anger which relate him, despite the more ludicrous elements of his behavior, to the passionate excesses of Loveit (207). And his excesses in good nature itself make him the comic dupe. At the end of the play his ready acquiescence in being outwitted by his son's secret marriage contrasts with Dorimant's ill-natured revenge on Loveit for temporarily outwitting him. Yet by the same impetuous good nature with which he accepts his son's marriage, he also indiscriminately accepts both the hero and his modish companion, Medley: "Mr. Medley, my sister tells me you are an honest man, and, adod, I love you" (257). Medley, of course, is indeed an "honest man," but not in the sense in which Old Bellair through the values of his own world accepts him. Like the hero, Medley is one kind of honest man while Old Bellair is another. But in terms of traditional honest-man values and those of the play they are mutually aberrant.

Among these obliquities, the world of Young Bellair, Emilia, and Lady Townley stands in most respects as the true perpendicular.[7] That they are to be distinguished from the hero is repeatedly made clear in the opening scene. To Dorimant, Young Bellair is "handsome, well-bred, and by much the most tolerable of all the young men that do not abound in wit" (201). The alleged deficiency in wit lies partly, of course, in Bellair's desire to marry:

BELL. You wish me in heaven, but you believe me on my journey to hell.

MED. You have a good strong faith, and that may contribute much towards your salvation. I confess I am but of an untoward constitution, apt to have doubts and scruples, and in love they are no less distracting than in religion; were I so near marriage, I should cry out by fits as I ride in my coach, *Cuckhold, Cuckold,* with no less fury than the mad fanatic does *Glory* in Bedlam.

BELL. Because religion makes some run mad, must I live an atheist?
(199)

7. Dobrée, *Restoration Comedy,* p. 75, has seen that Young Bellair (presumably Emilia and Lady Townley would also be included) presents "the happy mean, or an indication of the most comfortable way to live." But this aspect of their role is not explored; and the interpretation offered for the play as a whole is very different from the one here proposed.

Though the wit of Medley, like that of the hero, seems to have more "art," Bellair's wit in the view of the play is the more nearly "true." It is not only a "happy mean"; it takes cognizance of Nature's diversity as neither Dorimant's libertine assumptions nor, at an opposing extreme, Loveit's courtly expectations do. And in the face of this diversity, the significant word is "faith." Dorimant initially has no faith. Like Medley, he is an "atheist." Loveit originally has too much and none at the end.

This same common-sense moderation continues to distinguish the world of the traditional honest man from that of the libertine-Machiavel. Thus when Young Bellair offers to "vow" his constancy—as the hero is throughout the play doing—he is prevented by Emilia:

EMIL. Do not vow—Our love is frail as is our life, and full as little in our power; and are you sure you shall outlive this day?
BELL. I am not, but when we are in perfect health 'twere an idle thing to fright ourselves with the thoughts of sudden death. (205–6)

In light of the play's own values, Emilia's awareness is an essential one. It constitutes a principal source of dubiety in the problems of love as viewed by the Restoration comedy of manners. It also bears an obvious relationship to the convictions of the libertine.[8] But Bellair's reply provides the common-sense complement. And here love is "health," not as for the hero a "fit" or, in the case of a prolonged seizure, a "disease." As a result, while the "passion" of the honest-man lovers is markedly less intense than in the other worlds of the play, it is far more stable and secure. Except for parental interference, Emilia and Young Bellair remain a point of calm in the midst of more violent extremes around them. While Dorimant and Loveit bitterly argue the relative merits of modish "wits" and "fools" as lovers, the honest-man world establishes the merits of lovers who are neither of these. And while Dorimant and Harriet exchange barbed accusations and establish elaborate conditions for "proof of passion," Emilia and Bellair quietly accept their faith in each other.

In other areas of professed value, however, the world of the traditional honest man and of the hero appear to be and to an extent are one. Young Bellair is "ever well-dressed, always complaisant, and seldom impertinent." Emilia "has beauty enough to provoke detraction; her carriage is unaffected, her discourse modest, not at all censorious nor pretending, like the counterfeits of the age" (202). These praises come from the "honest-man" world of Dorimant and Medley—with

8. The problem, of course, was also a subject of constant debate in the traditions of courtly love. This point is discussed in our subsequent inspection of pre-Restoration comedy.

what comic inconsistency will be apparent. Together with a long list of ethico-social characteristics such as "good humour," "kindness," "obligingness," they represent values subscribed to by both worlds, though in the world of the hero they are consistently corrupted by disparate assumptions and practices. They are values for the play only when, as in Emilia and Young Bellair, they establish a harmony between appearance and reality rather than a discrepancy. And in these terms they also serve to establish a harmony among Nature, Reason, and Art. They are part of the play's assumption not only that Nature's "degrees" must be kept by the restraint of Reason but that the "natural" balance and harmony of those degrees within the body social is also a matter of art. "Good breeding" in the face of Nature's diversity is an essential if social intercourse is to be "natural and easy." The code of manners for the honest-man values of the play, accordingly, is "Nature still, but Nature methodised." Terms like "unaffected" and "impertinence" look to the need of keeping degree. Others like "complaisance," "civility," "good nature," and lack of censoriousness reflect the need of tolerance in a natural harmony that encompasses diversity. In all these respects the world of Emilia and Young Bellair provides for *The Man of Mode* a norm in manners, wit, passion, and control which helps to define contrasting divergencies in the several worlds about them. They continue this role in the comedy which develops between the play's two "men of mode," Dorimant and Sir Fopling. But here they reveal also the fact that their world does not escape the perspective which sees them too as in certain ways defective.

In the hero and the dupe, the wit and the fool, the gentleman and the fop, Nature's diversity seems to exist at its most obvious extremes, though the extremes again reflect the play's shifts in concern. The ludicrous excesses of Sir Fopling look more to the manners and values of the honest man than to the libertine. The grossly libidinous predilections of the country knight are replaced by the sterility of the city fop in his overrefined devotion to the surfaces of clothes and social ritual.[9] These alterations have still a place, however, in the comedy of love. As the universally acclaimed "fool" in the total world of *The Man of Mode,* Sir Fopling involves a thematic term which works in many directions. But among them is the fact that he plays the fool in love. His attempted "intrigue" with Loveit—prompted by the hero as part of his own undertaking—ends, as we expect from the hero's dupe, in fiasco. Apart from his evident witlessness, he has played the fool because his only real desire in his undertaking was to conform to the ritual of the "mode." He is incapable of either "heroic" appetite or love. Yet his

9. Both types of dupe had, of course, been conspicuous features of Restoration comedy from its beginning, and are among the most obvious aspects of the traditions inherited from Jacobean and Caroline drama.

lack of both keeps him from playing the fool in other ways—as it has
been played by Loveit and Belinda and is perhaps being played by
Harriet or, from the libertine point of view, as it is possibly being
played at the end by the hero.[1] Since he is incapable of "passion," he
is also incapable of "the fall." When Loveit rebuffs his advances at the
close of the play by calling him a fool, he happily decides that "An
intrigue now would be but a temptation to me to throw away that vigour
on one which I mean shall shortly make my court to the whole sex in a
ballet" (285).

By his freedom from passion, Sir Fopling as fool acquires further
implications. Critics have long commented upon his "delightfulness."
"He is in himself a delight, presented from pure joy of him, and is not
set up merely as a target for the raillery of wiser fools." [2] But it would
seem to be very much as a target for wiser fools that he is "set up." A chief
source of his delightfulness is that of all the characters in the play he is
the most fully and naturally good humored. His open pride and vanity,
unlike these covert traits in the hero, are both innocuous and free of
guile. In his nature there is no drive for power and no Machiavellian
cunning. Yet he is repeatedly rejected by the wiser fools as they acclaim
the hero, whose surface good humor conceals his natural malice.[3] The
irony is heightened by the hero himself. Concerning the fool he suggests to an approving audience that "Nature has her cheats, stums a
brain, and puts sophisticate dulness often on the tasteless multitude for
true wit and good humour" (232). But it is clear at the moment and
throughout the play that Nature has her cheats in sophisticate charm as
well as dulness.

The comedy of values takes accordingly still another turn. Sir
Fopling's chief offense in terms of his relations to others is his "impertinence." He fails in his lack of restraint to keep decorum or degree.
But beneath the hero's surface control lies, of course, the most extreme
"impertinence." The fool and the hero are the only two characters in the
play who are persistently guilty of aggression—the one open, bump-
tious, and repelled, the other covert, mannered, and successful. We are
reminded thereby that for the hero the essential purpose of his restraint
is not moderation but indulgence, not the keeping of order but its violation. And while the fact enhances the comedy of appearance and reality,

1. Thus Belinda's "Well, were I minded to play the fool, he [Dorimant] should be
the last man I'd think of" (226) ; Loveit's "He [Dorimant] shall not find me the loving
fool he has done" (239) ; and Fopling's "Women are the prettiest things we can
fool away our time with" (252) bring the play's women, hero, and fop together in the
enveloping comedy.

2. Dobrée, *Restoration Comedy*, p. 73.

3. One of the obvious points of comedy here is that Fopling affects "malicious-
ness" in an attempt to comply with the "mode" of the hero (see III.3, p. 243). But
as the naturally good-humored fool, he is incapable of it.

it also extends the comedy of values in which the hero conquers the worlds of honor in the minor plot.

The lines of conquest involved are established in the opening scene of the play. Emilia's marriage to Young Bellair is to be encouraged by Dorimant in the hope that thereafter he may more easily seduce her (202). In the meantime Young Bellair's friendship is being cultivated for an additional reason.

MED. You and he are grown very intimate, I see.

DOR. It is our mutual interest to be so: it makes the women think the better of his understanding and judge more favourably of my reputation; it makes him pass upon some for a man of very good sense and I upon others for a very civil person.   (202)

Meanwhile in the world of the parents there remains to be won over Harriet's mother who, as a member of "the last age," shares the opinion of those in the present that Dorimant is "an arrant devil" (193). As the hero's three undertakings—with Loveit, Belinda, and Harriet— develop in the major action of the play, his undertakings with the two groups of the minor plot develop also. After Belinda, as part of her own intrigue with Dorimant, has witnessed his first "cruel" treatment of Loveit, she engages in the following conversation at Lady Townley's:

BEL. Well, that Dorimant is certainly the worst man breathing.

EMIL. I once thought so.

BEL. And do you not think so still?

EMIL. No, indeed!

BEL. Oh, Jesu!

EMIL. The town does him a great deal of injury, and I will never believe what it says of a man I do not know again, for his sake.

BEL. You make me wonder!

L. TOWN. He's a very well-bred man.

BEL. But strangely ill-natured.

EMIL. Then he's a very witty man.

BEL. But a man of no principles.

MED. Your man of principles is a very fine thing indeed!

BEL. To be preferred to men of parts by women who have regard to their reputation and quiet. Well, were I minded to play the fool, he should be the last man I'd think of.   (225–6)

The situation for Belinda is clear. It involves both her struggle between passion and reason and the comedy in which the character of the hero is rendered more equivocal by the dissembling of his critic. The most potent comedy, however, lies in his being defended by Emilia, though this situation too remains in part ambiguous. The eventual success of Dorimant's designs upon Emilia is left in question at the end of

the play. That he has found a "little hope" was indicated in the opening
scene. And Emilia's change of mind concerning him presumably
provides a basis of the hope. Yet by his own grudging admission he has
found her "a discreet maid" (202). And the play makes clear not only
that she is that and much more but that she is altogether in love with
Young Bellair, whom she marries. Nevertheless, since one of the realities in the play which remains fundamentally elusive is the ultimate
nature of love, Emilia's marriage raises rather than settles the question
of Dorimant's eventual success. He had himself promoted the marriage
with the conviction that "nothing can corrupt her but a husband. . . . I
have known many women make a difficulty of losing a maidenhead who
have afterwards made none of making a cuckold" (202). But whatever the eventuality in this regard, Emilia's defense of Dorimant here
promotes his conquests and expands the comedy of appearance and
reality.

At the same time it sharpens the comedy of values. Emilia and Lady
Townley have lost perspective among the various values of the honest
man. To Belinda's charge that the hero is both "ill-natured" and "a
man of no principles"—which he, of course, is—they offer no direct
refutation. Nor do they to Medley's "Your man of principles is a very
fine thing indeed!" They only suggest instead that Dorimant is, nevertheless, "a very well-bred man" and "a very witty man." For this world
of the honest man, the importance of manners has obscured the importance of morals, even though that world itself is essentially moral in
its actions and convictions.

Immediately following the scene in which Emilia has defended Dorimant, Young Bellair does the same. He is in the Mall with Harriet. She
is about to meet Dorimant for the first time, but she has already seen
and been captivated by him. He is here the subject of conversation:

HAR. I never saw anything in him that was frightful.
Y. BELL. On the contrary, have you not observed something extreme
   delightful in his wit and person?
HAR. He's agreeable and pleasant I must own, but he does so much
   affect being so, he displeases me.
Y. BELL. Lord, madam, all he does and says is so easy and so natural.
HAR. Some men's verses seem so to the unskilful, but labour i' the one
   and affectation in the other to the judicious plainly appear.
Y. BELL. I never heard him accused of affectation before. (Enter
   Dorimant and stares upon her)
HAR. It passes on the easy town, who are favourably pleased in him
   to call it humour.   (234)

Harriet's criticisms, like Belinda's, are accurate though complicated
by her own dissembling and affectation. But here it is Bellair who, like

Emilia in the scene before, is the center of the comedy, not only in being fooled by Dorimant's friendship and in being the instrument for sustaining his reputation, but in the superbly equivocal and thematically central irony of his phrase "so easy and so natural." These are fundamental terms in the traditional criteria of the honest man. But what is easy and natural for Dorimant is to play the hypocrite in appearing to have an "agreeableness" and "pleasantness" which in reality are far from natural for him. The phrase places him and his particular "honest-man" mode in critical juxtaposition with true honest-man values. It also makes clear, as the previous scene had done for Emilia and Lady Townley, the essential confusion and debility of Bellair's own honest-man sense of values which permit him and his world to be conquered by the hero.

The discussion between Bellair and Harriet serves as preface for Dorimant's third and last undertaking, the attempted seduction of the heroine. While the development of that action follows Etherege's customary pattern, its resolution is merged with and modified by the larger denouement in which the hero's several conquests are completed. In the last scene of the play, Dorimant's entrance and the final conditions of acceptance between hero and heroine have as prelude a song written by the hero himself. In part it reads:

> None ever had so strange an art
> His passion to convey
> Into a listening virgin's heart,
> And steal her soul away.   (277)

The "satanic" posture embedded in the verses' synthetic pastoralism ("As Amoret with Phyllis sat") catches many of the play's comic tensions.[4] But it specifically prepares for the denouement that follows. With an art not totally strange to the reader of Etherege's earlier plays but now more consummate and deeply ironic, Dorimant conveys his "passion" into the listening heart of the virgin heroine as he vows his surrender and reform: "By all the hope I have in you, the inimitable colour in your cheeks is not more free from art than are the sighs I offer." And again "I will renounce all the joys I have in friendship and in wine, sacrifice to you all the interest I have in other women—" (278).

When this undertaking is interrupted by the untimely arrival of both Loveit and Belinda, all Dorimant's intrigues are simultaneously threatened with exposure and he, like the earlier heroes, is threatened with reduction to the status of a dupe. For Dorimant too, however, his wit saves his reputation and restores his heroic status.

4. It catches also many of the "comic tensions" in the society of Etherege's time. The song is typical of the period's "courtly" love lyrics.

DOR. (to Lov.). I had trusted you with this secret, but that I knew the violence of your nature would ruin my fortune, as now unluckily it has. I thank you, madam.

LOV. She's an heiress, I know, and very rich.

DOR. To satisfy you I must give up my interest wholly to my love; had you been a reasonable woman, I might have secured 'em both and been happy.

LOV. You might have trusted me with anything of this kind, you know you might. Why did you go under a wrong name?

DOR. The story is too long to tell you now—be satisfied, this is the business, this is the mask has kept me from you.

BEL. (aside). He's tender of my honour, though he's cruel to my love.

LOV. Was it no idle mistress then?

DOR. Believe me, a wife, to repair the ruins of my estate that needs it.

LOV. The knowledge of this makes my grief hang lighter on my soul; but I shall never more be happy.

DOR. Belinda!

BEL. Do not think of clearing yourself with me, it is impossible. Do all men break their words thus?

DOR. Th' extravagant words they speak in love; 'tis as unreasonable to expect we should perform all we promise then, as do all we threaten when we are angry. When I see you next—

BEL. Take no notice of me, and I shall not hate you.

. . . . . .

DOR. We must meet again.

BEL. Never.

DOR. Never?

BEL. When we do, may I be as infamous as you are false. [The aside conversation with Belinda ends here.]

L. TOWN. Men of Mr. Dorimant's character always suffer in the general opinion of the world.

MED. You can make no judgment of a witty man from common fame, considering the prevailing faction, madam.

O. BELL. Adod, he's in the right.

MED. Besides, 'tis a common error among women to believe too well of them they know and too ill of them they don't.

O. BELL. Adod, he observes well.

L. TOWN. Believe me, madam, you will find Mr. Dorimant as civil a gentleman as you thought Mr. Courtage.

HAR. If you would but know him better—

(282–4)

The comedy here, of course, is rampant. The lie to Loveit saves Dorimant's reputation in two ways: She no longer believes he has "barbarously" abandoned her; and she accordingly rebuffs the advances of

Sir Fopling, thus completing the hero's control and conquest of the dupes. Medley's consequent, "Dorimant! I pronounce thy reputation clear, and henceforward when I would know anything of woman, I will consult no other oracle" (286), furthers the hero's triumphs by reinstating his supremacy within his own world. Medley's praise, in turn, would indicate that he, who should best know, does not take the professed "conversion" as more than continued stratagem. Were Dorimant about to fall into marriage, Medley, as an "atheist" in such matters, would hardly consider his reputation clear. Next, Belinda's "He's tender of my honour" continues the comedy. It was his own "honor" and vanity of which he was tender, but an essential part of his reputation and conquest is thus salvaged from the affair with Belinda. Again, Dorimant's reminder to Belinda concerning the "extravagant words" men speak in love casts its light upon the words he has just spoken to Harriet in avowing his passion. Finally, while Belinda's realization that Dorimant is "false" is immediately followed by the general assertion that he is "civil," the comedy in the hero's successes is climaxed by Harriet's "If you would but know him better—." Unconsciously the heroine herself thus underscores the comedy of Medley's own "malicious" wit concerning the "common error among women." But the result of all this is that the hero conquers his last enemy, Lady Woodvil. And the way is prepared for the closing lines:

L. WOOD. If his occasions bring him that way, I have now so good an opinion of him he shall be welcome.
HAR. To a great rambling lone house that looks as it were not inhabited, the family's so small; there you'll find my mother, an old lame aunt, and myself, sir, perched up on chairs at a distance in a large parlour, sitting moping like three or four melancholy birds in a spacious volery. Does not this stagger your resolution?
DOR. Not at all, madam. The first time I saw you you left me with the pangs of love upon me, and this day my soul has quite given up her liberty.
HAR. This is more dismal than the country!   (287)

It is part of the comedy of the hero and of the play that neither we nor perhaps the hero himself can be entirely certain as to what his real intentions have by this time come to be. But Harriet's dissembling to the last, while it may seem to augur well for her success, works another way. Dorimant's pangs of love and his soul's surrendering its liberty are dismal in more ways than Harriet in her final affectation can be aware. One recalls that with the "pangs of love" for the heroine upon him, the hero successfully pursued his seduction of Belinda; [5] that the

5. See IV.I, p. 254: "The hour is almost come I appointed Belinda, and I am not so foppishly in love here to forget: I am flesh and blood yet."

"forty days" which he had vowed at his first meeting with Harriet would be "well lost to gain your favour" (236) have only just begun; that for one whose soul has quite given up her liberty, the behavior with Belinda immediately preceding that avowal was something more than curious; and that in general the dubious nature of Dorimant's soul qualifies the possibilities of future action implied in the resolutions of Etherege's previous comedies. The play in its totality and particularly in the closing scene suggests that if the hero troubles at all to undergo his "trial"—a temporary endurance of the country—he will do so more for conquest than for love and that the country accordingly is more likely to become the setting for a "ruin" than a romance. Yet if the hero's protestations should prove sincere, the basic dubiety of the play still exists concerning the ultimate nature of love. Harriet's "dismal" echoes the reticences of Etherege's previous heroines; and her affectation in this respect looks forward to the same affectation in Congreve's Millamant, to the explicit problem of *The Relapse,* and to the continuity of interest for Restoration comedy of manners as a whole.

In this regard one further point remains which distinguishes *The Man of Mode* from Etherege's previous works. In the context of the play, Harriet's "melancholy" picture of the "country" becomes in certain ways a possible and paradoxical "symbol of fertility." If Dorimant is finally drawn into the country by love, his passion will at least to some extent have transcended the element of sterility and triviality which characterizes the total "city" milieu of the play. It is surely wrong to assume that Etherege was not aware of this sterility.[6] In the first two plays the libertine worlds were fully conscious of their own frivolity. It was an aspect of their assertion to themselves and to the conventional world from which they revolted that the traditional ideals which they rejected had been invalidated by the realities of man. But in *The Man of Mode* Lovett can banish "poor Mr. Lackwit but for taking up another lady's fan" without seeing anything comical in the situation (210), a state of affairs foreign even to the befuddled Lady Cockwood. The condition of the hero is not greatly different from the dupe's. Though he may take up the lady's fan, his greater "pleasure" is in provoking her to break it.[7] And while he has, unlike the dupe, some sense of the absurdity involved, there is nevertheless beneath his posturing a compulsive malice and vanity which, given their milieu, are more deeply absurd than the hero is aware. The demonic passions of a Don

6. This is the assumption made in L. C. Knight's essay, "Restoration Comedy: The Reality and the Myth," *Explorations* (London, Chatto & Windus, 1946), pp. 131–49, which cites as a characteristic deficiency of Restoration comedy rather than its society several of the points mentioned in the following paragraphs.

7. "There has been such a calm in my affairs of late I have not had the pleasure of making a woman so much as break her fan, to be sullen, or forswear herself these three days" (195).

Juan are now comic in part because they so willingly vent themselves in the trivialities of the drawing room and the Mall.

The world of Emilia, Young Bellair, and Lady Townley, in turn, is, for all its value as a "happy mean," unworthy of being conquered by any but a comic hero. Lady Townley's house is, as she herself states, "the common refuge of all the young idle people" (228). But the idleness of this middle world is not a conscious or comic revolt against anything. There is simply nothing better to do. For Lady Townley, Medley is a "very necessary man." He knows "all the little news o' the town" (207). Emilia "loves" to hear him "talk o' the intrigues; let 'em be never so dull in themselves, he'll make 'em pleasant i' the relation" (207). The comedy of love, of nature and art, of wit, passion, and control is everywhere conditioned by this comedy of manners. The comedy has, of course, those other facets which we have inspected—in the hero, the libertine-Machiavel beneath the manners of the honest man; in the world of Lady Townley, the capacity of manners to corrupt their own value and the value of a sanctioned morality which they in other ways express. But the final comedy of both concerns is that the society of the play, whether it pursues pleasure or power, does so in an endless and sterile round of play houses, parks, drawing rooms, and "all the little news o' the town."

This comedy, however, is again ambiguous, though now in a somewhat different sense. If the play insists upon the frivolity of its society, it suggests no adequate set of values by which that frivolity may be judged. A temporary endurance of the country is at best a partial and tentative antidote.[8] As envoy to Ratisbon, particularly during the final months of crisis in James' reign, Etherege was to take up the cause of something besides pleasure with a devotion, skill, and even passion which easily give the lie to much that has been said and written about him as a man.[9] But for all that, his own and man's real worth remained a matter of doubt. The comic dramatist certainly did not at any time return simply to "traditional" orthodoxy. If he saw the sterility of an idle leisure class devoted to pleasure and politesse, he also saw, even as

---

8. The proviso scene in *The Way of the World* is in this respect also a point of culmination for Restoration comedy of manners. It involves the explicit attempt of hero and heroine to come to some kind of meaningful terms with the trivial "ways" of their "world."

9. From Ratisbon in November of 1688, Etherege wrote, "At such a time as this a man is not to wait for instructions, but to hazard all to save his King and Country. I should be glad of a word now and then to encourage me [he had virtually none in the closing confusions of James' reign] but the want of that shall never coole the passion I have to perform my duty." The passion was not "dissembled." On his own initiative Etherege tirelessly urged his fellow diplomats at other posts in central Europe to exert "every effort" to save their "King and Country." (The quotations and the information come from a manuscript of Etherege's correspondence which the Houghton Library at Harvard University has permitted me to inspect.)

he worked valiantly in the midst of it, the sterility—the hypocrisy, cunning, pettiness, and amorality—in the traditionally worthier realms of man's endeavor and aspiration. Indeed, in the maze of political intrigue and malice which surrounded him at Ratisbon he could perceive a comedy of power, of Machiavellian ruthlessness garbed in politesse, of nature versus reason, and of man in the dark which was not fundamentally very different from the comedy of the leisure society in his plays. And there is no reason to suppose that he found the one world more noble and worthy and less comic than the other. He himself served them both, but without, one can be sure, believing fully in either. Thus the fact that his plays offer no adequate alternative to the frivolity which they expose would seem to indicate for their author the final comedy of man.

6

The Comic Language

I

THE LANGUAGE of Etherege's plays and of the Restoration comedy of manners as a whole divides with peculiar clarity into two distinct sets of literary characteristics. Provisionally we may label these the metaphoric and the nonmetaphoric. This is not to say merely that the language has its "logical" and its "poetic" components of meaning. In such terms, both aspects of the language are "poetic." Indeed, we shall find that they organize the experience of the plays at much the same level of awareness, with much the same meaning, and fundamentally in much the same manner. But their precise rhetorical characters are distinct, and they complicate the logical surfaces of the language in somewhat different ways.

If, for the moment, we view the "nonmetaphoric" language as constituting a distinct mode of expression, we can see at once that it has several salient characteristics. We may briefly summarize them here before investigating them in detail.[1] The language is, first of all, prevailingly "substantive" in nature. The verbs, even when they are not merely connective or "copulative," seldom carry the weight of the meaning. The weight is consistently in the nouns or in adjectives derivative from them. As a result, the language at its surface does not characteristically seem to express movement or change. The components of experience seem fixed and discrete. The sense of experience expressed by the language appears to be more a matter of "being" than "becoming." Second, it is not a sensuous language. It is only sporadically interested in projecting the immediate and concrete surfaces of experience. As a rule it deliberately abstracts that level of experience into generalized classes and categories.[2] It is concerned, that is, to express

1. It is perhaps necessary to stress that the following statements are generalizations based upon predominant characteristics in the plays. For most of the generalizations here and elsewhere in this chapter, one can find, of course, specific exceptions. But careful inspection of the language will reveal, I believe, the justness of the observations made.

2. Among the exceptions to this generalization are a few passages often cited as Etheregean language at its "best"—usually with the implication that the passages are somehow typical. Conspicuous here is Medley's extended description of Harriet in *The Man of Mode* (p. 193). But in its degree of particularity and "sensuousness" the passage is not only exceptional but unique in Etherege's play.

directly and explicitly the generalized attitudes and values of the comic worlds which we have already examined: Nature, love, honor, wit, malice, passion, good humor, impertinence, and so on through a long list of constantly recurring terms with which we are familiar. Third, therefore, the language must be primarily concerned with establishing relationships among those terms. The tone and rhetorical structure thus become assertive, "indicative" in "mood." And since the realities and values of the comic world are pervasively schematized, both the words and the rhetorical patterns by which their relationships are expressed also assume a schematic and oppositional character. Wit and fool, gentleman and fop, reason and passion, good nature and malice, virtue and vice are, at the level of diction, the immediately expressed "raw stuff" of experience. And the shape and mold of the experience projected is the sum of their relationships. These relationships being schematic and oppositional, the whole movement of the language becomes one of persistent parallelism or balance: "He knows so much of virtue as makes him well accomplished for all manner of vice" (7). Or, with a double balance, "Blockheads are as malicious to witty men as ugly women are to the handsome" (211). Or, again, in a more elaborate and less precise balance, one of Dorimant's speeches to Loveit: "Good nature and good manners corrupt me. I am honest in my inclinations, and would not, were't not to avoid offence, make a lady a little in years believe I think her young, wilfully mistake art for nature, and seem as fond of a thing I am weary of as when I doted on't in earnest" (216). The parallelism is not at all times, of course, so pronounced.[3] But a continuous preoccupation with the generalized and schematized level of experience here noted results in a pervasive parallelism throughout Etheregean comedy. This characteristic, indeed, becomes more prominent with each successive play.

It is not to our purpose to anatomize the precise rhetorical nature of this parallelism or to examine the kinds of variation which the language manifests within this general characteristic. The point here is simply that the movement of the language, like the diction, is not concerned with the immediate and sensory world of experience. It is part of an impersonalized and highly formalized ordering of general classes and abstractions. And its chief business is to establish relationships in nonsensuous and rational terms.[4] At the same time, the direct and relatively uninvolved form of the parallelism, together with a highly normalized syntax and general word order, establishes an insistent,

3. It is less pronounced in Etherege than in any other major comic dramatist of the Restoration.
4. It is important to note how this abstracting quality of the language works in projecting the presumably personal emotions of the characters. Thus Loveit's rage when Dorimant proves "unfaithful": "Faithless, inhuman, barbarous man"; "Without sense of love, of honour, or of gratitude," etc. (214).

repetitive movement in the language. We may note this even in a passage having less marked parallelism and balance than most. (The passage is from the opening scene of *The Man of Mode*.)

MED. He is like many others, beholding to his education for making
  him so eminent a coxcomb; many a fool had been lost to the world
  had their indulgent parents wisely bestowed neither learning nor
  good breeding on 'em.

BELL. He has been, as the sparkish word is, brisk upon the ladies
  already; he was yesterday at my Aunt Townley's, and gave Mrs.
  Loveit a catalogue of his good qualities under the character of a
  complete gentleman, who, according to Sir Fopling, ought to dress
  well, dance well, fence well, have a genius for love-letters, an
  agreeable voice for a chamber, be very amorous, something discreet, but not over-constant.   (200–1)

We shall later see that the character of this general movement contributes in a particularly important way to the comic expressiveness of the language. What we need here to note is that in this and the other verbal characteristics mentioned we have what are usually considered classic nonmetaphoric qualities of prose. But in that case we must ask how the prose is "literary"—or, more to the immediate point, how it is dramatically expressive. To answer the question we shall need to drop the term "prose" and take up the distinction between the language of logic and the language of literature. The distinction is sufficiently commonplace not to require elaboration. But the emphases we shall wish to make prompt one observation.

It is the peculiar characteristic of literary language, not so much to displace words from their established and referential frames of meaning —since it is in the nature of words that their referential meanings persist—as to "disturb" the conventional frames of reference through new or more extended signification. It is in these terms that the language of metaphor is considered the language par excellence of literature, though the fact raises the question as to whether all literary language —and therefore literature—is not finally "metaphoric." At any rate our present concern is to note that while the "nonmetaphoric" language of Etheregean comedy is ordering the comic experience of the plays in a fashion which at its surface seems to be, and to an extent is, that of logical discourse, it is also ordering it in a distinctly literary way. More precisely, while the terms of the language, together with surface line and texture, are establishing what seems to be a clear and logically coherent order of experience, the language at another level is consistently confusing that order by "disturbing" the ordinary referential frames of meaning. Out of this situation comes a new and final order of meaning which at the verbal level is the play. It has emerged from the

interplay between the logical surfaces of the language and forces working across it. And this general situation corresponds to the dramatic
structure and meaning of the play, since, we have seen, Etheregean
comedy as a whole is concerned with disturbing and reordering the
apparently logical order of its comic world. We shall return to this
situation in more detail. For purposes of clarification, however, we may
note here a relatively simple case.

   In the opening scene of *The Man of Mode,* Dorimant tells his friend,
Medley, "Next to the coming to a good understanding with a new
mistress, I love a quarrel with an old one" (195). At the surface of the
language the statement seems in its clear, assertive balance, to contribute in an explicit and logical way to the portraying of the "honest-
man" world of the comic hero. It announces, for example, the libertine's
"variety" in love as an aspect of the pursuit of pleasure. It also establishes, as twin aspects of that pursuit, the pleasure of the senses and the
pleasure of "warfare." But in the context of the play the full meaning
of "good understanding," apart from a possible phallic pun, is highly
equivocal. It cuts across the logical order of the statement in such a
way as to undermine the surface relationships and schematic distinctions of the terms "new mistress" and "old one," "good understanding"
and "quarrel." And out of this disordering emerges a new and final
order at the level of the play's comic meaning.

   By "good understanding" Dorimant means, of course, that the new
mistress—like the old one previously—yields to his persuasions. The
first equivocation concerns the terms on which the "good understanding" is reached: whether, for example, they are libertine ("follow nature," "appetite," gratification of the senses, liberty, the philosophy of
"use," etc.) or whether they are "courtly" ("honor," "passion," "soul,"
constancy, obligation, gratitude). In either event, however, the fact
of Dorimant's libertine convictions and actions within a double-standard
society makes clear that there can be no good understanding on the
part of the lady if she is foolish enough to yield on either set of terms.
The play's exposition, in fact, has already made sufficiently clear that
the good understanding in Dorimant's winning a new mistress must
be as much a quarrel as his breaking off with an old one. We are accordingly prepared for the "witty sex battles" which will ensue in the
play's development. Dorimant's three "mistresses" in the play ex-
haustively explore the implications of these equivocalities. Loveit's
"good understanding" on courtly terms proves to be ignorance. Belinda's yielding proves not to be a matter of coming to an understanding
at all, but the weakness of reason yielding to passion. Harriet's wiser
understanding, together with her control, produces a situation of at
least temporary if not permanent stalemate. But further, and as a part
of all this, the play's exposition before Dorimant's speech has prepared

us to ask whether, on the part of the hero himself as well as his mistresses, there is not bad rather than good understanding. Working across the apparently logical surfaces of the statement, in other words, is a set of questions concerning not only the fashionable "mode" but man: the question of true understanding, the relationship of reason to passion, of nature to social and moral order. The reordering and final comic meaning which emerges from these equivocalities relates not only to the "honest-man" world of the hero but to the comic world of man. It suggests, for example, that true understanding and true fulfillment are incompatible with unrestrained liberty and "warfare."

To an extent in the preceding chapters, we have seen this verbal tug-of-war in progress in the plays; and the instances of verbal irony and ambiguity which we have inspected make clear its chief structural source. The alleged realities and values in the "honest-man" world of the comic heroes are expressed in large part by terms which draw upon other realities and values very different from those of the libertine "honest man." Consequently these other frames of meaning—the traditional honest man, the courtly, the heroic, the Christian and classical humanist—provide, in effect, a constant reservoir of ambiguities upon which any of a vast number of words may draw, but the precise meaning of which will be conditioned by the particular verbal and dramatic context. Nature, art, reason, passion, love, honor, wit are a few of the more central terms in which we have seen something of this operation. Thus the equivocalities of this nonmetaphoric language create a literary situation which has certain properties resembling the metaphor. A chief difference is that, though the "vehicles" (the nonlibertine references) are never overtly expressed, there may be as many as four or five brought simultaneously into relationship with the "tenor" (the surface libertine assertion). Consequently the tensions among the several frames of reference and the synthesis which resolves them frequently become highly complicated and charged with comic meaning. The result in a general way, of course, is an emerging definition of the libertine "honest-man" world in terms of its relationship to all the other worlds which the language juxtaposes with it. But this means of definition has a peculiarly comic value. For the characters in the play, it provides repeatedly a kind of comic reversal—the strong, direct, assertive movement of the parallelism and balance, broken by the disruptive intrusion of the meaning in depth. For the play, the final effect is a synthesis of meaning which has something of the order, clarity, and logic of one and the density and complexity of the other.

To illustrate more fully this thus far largely abstract account, we may briefly return to Dorimant's speech, quoted above: "Good nature and good manners corrupt me. I am honest in my inclinations, and would not, were't not to avoid offence, make a lady a little in years believe I think her young, wilfully mistake art for nature, and seem as fond of a thing I am weary of as when I doted on't in earnest" (216). The speech is typical of the language of the play, though the extent to which the particular character and situation add their influence will be apparent. For example, Dorimant has himself, of course, consciously inverted some of the terms. He asserts that he is "corrupted" into being too kind, though he knows—and wishes Loveit to know—that in asserting his kindness, he is actually asserting his malice. Consequently, in the surface sense, he is not corrupt. But beneath the surface inversions lies a network of further implications. Though they still have distinctive meaning for Dorimant as a particular character, they involve his entire "honest-man" world in a series of searching equivocalities. At one level "Good nature and good manners corrupt me" remains a simple inversion for that world. It could never be "kind," as Dorimant is here pretending he is. Further, the whole speech, like Dorimant's general treatment of Loveit, is sufficiently malicious to make clear that he and his world have no real good nature and good manners by which to be corrupted. Yet the very skilled expression of the speech itself provides ample evidence that Dorimant, and his world, have an abundance of "good manners," but carefully corrupted in use. The traditional and the modish honest man are here illuminating each other; and in doing so, they define at a new level of meaning the modish world of the play.

The speech also raises the whole involved question of nature and manners, so central to Dorimant, the play, and Restoration comedy. Since there are at least two very different "natures" in the play, their diverse relationships to manners play upon the equivocalities of Dorimant's general assertion and upon the question of corruption. And this, in turn, leads to "I am honest in my inclinations." He isn't honest, of course, in the traditional sense; he is only "honest." Yet—though here Dorimant and his world have less of a case than the earlier Etheregean "heroes"—he might assert that he *is* the most honest man in acknowledging that the world is made up of "villains and fools" and in acting accordingly. The play's entire set of value oppositions, based upon opposing postulates concerning nature, comes here into focus.

But now "inclinations" comes into the picture. The term reminds us that from one point of view Dorimant is by real inclination honest neither in the traditional nor the modish sense. Even in his own "world" he must conceal his natural inclination to malice beneath the modish surface of "honesty" in order to give the malice outlet. Thus his surface civility is the result of restraint acting as stratagem—not direct inclination. At the same time the term focuses upon the inconsistency of surface good nature as a modish requisite in this world. For we have seen that the insistence on good nature was not entirely a Machiavellian device. It looked to a set of values curiously at odds with the libertine-

Machiavel assumptions concerning nature. This in turn reminds us that Dorimant's "wilfully mistake art for nature" is a final summing up not only of the problem of art and nature, but of all the other questions raised by the earlier terms of the speech. Dorimant confidently assumes, beneath his own conscious irony, that he has not mistaken art for nature—with respect either to Loveit's beauty or to his own ideas of reality and value—but that his own art is so skillful that others will. Thus he has at least willfully divorced art from nature, if not mistaken one for the other. He has used art, that is, to conceal nature.[5] The play, however, has long before this made clear that Dorimant in doing so has in a fundamental sense mistaken art for nature also. Good manners and good nature are a *part* of nature when the inclination is truly honest.

The intricate verbal situation in Dorimant's speech does not, of course, prevail at every point in Etherege's plays.[6] But in kind, if not in degree, it typifies the most conspicuous "literary" characteristic of the nonmetaphoric language. And there are throughout the plays passages at least as involved as the excerpt which we have examined. In the simplest cases the situation frequently appears to be nothing more than an inversion. The constant reference to the "good-natured town," for example, seems simply an assertion that the "town" is really malicious. Yet the town *is* "good-natured" at its surfaces, partly as a Machiavellian device but partly because it does, paradoxically, consider good nature to be an absolute value—even though, in effect, its demands stop at surface requirements only. What, therefore, appears at first glance to be a simple verbal inversion actually sustains and defines many of the central concerns of the play—among them, of course, the comedy of appearance and reality.

Beyond this simplest type of situation the degrees of involvement vary. But the verbal comedy at some level of intricacy repeatedly cuts across what at first glance appears to be the clear and logical order of the language. Thus Dorimant's laconic "Kind," when he has finally won Belinda's consent, brings the "mode," the traditional honest man, and courtly love into an elaborate interplay of comic meaning (227). An extended set of terms draw in a similar manner upon these three frames of reference and frequently upon the less specialized ones of general Christian and classical values as well—"obliging," "goodwill," "gratitude," and so on. But there are other terms which relate to

5. In the particular case considered here, he has also in a sense used art to reveal nature. That is, he has wished to let his natural malice "shine through" the polished surfaces of his "good manners." But except with Loveit, to whom his nature is already known, this is seldom the use to which Dorimant puts his art. Its general function, we have already seen, is to conceal.

6. It is least prevalent in the first play and most prevalent in the second. In the third, the comic irony and ambiguity in the characters' speeches depend to a larger extent than in the earlier plays upon the dramatic situation.

virtually all the major frames of reference and which can repeatedly
create, therefore, a still greater density than that in the speech of Dorimant just examined. Perhaps the most persistent and central of those
terms is "honor." In *She Would If She Could,* we have seen that this
word is thematically the central one. It reticulates throughout the play
in verbal situations of the type we have considered. The following
example of its use will indicate how a single word in dramatic context
can acquire the subtlety, counterpoint, and overtones of an extended
"conceit."

In the second act of *She Would If She Could,* Lady Cockwood awaits
impatiently the arrival of Courtal. Through his stratagem of "flight-in-
pursuit" he has been obliged to make an appointment with her—at
which, it is her intention, he shall have the opportunity of cuckolding
her husband, who is also Courtal's professed friend. Courtal's failure
to arrive at the appointed hour gives rise to Lady Cockwood's fear of
disappointment and to her "courtly" conviction that her "servant" is
"ungrateful," "insensible," "perfidious." A knock, however, revives
her hopes, and she sends Sentry to the door with "Peace, he may yet
redeem his honour" (110).

The ambiguities of the word "honour" reflect in epitome here again
certain ironies and oppositions that are fundamental to the play as a
whole, to Etheregean comedy, and to the Restoration comedy of manners. What appears at first glance to be merely an inversion ("dishonor" would seem the proper word) must actually be taken as at once
inverted and not inverted. And in each position the word brings into
significant relationship a variety of conflicting references. In the
"courtly" pose of Lady Cockwood, Courtal has avowedly confessed
himself her "servant," so that an entire set of specialized values and
assumptions—"gratitude," "constancy," "devotion," etc.—do indeed
oblige him in "honor" to fulfill his "lady's" expectations. But these
considerations are tangentially related to a less specialized set of values.
Courtal has made an explicit commitment, and the honor simply of his
"word," of fulfilling an assumed obligation, is also at stake. This consideration, in turn, extends into the specialized honor of the modish
"honest man." "Barbarousness," as a matter of purely expedient policy,
of efficacious "reputation," is to be avoided. Fidelity to a commitment
is even in this frame of reference a necessary point of "honor."

But the word, of course, looks the other way, too—not only in the
obvious and conventional senses, but in terms of the inverted "heroic"
and "honest-man" values in the world of the play. For if Lady Cockwood's stratagem succeeds, not only will Courtal's fail, but those dis-
criminations of appetite and taste by which the hero and the dupe are
distinguished will have been violated. In both instances the hero-dupe
relationship will, in fact, be reversed, with an obvious destruction of

"honor" for the hero. Thus once more the implications of a single word reflect microcosmically a central insight and a fundamental aspect of structure for the play as a whole. Beneath a superficial opposition and equivocality, the word establishes a paradoxical similarity in reality and value. Implied as a "synthesis" of the terms, in other words, is the inescapable necessity of honor, of obligation, whatever the particular "world" may be. The implications propose that in any context of values sheer individualism, unencumbered by duty or obligation, is a social impossibility. The practical necessity of restraint for fulfillment—at whatever level—is asserted. Some of the basic inconsistencies of the "honest man" mode are accordingly projected through a verbal complexity in depth. The logical surface of the language has been disturbed by a set of ambiguities which resolve into a kind of comic synthesis.

II

The prominence of certain types of imagery in the Restoration comedy of manners has been customarily noted by students of the plays. But the contributions of that imagery to the comic expressiveness of this body of drama has not been much explored. We may begin such an exploration by noting in the world of Etherege's plays, as in the Restoration society which it reflects, the fashion of the "comparison" or "similitude." As employed in both the drama and its age, the term included types of comparisons which are not commonly considered to be strictly metaphoric: fools are to wits as ugly women to handsome. This type of comparison accounts for much of the persistent balance and parallelism in the general structure of the language, and is a principal means of constructing at the verbal level the play's comic world of logically schematized and abstract terms. We should note, however, that while this particular class of similitudes is not strictly and overtly metaphoric, it frequently involves by the nature of its terms a metaphoric process which cuts across the logical surfaces of the comparison.[7] In Harriet's statement—"Women then [when they are ugly] ought to be no more fond of dressing than fools should be of talking" (219)—the explicit comparison involves merely two examples of violating "decorum" or "degree." But there is an implied relationship between the terms which brings them together in a metaphoric synthesis. The dressing in one case becomes a kind of talking, the talking a kind of dressing; and the fools and the women are brought

7. This situation will, of course, exist to some extent in any comparison where the terms are at all susceptible to such a process. The point here is that Etherege's plays and the Restoration comedy of manners deliberately employ comparisons whose terms can so interact.

together in a way which enlarges and particularizes the general relationship explicitly asserted.

Most frequently the type of comparison or similitude which is not
overtly or entirely metaphoric in nature serves one of two general functions. First, for a variety of comic purposes, it may compare aspects of
the world of the play to other "worlds" outside the general milieu of
the comedy—as, for example, in Gatty's similitude, "I perceive he
[Freeman] runs in thy head as much as a new gown uses to do in the
country the night before 'tis expected from London" (168). Explicitly,
the comparison twits Ariana for a "country-like" enthusiasm for her
"gallant." But the most trenchant comparison lies outside the explicit
logic of the statement, and implies, of course, that gallants are like
gowns, with a host of significances for the characters and the play which
are too obvious to require elucidation. Frequently the metaphoric
process is more apparent: Courtal is aware that Lady Cockwood's
promoting the acquaintance of the heroes and heroines is as unlikely as
"that an old rook should bring a young snap acquainted with his bubble" (104–5). Here, of course, the function in part is to suggest the
comic "value" to Lady Cockwood of her "gallant." But, like many of
the comparisons which relate outside worlds to those of the play, the
function is more extended. It establishes the conniving and trickery
which are part of the world of the play; but it also suggests that
these are only aspects of man and society at large—not merely of a
specialized world. The character and import of the play's world tends
thus to be generalized into larger areas of experience. The conniving
within the play becomes one aspect of the larger reality of "rooks"
and "snaps."

The second common employment of the similitude which is not
strictly metaphoric in form is to define aspects of the comic world's
general milieu which cannot be or are not objectified in the play:
"Beauty runs as great a risk exposed at Court as wit does on the stage,
where the ugly and the foolish all are free to censure" (249). At the
logical level the addition of Court and stage to the comic world is
important, together, of course, with the emphasis upon malice. But the
metaphoric implication which cuts across the logical surface is that
the Court is like a stage, with consequent suggestions which support
major images and concerns of the play: the "game," appearance and
reality, and so on. In point of number, these types of comparisons are
conspicuous among the metaphoric or quasi-metaphoric aspects of the
language. But their main task is to assist in constructing the comic
worlds of the plays at the logical level of meaning. Their contribution
to the "disturbing" or complicating of that level is relatively slight.

When we come to the fully metaphoric language, we find that it brings directly into the play all the traditional frames of thought and value in terms of which the "honest-man" world is formed. It accomplishes overtly what the "nonmetaphoric" language accomplishes by implication. Like that language, too, but again overtly rather than by implication, it defines the character of the comic world by bringing two or more frames of reference into ironic juxtaposition. The logical surfaces of the language are thus once more "disturbed," but now the complicating process is "lineal" as well as in "depth," since the metaphoric relationships tend to be rhetorically extended rather than compact. And the imagery tends, in its extension, to assume much the same marked balance and direct, repetitive movement as the nonmetaphoric. In this movement it provides concreteness for the abstract terms at the other level of expression; and here again a comic irony is likely to be established between the suggested "realities" of the abstract language and the specific body given to them by the imagery. For example, the "passion" proposed at the abstract level characteristically becomes mere animal appetite at the level of metaphor. Or "honor," in its suggestion of the "heroic," becomes a matter of the hero's marching "bravely at the rear of an army of link-boys" (6). Some of these general characteristics of the imagery require further comment.

One of the most frequent types of image in Etheregean comedy expresses naturalistic attitudes toward love, women, marriage. This, of course, is part of the libertine's postulates concerning nature. But the naturalistic imagery of the plays persistently makes clear that libertine nature has also become Hobbesian or "Machiavellian"—of however comic variety: [8] "Since we know the bush, why do we not start the game" (104); "These deer cannot herd" (106); "Who the devil that has common sense will go a-birding with a clack in his cap" (155). The lover is a kite hovering about a "backside, watching an opportunity to catch up the poultry" (154). Or the two lovers may "fall to and love, as gamecocks fight" (224). In general, the first and most obvious comic incongruity in such images lies merely in their violation of conventional expectations. And their comic expressiveness in this respect would be much the same with or without the specific context of the plays. Within that context, however, the incongruity becomes important as an expressed awareness of conventional ideals violated by reality. And it takes in this respect an extra turn, since it consciously expresses the fact that the sensual pursuit of pleasure by the libertine

8. The naturalistic sex imagery is, as one might expect, considerably less common in *The Man of Mode* than in the earlier plays. Sex, as we have seen, is in Etherege's final comedy more a matter of power than of sensual gratification; and the imagery reflects the fact. Further, Dorimant's more persistent posture and guile as a courtly lover tend to keep the libertine's naturalistic convictions concerning sex submerged beneath the verbal surfaces of the play. Finally, the presence of three nonnaturalistic "worlds" conditions, of course, the total imagery of the play.

is no naturalistic state of bliss, but a very Hobbesian state of war. While the imagery, then, expresses the revolt of the modish "honest man" from conventional ideals, it makes clear his awareness that his own espoused "reality" is also far from ideal. The imagery can, therefore, at once deprecate conventional assumptions and the assumptions of the libertine "honest man."

Much the same situation exists for the "heroic" imagery. We have seen that the comic "undertaking" is given an inverted heroic or mock-heroic caste. This aspect of the play in terms of character and action is supported by the imagery: Sir Frederick "vanquishes" the constable and "massacres" the windows—"most honourable achievements, such as will be registered to your eternal fame by the most learned historians of Hick's Hall" (6). In the heroic battles the "trumpet sound[s] a charge to this dreadful foe" (16); the heroes become "men-of-war . . . cruising . . . for prizes" (106); or, in completely stock images, they lay "sieges," storm "cities," and send and receive "challenges" which "must not in honour" be ignored (156). The consistent stress here, of course, is upon the "heroic" in "warfare." And the conscious irony by which the plays' "honest men" at once deprecate their own and the traditionally heroic values modulates into the ironies of the Hobbesian-Machiavellian natural state of war. Consequently at the non-metaphoric level of the language, the abstractions which define the character of the comic world in terms of the heroic are further complicated by the intrusion of the "nature" of the beast. Such terms as "courage," "valor," "defiance," and above all, "honor" become not only mock-heroic aspects of the "undertaking," but inverted terms for Hobbesian warfare and Machiavellian intrigue.

In the Christian imagery of the plays the same general situations prevail. Most commonly at the overtly metaphoric level, the Christian imagery assumes implications also of the courtly in defining the character of the "honest-man" world.[9] To Harriet's question, "Could you keep a Lent for a mistress?" Dorimant replies, "In expectation of a happy Easter" (236). In some respects the imagery in this particular instance is not typical of the general metaphoric language of the plays. "Lent" and "Easter" have a density which is more like the abstractions of the nonmetaphoric language. In terms of comic meaning, the force of the images operates in precisely the same way. But as in the less intricate Christian imagery also, they support and give specific body to a large set of ambiguously charged abstractions operating throughout the plays: "heaven," "hell," "sin," "grace," "fall," "faith," "fa-

9. Generically speaking, the use of Christian imagery to express courtly love attitudes and values had, of course, been traditional since the Middle Ages. Much of the Christian-courtly imagery in the Restoration comedy of manners reveals this traditionalism. But the dramatic contexts serve to specialize the significance of the juxtaposition in ways which are here explored.

natic," "atheist," "devout." The Lent-Easter witticism embodies, in fact, the whole ironic grace-fall-regeneration archetype which characterizes the total comic structure of the plays. And the comment it makes upon the world of the play summarizes the general import of both the Christian abstractions and the Christian imagery. It summarizes, indeed, the central import of Etheregean comedy. It deserves, therefore, to be considered in more detail.

At the surface of the image is, of course, a set of courtly assumptions with Christian overtones : The devoutness of the lover, the self-sacrifice, the final and transcendent fulfillment. But combined with these are a set of distinctly Christian assumptions which also have courtly applications : repentance, atonement, and rebirth. At these levels alone, the point is obvious. The application of either courtly or Christian values to the world of Dorimant makes a sufficient comment in itself. But the customary inversions are again in the imagery. Harriet is obliged, like the earlier heroines, to qualify expectation and desire with libertine reality. And Dorimant's "Easter" is scarcely, at this stage at least, either courtly or Christian. The disparity underlines with greater firmness than in the earlier plays the unquestionable deficiencies of the comic world projected. And it catches the central ironies of character, action, and values in the play : the definition of the comic world by traditional frames of value which reveal not only its character but its inconsistencies and its deficiencies ; the ambiguity of the curve of action (from grace to fall, or from fall to grace) ; the comic uncertainty of man as to either his own nature or his own desires.

III

It is apparent that what we have here been discussing as a "literary" use of language in Etherege's plays is a matter of wit. The language, in other words, is most conspicuously literary by virtue of being witty. From Aristotle to Freud, wit has been considered as the perception of similarities in things dissimilar.[1] What is implied in such a definition is that the dissimilarities are superficially much more marked than the similarities (Dr. Johnson's "occult" resemblances), so that a distinct sense of incongruity exists in the comparison. Consequently the force of the wit may lie merely in the marked differences of the objects. But better still, it may lie in the extent to which both likeness and difference are insisted upon at once. Thus the question of wit impinges upon the question of metaphor.[2] And the two become merged points of interest in the poetry of such a writer as Donne.

1. Or of dissimilarities in things similar. See "Spectator #62," *The Works of . . . Joseph Addison,* ed. Henry G. Bohn (London, 1856), *2,* 357–62.

2. See I. A. Richards' discussion of the metaphor, *The Philosophy of Rhetoric,* (Oxford Univ. Press, 1936), p. 125.

As the term "wit" is most currently used today, however, and as it has been generally applied to the Restoration comedy of manners, it means essentially comic wit. And that in turn would seem to mean that in the wit, as in comedy at large, the incongruities involve a minification which operates upon one or both of the objects compared.[3] The point will help to distinguish comic wit from wit that is not comic. The peculiar power of much of Donne's wit, for example, lies to a considerable extent in the fact that a comparison which by conventional associations and values would be expected to minify the "tenor," serves instead to enlarge it. One should not, presumably, have much trouble in being comically witty about a pair of lovers and a pair of compasses. But Donne has established by his comparison a kind of sublimity in the realm of the potentially ludicrous. The wit is not comic because the poet has kept the minifying power of the "vehicle" suppressed or, as it were, just beneath the surface. Had he permitted some of the potentially ludicrous to materialize, he might then have had comic wit of some complexity.

For, again as with comedy in general, the simpler forms of comic wit merely diminish the object of the witticism. But a more complex form will establish an ambivalence which derives from a simultaneous movement toward diminishment and augmentation. In the field of comedy at large, the distinction will mark a central difference, for example, between Jonson's most characteristic comedy and that of Shakespeare. In terms of character it separates in one essential way Bobadil and Falstaff. Indeed, it is quite apparent that those comic characters whom we instinctively choose as greatest possess almost invariably a marked ambivalence—Falstaff, Don Quixote, Alceste, Parson Adams, Emma, and so on through the list. It is an essential of the comic hero (or comic heroine), in fact, that he have this ambivalence. His attitudes and actions serve, on the one hand, to criticize his society; but they serve on the other to criticize himself. If they do only the former, the character is not comic; if they do only the latter, he is no hero. As an aspect of his ambivalence of character his wit, if he has any, will also be ambivalent. It may sometimes operate to minify his society—and then we laugh with him. Or it may sometimes serve to minify him—and then we laugh at him. But it may simultaneously do both, and then the comic

---

3. This minifying factor seems implicit in much theorizing about the nature of comedy. One may, for example, interpret Aristotle's definition in the *Poetics* (the "Ridiculous" as "a species of the Ugly") as based essentially upon the element of minification in the comic object or situation. (*The Art of Poetry,* trans. Ingram Bywater [Clarendon Press, 1920], p. 33.) Again Bergson's concept of the "mechanical" in *Le Rire* might be interpreted as proposing—though the author's emphases are elsewhere—a special type or "area" of minification as the essential element in comedy. In these and other familiar theories of the comic, however, minification, to the extent that it seems implied, is entirely one directional. The concepts do not take adequate account of the situation discussed in the following observations.

complexity and force of both character and language is at its peak. Most of Falstaff's wit is of this variety (for example, the "honor" speeches in the last act of *Henry IV*, Part I). Without in any way proposing, of course, an equality of literary merit, we may note the similarity in these respects to the Etheregean comic hero.[4]

But along with the general similarities, the comparison of Falstaff with the Etheregean hero serves also to mark essential differences. We need not here investigate the comparison in detail. But it is clear that one of the easiest and most obvious distinctions—the highly individualized character of one, the severely typical character of the other—points to a fundamental distinction in every aspect of comic structure. The Etheregean hero is the explicit and direct embodiment of an abstract and generalized system of attitudes and values. The sum of his characteristics, therefore, is little more than the sum of the abstract system which he embodies. In this respect he is essentially like all the other members of his comic world. And it is precisely therein that the characters most fully serve their comic roles. For the immediate as well as ultimate comedy of Etherege's plays is the comedy of one set of assumptions concerning reality and value playing out its merits, defects, inconsistencies, and equivocalities within a frame of other conflicting sets of assumptions.

The first purpose of the wit, then, is to project the nature, conflict, and relative values of these several sets of assumptions. And it is precisely therein that its comic complexity lies. For at a single instant and with a single word it characteristically serves both to minify and enhance not merely one object but several opposing ones. Lady Cockwood's "Peace, he may yet redeem his honour," is not a witticism on the part of Lady Cockwood. But it is comic wit on the part of the play, and from two points of view: First, it univocally diminishes Lady Cockwood by exposing her comic confusion and inconsistency. To this extent it diminishes also the entire world of conventional hypocrisy which she represents. But, second, it at once comically diminishes and enlarges, though in different ways and to different degrees, the unspecialized Christian and Christian humanist traditions, as well as the courtly, the heroic, and the specialized "honest-man" worlds by placing them in comically illuminating positions vis-à-vis each other. The same essential situation prevails for Dorimant's "art" and "nature," Gatty's "challenge," and so on through the comic wit of the play. When the wit of the play is also the wit of the speaker—normally hero or heroine—the situa-

---

4. As with the Etheregean hero, Falstaff's wit—like his general comic nature—has still an additional dimension through his ironic awareness of his own ambivalence. As "comic hero," then, he—and the Restoration comedy of manners heroes—are to be generically distinguished as at a more involved level of comic form from, say, Don Quixote, Alceste, and Parson Adams.

tion, of course, takes on a special complexity. But in any event, the final comic meaning of the wit, like that of the total play, is to express the confusion, uncertainty, and ambiguity of human life.

IV

The characteristics of language which we have here discussed suggest, like the total comic structure of the plays, relationships with certain general characteristics of the age. It is not part of our intent to pursue these suggestions in detail. But it is relatively easy to see what the salient connections might be. In the abstract, generalized, logically schematized structure of the comedy, one may see reflected the so-called "rationalism" of the age, or even the Cartesian and scientific preoccupation with "primary qualities." In the abstracting of human experience into the set frames of various traditions of thought, one may perhaps see the intellectualizing force and consciousness of an aristocratic society. Or in the pervasive opposition between two broadly opposing sets of thought concerning nature and man—Hobbes, Machiavelli, the libertine, versus Christian and classical, the courtly, and the traditional honest man—one may see the age's consciousness of an increasing conflict between an older orthodoxy and an emerging individualism which looks to our own age. These and other factors may very well have exercised an influence on Etherege's plays. If they did, so, too, did the comic awareness which—as comic awareness has a way of doing—confounded them. For we have seen in sufficient detail that the plays set up their own and their comic worlds' traditions, rational order, and primary classifications largely for the purpose of violating them at every turn. The hero and the dupe have their relationships blurred; the libertine-Machiavel is threatened, at least, with something approaching a Christian-classical—if not quite courtly—heart; the refinement of a quasi-aristocratic society becomes a maze; a state of grace may prove to be a fall, or a fall a state of grace.

The result of all this, we may once more remark, is not, at the level of the plays' meaning, simply confusion or cynicism or despair. Particularly with *The Man of Mode*, Etheregean comedy proposes its own order—its own set of realities and values. But as with all thoughtful comedy, the order emerges from the comic fact and form of man's inveterate disorder. The disorder is surely not confined to that of a specialized society. On the contrary, the wit by which that society most clearly announces its own special character becomes the principal vehicle for universalizing the comic ritual which the plays project. For the comedy, finally, is one in which not merely libertine but Christian, classical, "heroic," courtly, and honest-man postulates concerning the nature of man are brought to the test of human experience. And from this point of multiple vision, the comic ritual of the plays is primarily one in which man in the pride and assertiveness of his wit progressively reveals its and his own general insufficiency and confusion.

Even from this view, however, the wit is equivocal. In terms of the play we can, on the one hand, see the comic and ritualistic formalism as distancing experience in order to look at it more closely.[5] Yet, on the other, the insistent, repetitive balance and parallelism, both of language and general structure—although highly expressive in their comic tensions between order and disorder—suggest a certain inflexibility. One eventually comes to feel that the persistent irony is somewhat overbrittle, even for the type and level of experience with which the plays deal. But one feels, with whatever difference of degree, something of the same quality in the sterner and more searching irony of Swift, or in the broader and more flexible wit of Pope. The sense of insufficiency derives in part, perhaps, from the Restoration and Augustan refusal, as Herbert Davis has noted concerning Swift, of "the happiness of being well deceived." [6] "I hope," said Swift, in his "Letter to a very young Lady on her Marriage," "you do not still dream of charms and raptures, which marriage ever did, and ever will, put a sudden end to." [7] Etheregean comedy takes a somewhat less categorical view of the matter; but the unyielding intellectualism of its surfaces seems to reflect something of the same disenchantment. To this extent it reflects also something of the ambivalence in the ritual of wit which characterizes its comic world. For if that ritual for hero and heroine took away too much, it also guarded against the expectation of too much and the realization of too little. The comic vision and expression of Etherege's plays keeps, in a generic sense, something of the same middle ground.

5. Dobrée has suggested that aspects of structure and comic texture in Etherege's plays are like a ballet: "It is all a dance; the couples bow, set to partners, perform their evolutions, and bow again." (*Restoration Comedy,* p. 63.) There is some justness in the observation if one avoids the idea that the comedy is, therefore, merely "gay," "uncritical," "artificial." Certainly the persistent elements of music, dance, song add to the highly formalized structure and suggest an abstraction something like the dance. The comedy is, indeed, a kind of dance, but a ritualistic dance—an ironic and ambiguous version of the dance of life.

6. Herbert Davis, *Stella. A Gentlewoman of the Eighteenth Century* (Macmillan, 1942), p. 24.

7. See *ibid.,* p. 47.

Part III

ETHEREGEAN COMEDY AND THE TRADITION

7

The Comedy of Love

Lyly and Shakespeare—the Questions

THE most immediate question in Etherege's comedy of love—whether sexual desire is only physical appetite or something more —is presumably as old as the concept of body and mind or spirit. As old presumably is the comedy of man caught in the grip of an appetite or passion which he believes to run counter to reason and which, therefore, he struggles successfully or unsuccessfully to control. The hunching males of Aristophanes' *Lysistrata* are in some ways only a more earthy version of Lyly's courtly lovers or of Tanner in *Man and Superman*. For Western culture, however, these problems were intensified and reformulated by the lyrists of Provence. And with them, too, the distinctions were sharpened, if not entirely created, between fact and fancy, the experience and the expectation, what is transient and what if anything endures. For the late sixteenth and early seventeenth centuries, an awareness of these problems had been sufficiently assured by the mixed and varied nature of their heritage—the lyrists of Provence, Dante, Petrarch, Castiglione and Bembo, Ovid, the fabliaux, Jean de Meun, Chaucer, Aretino, Montaigne. But the awareness was further intensified by the general character of the time—the historical position between an old order and a new ; the prevailing critical temper ; the impulses at once toward orthodoxy and iconoclasm, doubt and affirmation.

In the "romantic" comedies of Lyly and Shakespeare, as in the poetry of Sidney, Greville, Drayton, Shakespeare, Marston, Donne, these problems and conflicts recur in varied form. With Lyly, in fact, the comedy of love as a central concern in English drama begins. The perceptions, interests, and form of his plays are in many respects far from new.[1] But in the field of English drama they acquire an original and distinct dramatic expression, certain characteristics of which have

1. Most of the important studies on Lyly's general sources and antecedents are listed by David Lloyd Stevenson, *The Love-Game Comedy* (Columbia Univ. Press, 1946), in the notes to ch. IX, "Lyly's Quarreling Lovers." The following comments on both Lyly and Shakespeare cover to a considerable extent material also discussed by Stevenson, and from something of the same point of view. There are, however, significant differences in emphases and interpretation.

significance for this study. First of all Lyly's plays are centrally concerned with the nature of love. They project not only the inner complexities, contradictions, and ambiguities of its nature but the conflicts which it generates in social action. Further, the plays provide a consistently critical examination of courtly love assumptions in particular and of romantic love at large; and their treatment of these assumptions is expressed in Christian-classical terms of body and mind, passion and reason. At the same time they employ contrapuntal groupings of characters who possess contrasting attitudes toward love. Within these contrasts is a comedy of antagonism between the sexes based both upon disparate attitudes toward love and upon the disparity in social status between the sexes. These sex combats in turn employ an elaborately patterned wit as instrument of attack and defense, as well as what in our inspection of Etherege's plays we have called the comedy of "disciplined feeling." Finally, embracing all these characteristics, is the plays' heightened formalism and intellectualized schematization of comic structure. Each of these attributes supplies the currents of English drama with forms and interests which lead ultimately to the Restoration comedy of love. Some of the more important require comment.

The attack which Lyly's plays make upon courtly and romantic assumptions concerning love has an especial interest for us. The attack takes several forms. First, the world of Lyly's plays is as aware as the Restoration that the courtly paraphernalia of sighs, tears, and protestations may be used as a "Machiavellian" disguise for simple concupiscence, and that in love, consequently, as in other aspects of human activity, art and nature may be quite asunder. "Love, faire child," says the aged Soothsayer in *Sapho and Phao,* "is to be governed by arte." And she introduces a lengthy discourse on Ovidean precepts of expediency with, "Flatter, I meane lie; litle things catch light mindes, and fancy is a worme, that feedeth first upon fenell." [2] Consequently, the witty sex antagonism in Lyly's plays takes repeatedly a Restoration turn. Nisa, in *Love's Metamorphosis,* spurns the protestations of her suitor with the assertion that she would rather be "worne with the continuall beating of waves, then dulled with the importunities of men, whose open flatteries make way to their secret lustes, retaining as little truth in their hearts as modestie in their words" (v.4.68–71). And Campaspe counters the vows of Apelles with, "If your tongue were made of the same flesh that your heart is, your wordes would bee as your thoughts are: but such a common thing it is amongst you to commend, that oftentimes for fashion sake you cal them beautifull, whom you know black" (*Campaspe,* IV.2.24–7).

At the same time Lyly uses the machinery of courtly sighs and tor-

2. *The Complete Works of John Lyly,* ed. R. Warwick Bond (Clarendon Press, 1902), Vol. *2,* II.4.55–61. All following references are to this edition.

ments as an indication of the power which sexual desire has to overrule
man's reason. Characteristically the desire has little of Petrarch's
idealism or the Platonic spirituality of Bembo. The lovers themselves
may be beguiled into espousing some form of courtly idealism. But their
passion predominantly is viewed as a matter of the "blood."[3] "I doe
not thinke," says one of the characters in *Love's Metamorphosis,* "Love
hath any sparke of Divinitie in him; since the end of his being is
earthly. In the bloud he is begot by the fraile fires of the eyes, &
quencht by the frayler shadowes of thought. What reason have we
then to soothe his humour with such zeale, and folow his fading de-
lights with such passion?" (I.I.9–13) Hephestion warns Alexander
that "time muste weare out that love hath wrought, and reason weane
what appetite noursed" (*Campaspe,* III.4.120–1). Sapho, having conquered her passion, comes to see her "disease" as merely "appetite"
which had yielded to "reason" (*Sapho and Phao,* v.2.30–7). And
Alexander himself, having also conquered his passion with reason, can
dismiss the lovers, Apelles and Campaspe, as "Two loving wormes"
(*Campaspe,* v.4.127). "Loving wormes," indeed, is a favorite image
in Lyly's plays, and man irrationally wriggling in the torments of his
passion a favorite comic view.[4]

It is not, however, the total view. As Stevenson, among others, has
pointed out, "Lyly regarded the two worlds of romance and real life
as irreconcilable."[5] But they are irreconcilable in a number of different
ways. If Lyly was not in the Etheregean libertine's sense a "naturalist,"
he was aware that love, as a matter of the "blood," might sate with
feeding. And his quarreling lovers, like those of the Restoration, bring
this awareness to their sex antagonism. Yet their most characteristic
comedy lies another way. Lyly's favorite comic curve, in his dramas
as in *Euphues,* traces the disillusion and frustration of lovers with
courtly or romantic assumptions about love—most frequently the males
—through the failure of experience to justify expectations. In *The
Woman in the Moone,* the courtly attitudes and expectations of the
three shepherds are violently routed by the "reality" of woman, sym-
bolized in the fickle and chameleon Pandora, and by Venus herself
who counsels,

> Away with chastity and modest thoughts,
> *Quo mihi fortunam si non conceditur uti?*
> Is she not young? then let her to the worlde.
>
> (III.2.16–18)

3. Among Lyly's assorted lovers the most conspicuous exceptions to this statement
occur when the allegory of the plays, as in *Endimion,* makes Elizabeth the object of
the lover's adoration.
4. The fact that "worm" is for Lyly as for the Renaissance in part a term of endear-
ment conditions but does not basically alter the nature of this view.
5. *Love-Game Comedy,* p. 171.

And Phao, having been frustrated by the guile and deceit of Venus, concludes that "Loves are but smokes, which vanish in the seeing, and yet hurte whilest they are seene" (*Sapho and Phao,* v.3.11–12). In a sense, therefore, the characteristic curve of action in Lyly's plays is the inverse of Etherege's. Moving like the Etheregean hero from conviction through experience to a new awareness, Lyly's lover finds love to be less instead of more than he had expected. And the distinction marks a significant swing of the pendulum. For Lyly and his time, the comedy lay in the fact that the courtly ideals of his society were inconsistent with reality. For Etherege the comedy lay in the fact that the libertine convictions of his "heroes" might possibly be likewise inconsistent with reality. We shall want, then, to see how the seventeenth-century comedy of love marks the transition between the two extremes. But we shall want to see first how, within the total context of Lyly's plays, the comedy of love proposes a further view which in some ways resembles more clearly Restoration comedy than it does the Jacobean and Caroline drama which intervenes.

If Lyly, like Etherege, considered the romantic and idealistic extremes of courtly love inconsistent with reality, he too did not therefore entirely dismiss the possibilities of something more than physical hunger. While one course of action in Lyly's plays is the disillusion of a courtly lover, there is also the comic curve in which lovers are married. It has frequently been asserted that such marriages settle none of the issues which the conflicts of the lovers have raised, and that they are, therefore, to be considered as weaknesses in Lyly's comic structure. The assertion perhaps is not without some justness. But in such plays as *Campaspe* and *Love's Metamorphosis,* the inconclusiveness of the marriage would seem to be precisely the comic point. The resolution of love opens out, much as in Etherege's comedy, into future possibilities of transitoriness, discord, and disillusion. Nevertheless, within the resolution is also the possibility of a fulfillment beyond that of animal appetite. In *Love's Metamorphosis* the love of Protea and Petulius seems idyllic once the latter has been rescued from the clutches of the siren. And in the terms of their union is announced a theme recurrent in Lyly, as in Etherege—the necessity of control for any true fulfillment in love (v.2 and v.4.24–7). But the promises of their union are hedged about by the equivocal character of the presiding goddess, Venus, whose faithful devotees they are, and by the forced and quarreling marriage of the nymphs and shepherds at the end.

In the resolving marriage of Apelles and Campaspe, too, there is the possible promise of fulfillment beyond Alexander's "two loving wormes." Yet Apelles himself is aware that he has endured "intollerable passions, for unknowne pleasures" (*Campaspe,* v.2.10–11). And the choral disenchantment of Diogenes casts its shadow upon the lovers somewhat as does the comic reconciliation of the Cockwoods in *She Would If She Could*. Apelles' own conclusion that it is better to "melt with desire, than wrastle with love" (lines 11–12), is a persistent and ironic "resolution" to the conflicts and contrarieties of passion in Lyly's plays. It is, indeed, the spirit in which the shepherds at the beginning of *Love's Metamorphosis* undertake the pursuit of the nymphs: "We have bodies, Silvestris, and humane bodies, which in their owne natures being much more wretched than beastes, doe much more miserably then beasts pursue their owne ruines: and since it will aske longer labour and studie to subdue the powers of our bloud to the rule of the soule, then to satisfie them with the fruition of our loves, let us bee constant in the worlds errours, and seeke our owne torments" (1.1.14–20).

In this dubious spirit of capitulation to the demands of the flesh, they chart their campaign against the nymphs. It becomes, both in method and resolution, the most nearly "Etheregean" of all Lyly's plays. The shepherds assume the pose of idealistic courtly lovers. Ramis protests to Nisa that ". . . my thoughts are as holy as thy vowes, and I as constant in love as thou in crueltie; lust followeth not my love as shadowes doe bodies, but truth is woven into my love, as veines into bodies: let me touch this tender arme, and say my love is endlesse" (III.1.3–7). The sincerity of Ramis' protestations are challenged by the witty Nisa, as of course, they should be. But by the end of the play the shepherds, like the reader, are somewhat less sure of the nature and intent of their desires. They willingly espouse the reluctant nymphs. Yet both are obviously unsure of the course of their love in marriage. "I consent," says Celia, "so as Montanus, when in the midst of his sweete delight, [he] shall find some bitter overthwarts, impute it to his folly, in that he suffered me to be a Rose, that hath prickles with her pleasantnes" (V.4.140–3). Yet the suggestion that the pleasantness may possibly prove to be beyond that of the worm is certainly present.

The resolution here, as in *Campaspe*, is but an aspect of the ambiguity which pervades the total comic structure of Lyly's plays. And that structure—in a generic if not a precise sense—again looks more toward Etheregean comedy than toward the intervening seventeenth-century comedy of love: the imperfectly resolved conflicts among the characters concerning their disparate attitudes toward love; the highly formalized structuring of character, action, language, which on the one hand seems to remove the comic experience from the level of reality, yet on the other suggests by its very artifice the central reality—the charm and, in Chaucer's term, "brotelnesse"—of the experience it depicts; the tension, at the same time, between the formal distance and the gross nature of an all too real component of the experience—the treachery, conniving, moral shallowness and corruption; over all, the power of the formalism to suggest "the game," not only of love, but of life, with something of the same involved ambivalence of implication for the image as in the comedies of Etherege; and finally, something too of the same ironic balance, detachment, restraint, and indirection of attitude on the part of the author.

In their concern with the nature of love, the early romantic comedies of Shakespeare involve much the same range of problems and values as do the plays of Lyly.[6] There is again little of the exalted spirituality of Spenser's *Four Hymns* or of Bembo in *The Courtier*. And there is even less of that homely blend of Christian-courtly "virtue" which we shall presently examine in the Jacobean and Caroline comedy of love. On the contrary, "wisdom and blood combating"[7] is the persistent comic theme. And as in Lyly both the theme and its resolution are expressed in a structure of pervasive ambiguity. That man by his nature should be subject to the "almighty dreadful little might" of love (*Love's Labour's Lost,* III.1.205) and to the irrational and insubstantial illusions which it induces is part of the comic view. But whether he should wish to escape it is more fundamentally and insistently than for Lyly a part of the comic question posed. In the two plays which we shall here briefly examine, the resolution leaves these questions suspended much after the fashion of *Campaspe* and *Love's Metamorphosis*. But in this respect as in others, they bring the comedy of love to a form and focus still more closely resembling the later plays of Etherege.

The denier or scorner of love who becomes its victim was, of course, a commonplace figure in medieval and Renaissance courtly love literature. This did not mean that the character was necessarily either a misogynist or a celibate. On the contrary, he might have a very lusty interest in the ladies. At the beginning of *Love's Labour's Lost,* Biron, like Chaucer's Troilus, and—though somewhat less busily—like Etherege's heroes, could "study where to meet some mistress fine" (1.1.63) and could

> . . . please the eye indeed
> By fixing it upon a fairer eye.   (lines 80–1)

In each case, the scorn was aimed at idealistic and romantic concepts of love and at those who, in the phrase of Dorimant, permitted themselves to become "so foppishly in love" that they could be "bound" or

---

6. Among the many studies of Lyly and Shakespeare, the following (in addition to Stevenson, *Love-Game Comedy*) have a particular bearing upon the general area of relationships here discussed: Bond, *Works of John Lyly, 2,* "Lyly as a Playwright," 231–99, especially Sec. 6; E. C. Pettet, *Shakespeare and the Romance Tradition,* London, Staples Press, 1949.

7. "Much Ado," II.3.170–1, *The Complete Plays and Poems of William Shakespeare,* ed. William Allan Neilson and Charles Jarvis Hill, New Cambridge Edition, Houghton Mifflin, 1942. All subsequent references are to this edition.

"enslaved" by its power. The issues, in other words, involved a skeptical
and broadly naturalistic attitude toward the nature of love as opposed
to more romantic concepts and expectations; the enjoyment of many
as opposed to "devotion" and constancy to one; and the mastery over
as opposed to the surrender to desire. In each case the scorner is obviously guilty of *hubris*. The peak of Biron's hubris lies beyond the
opening of the play; but like Troilus and all Etherege's heroes, he has
been "love's whip,"

> A very beadle to a humourous sigh;
> A critic, nay, a night-watch constable;
> A domineering pedant o'er the boy.   (III.I.177–9)

And in each case, the fall from hubris is a comic mocking and exposure
of oversimplified convictions concerning man's nature and an awakening
to the paradoxes, inconsistencies, strengths, and weaknesses to which
man by his nature is heir.

Unlike Troilus, however, but very much like Etherege's characters,
Biron is never really blinded by his desires. More sharply and consistently than Lyly's characters, he keeps before him a comic awareness
of the incongruity between the impulses of his desire and the reality
that may lie beneath. As a result the conflict between passion and
reason, expectation and desire, is more fully and consistently expressed.
Dan Cupid is the

> Dread prince of plackets, king of codpieces,
> Sole imperator and great general
> Of trotting 'paritors.   (lines 186–8)

And again,

> What! I love! I sue! I seek a wife!
> A woman, that is like a German clock,
> Still a-repairing, ever out of frame . . .
> Ay, and, by heaven, one that will do the deed
> Though Argus were her eunuch and her guard.
> And I to sigh for her! to watch for her!   (lines 191–202)

Biron's conclusion,

> Well, I will love, write, sigh, pray, sue, groan:
> Some men must love my lady, and some Joan,
>   (lines 206–7)

is much like the resignation of Lyly's shepherds, who conclude that it is
simpler to yield to love than to struggle with its irrational impulses.

But the relation between impulse and realization, fact and fancy is not
thereby settled. If love is a matter of the blood and if Cupid is, on the

one hand, "king of codpieces," to what extent may Cupid and the blood be also the source of "the right Promethean fire" (IV.3.351)? Biron's famous eulogy of love and woman at the conclusion of the fourth act is, of course, in part a consciously ironic and clever rationalization. In its context the speech provides one of the play's most telling pieces of satire upon traditional courtly idealism. But it provides also one of the principal points of reference in the play's concern with the nature of love. To what extent precisely is it false? Biron's subsequent and familiar "kersey noes" place his emotions and expectations on some kind of middle ground between codpieces and Promethean fire:

> . . . these summer-flies
> Have blown me full of maggot ostentation
> I do forswear them, and I here protest,
> By this white glove,—how white the hand, God knows!—
> Henceforth my wooing mind shall be express'd
> In russet yeas and honest kersey noes;
> And, to begin, wench—so God help me, la!—
> My love to thee is sound, sans crack or flaw.
>
> (v.2.408–15)

This is presumably about the ground on which Sir Frederick stands —or thinks he stands—at the end of *The Comical Revenge*, when, having derided the courtly excesses of Beaufort's world and having foresworn the libertinism of his own, he disposes of his "household stuff, my dear Mrs. Lucy," and resolves "to lead a virtuous life" with Mistress Rich (84). But precisely what Biron's love, however "sound," may be or ultimately prove to be, he is clearly as unsure as Sir Frederick. "How white the hand, God knows!" looks to the central question in the resolution of the play.

Meanwhile the question has been further defined. The varied and conflicting postures of wit have, as in both Lyly's and Etherege's plays, explored in part the relation of language to reality or of Art to Nature. But with the announced death of the Princess' father at the end of the play, "the scene begins to cloud" (v.2.730). The intrusion of the reality of death shatters the charming but brittle world of wit with which the characters have at once explored and distorted the realities of their emotions. Biron's confession,

> Your beauty, ladies,
> Hath much deform'd us, fashioning our humours
> Even to the opposed end of our intents,   (lines 766–8)

reduces to a level of sobriety the "[strange] shapes . . . which particoated presence of loose love" had wrought among the company (lines 773–6). It reasserts, in other words, the element of rational control with which all Shakespeare's plays are so integrally concerned. But it does not thereby answer the final questions in the comedy of love, some details of which have further interest for us.

Navarre and his followers are not, of course, Restoration libertines and do not attempt to satisfy their desires through seduction. The initial bases for the duel of wits are consequently different. For the Princess and her ladies there is no question of a double standard of sex relations or of Machiavellian masquerade. Though they are quick, like Etherege's heroines, to detect the falseness in the courtly postures of their wooers, they assume that the manner of the wooing is but "mocking merriment" (line 139), part of an idle "courtship, pleasant jest, and courtesy" (line 790). When they perceive, however, that the wooers are in earnest, they face some of the same problems as Etherege's women, and handle them in much the same way. The suitors are "attaint with faults and perjury" (line 829). Further, their now professedly earnest oaths are made "in heat of blood" (line 810), and in such cases "no words that smooth-fac'd wooers say" are to be trusted.[8] The women's recourse is to the same probationary trial that marks the close of Etherege's last two plays, and for much the same purpose:

> If frosts and fasts, hard lodging and thin weeds
> Nip not the gaudy blossoms of your love.   (lines 811–12)

Etherege's ladies, to be sure, would have considered frosts and fasts a dangerous extreme. But whether the demand be for thin weeds or a temporary endurance of the country, the problem is essentially the same. It concerns not only the nature and permanence of love in itself but its capacity to come to terms with and to survive in a world where realities of a very different nature also exist.

Benedick's concluding resignation in *Much Ado*, "There is no staff more reverend than one tipp'd with horn" (v.4.125–6), continues the comic theme. In the parallels and contrasts between the romantic world of Claudio and Hero and the skeptical disenchantment of Benedick and Beatrice, in the manner, too, in which these extremes of conviction and attitude qualify and balance each other, *Much Ado* at once looks back to Lyly and forward through innumerable seventeenth-century comedies of love to *The Comical Revenge*. With that particular point, however, we shall be later concerned. Our interest for the moment is confined to Beatrice and Benedick and the ways in which their own comedy of love continues some of the problems with which the Restoration plays are integrally concerned.

That the "warfare" between Shakespeare's couple is to some extent a

---

8. *Ibid.*, line 838. Compare the denouement of *She Would If She Could:*

GAT. Marrying in this heat would look as ill as fighting in your drink.
ARIA. And be no more proof of love than t'other is of valour.   (p. 178)

matter of individual personalities is clear. It is clear also that the comedy of that warfare involves a mutual attraction which has existed well before the play begins (1.1.44–64). Consequently the comic curve of action in Etherege's plays and *Love's Labour's Lost*—from conviction to experience to new awareness and doubt—is modified. The impediment to Beatrice and Benedick's acknowledgment of love is from the beginning a matter in part of private pride. And the wit with which they attack each other, the nature of man, and the follies of love must be judged accordingly. But the antagonizing force of conviction is also present. The awareness of man's lack of "divinity," which so largely informs the consciousness of Etherege's heroes and heroines, constitutes for Beatrice and Benedick as well a principal basis for their skepticism toward love and marriage. Beatrice will not be fitted with a husband "till God make men of some other metal than earth. Would it not grieve a woman to be overmaster'd with a piece of valiant dust? to make an account of her life to a clod of wayward marl? No, uncle, I'll none. Adam's sons are my brethren; and, truly, I hold it a sin to match in my kindred" (11.1.62–8). Benedick is equally aware of what Adam's "transgression" has meant for man (line 258–60). And putting his "neck into a yoke" is as much a matter for him as for Etherege's heroes of wearing his "cap with suspicion" (1.1.200–3). Therefore, he will "trust none; and the fine is, for the which I may go the finer, I will live a bachelor" (lines 246–8).

But the force of love catches up both of Shakespeare's characters much as it does the quarreling skeptics of Etherege's plays. With comic inconsistency Benedick suddenly finds "all graces" in Beatrice (see 11.3.30 and 239–44), and Beatrice with equal suddenness is ready to believe "better than reportingly" that Benedick is worthy to be loved (111.1.116). As with Biron, however, and all Etherege's heroes and heroines, the reversal is enriched by a full awareness within the characters themselves of the inconsistencies of their position. Benedick's rhymes—"lady" and "baby," "scorn" and "horn," "school" and "fool" —have "very ominous endings" (v.2.36–9). On one hand they satirize the courtly conventions of love. But on the other they throw into mocking question the relation of Benedick's impulses and desires in love to the possible reality which may lie beneath. In his request that the Friar "bind me, or undo me; one of them," the image of "binding" has the same equivocal implications as in Etherege's plays.[9] It may lead to Benedick's staff "tipped with horn" or it may lead to a fulfillment more nearly answering to the emotions which the two characters so furtively acknowledge. Meanwhile, as in the plays of Lyly and of the Restoration, the wit of the lovers has explored the possible nature of love within a

9. v.4.20. See *She Would If She Could*, p. 176.

frame of reference that ranges from naturalistic appetite to courtly exaltation. If in the process their wit has in some ways falsified their emotions it has also served to protect them from a too ready acceptance of expectations which may prove unfounded. They have been as reasonable as man may be when faced with the paradoxes of love. And the range of their awareness is viewed by Shakespeare's play as by those of the Restoration as the best possible insurance against the horns.

The Jacobeans—Frames of Reference

In moving from Lyly and Shakespeare to those lines of Jacobean and Caroline practice which prepare most clearly for the Restoration comedy of love, one notes at once certain fundamental differences. The quality and range of experience become more stringently circumscribed and doctrinaire. There is now a schematization of behavior, attitudes, and values which increasingly as one moves from the beginning to the middle of the century converts experience into dialectics and reduces to codification much that in the earlier dramatists had remained elusive and unsure. At the same time the terms of the schematization involve a specific frame of moral and social values with which the Restoration is basically concerned. The most essential difference is that while in the Jacobean and Caroline comedy the points of opposition are mutually exclusive, in the Restoration they are equivocally merged. This means that with much the same materials by which the Jacobean and Caroline dramatists simplified and dogmatized the problems of Lyly and Shakespeare, the Restoration restored something of the complexity and comic questioning which distinguishes the earlier plays.

In the second chapter of this study it was suggested that the society of Restoration comedy of manners derives much of its character from traditions which had developed throughout the seventeenth century. It was also suggested that the opposition in Etherege's plays between the libertine-Machiavel and the world or worlds against which he revolted grew out of the opposition in the preceding periods between what was often called the "epicure" and the "stoic." By the beginning of the seventeenth century the terms of this opposition had become firmly established in the comic drama. The "man of fashion" had become not only a "gallant" but an "epicure." Jonson's Truewit gives a familiar portrait: "What, betweene his mistris abroad, and his engle at home, high fare, soft lodging, fine clothes, and his fiddle; hee thinkes the houres ha' no wings, or the day no post-horse." To Truewit's admonitions, Clerimont replies: "Foh, thou hast read *Plutarchs* moralls, now, or some such tedious fellow; and it showes so vilely with thee: 'Fore god, 'twill spoile thy wit utterly. Talke to me of pinnes, and feathers, and ladies, and rushes, and such things: and leave this *Stoicitie* alone, till thou mak'st sermons." [1]

This opposition persists through pre-Restoration comedy. In Nabbes' *Covent Garden* (1632) Hugh Jerker, contrasting his pursuit of "pleasure" as an avowed "epicure" to the "virtue" and "honor" of Artlove as a "stoic," attempts the conversion of the latter: "My little Cos, here shall prove with undenyable arguments that drinking and wenching are the onely vertues in a gentleman of the last edition: to be excellent at them is a master-piece of education. Besides, they are the onely acumens of wit." [2] In Nabbes' play the contrast between the epicure and the stoic provides the opposition of attitudes and behavior around which the entire play is structured. The work thus lies in a line of development which prepares for Etherege's first play, *The Comical Revenge*.[3] And like the Restoration comedy, the point of central interest in the contrast concerns the question of love. Jerker, like Etherege's Sir Frederick, is until his conversion at the end a "naturalist" or libertine. Artlove is, like Etherege's Beaufort and Bruce, a "courtly" lover. Around these opposing terms and values the Jacobean and Caroline dramatists developed an increasingly prominent line of interest for the comedy of love. The epicure characteristically represents the order of the beast—in his naturalistic attitudes toward love, his sensualism, his stress on individualism, pleasure, indulgence. The stoic represents a rational order of moral and social law into which a quasi-courtly view of love has been incorporated and at least superficially harmonized with the emphasis on reason, virtue, honor, and restraint. He reflects, accordingly, the established or orthodox moral order of his time; and until the Restoration he prevailingly reflects the convictions and values of the dramatist as well.[4] The epicure, in turn, becomes an unequivocal corruption in Nature and in the sanctioned order of the plays. The possible range of meaning for his role is thus highly circumscribed. But his

1. *Ben Jonson*, ed. C. H. Hereford and Percy Simpson (Oxford Univ. Press, 1925-41), Vol. *5*, 1.1.24-7 and 62-6. This edition is used for all subsequent references to Jonson's plays.

2. *Works of Thomas Nabbes*, ed. A. H. Bullen (London, 1887), Vol. *1*, 1.4, p. 17.

3. In Nabbes' play as elsewhere in 17th-century drama, the specific terms "epicure" and "stoic" are employed for those oppositions with which this and the following chapter will be concerned. But the terms are by no means so conspicuous and persistent as are the oppositions involved. Our adoption of the terms here is in part for convenience of reference, but also in part as a reminder of the drama's relations to the traditions of thought reviewed in Ch. 2. In this regard Comus' reference to "those budge doctors of the Stoic fur" is of interest. See Ch. 2, p. 18, n. 7, above. The opposition between Comus and the Lady in Milton's masque has many similarities to the Caroline comedy which we shall presently inspect.

4. The sense in which certain plays of Fletcher constitute an exception to this statement will be presently discussed. The exceptional nature of some Caroline comedies will be considered in the following chapter.

opposition to the stoic involves further problems which are relevant
to our concerns.

In Jacobean comedy, the epicure's attitudes toward love commonly
reveal one or more of three components—Ovid, the medieval and
Renaissance naturalism espoused by the libertines, and the sensualism
of such Italian Renaissance writers as Aretino.[5] Occasionally the
specific and direct influence of these several sources is apparent.
Marston's indebtedness to the naturalism of Montaigne is especially
clear in *The Dutch Courtezan*.[6] In *Epicoene* the influence of Ovid
and Aretino is equally apparent. More often the convictions of the
epicure have the blurred and eclectic character of popular thought,
though significant differences continue to appear. The perfervid sensualism of Volpone's address to Celia [7] contrasts with the lighthearted,
casual, and purely animal appetite of Fletcher's Monsieur Thomas.[8]
In the Caroline period the Jacobean influences still in theory persist.
Glapthorne's Thorowgood cites "Aretius politicks" and "Ovid's Art"
as essential knowledge for a "gentleman." [9] Marmion's Philautus uses
Ovid's "art" and "the law, and the command of nature" as authority
for his libertinism.[1] But the voluptuousness common in the previous
period becomes, so far as it continues, a stilted formalism. The earlier
glow of a genuinely sensuous vitality is replaced by a self-conscious
dialectic. The comedy thus moves toward the drily ironic intellectualism of the Etheregean libertine, for whom sensuality is less a positive
pleasure than a means of mocking man's conventional pretensions.
But whatever the precise complexion of the epicurean lover, his love
was still of the body only. Virtue and honor were not merely irrelevant
to his pleasure; they were empty and artificial impediments to it.

The "stoic" opposition to these attitudes displays, in its turn, a
mixed and varied composition. It manifests everywhere the influences
of courtly love traditions; but its central emphases are modulated to
the moral and social values of the Christian humanist. Against the
sensualism of the epicure, it poses the love and beauty of the mind—
of woman's virtue and honor rather than the merely physical beauty

5. These distinctions are useful for analyzing certain variations in the drama. But
historically the separate components here suggested consistently overlap and merge.
Aretino, for example, reveals everywhere the influence of Renaissance naturalistic
thought, at the same time that he reveals also the direct influence of Ovid. In Aretino,
indeed, the 17th-century epicure had an important—and rampantly scurrilous and
cynical—example of Ovid, Machiavelli, and libertine naturalism combined. See his
La Cortigiana, an obvious satire on Castiglione's *The Courtier*.
6. See the following discussion of the play. See also J. Sainmont, *Influence de
Montaigne sur Marston et Webster*, Louvain, 1914.
7. *Volpone*, III.7.188-239.
8. See following discussion of *Monsieur Thomas*.
9. *Wit in a Constable* (London, 1640), I.I, B3r.
I. "Holland's Leaguer," III.4, p. 59, *Dramatic Works of Shackerley Marmion*, ed.
James Maidment and W. H. Logan, London, 1875.

which might titillate the senses. Indeed, unlike the orthodox courtly lover but very much like the critical poet from Shakespeare to Pope, the stoic is aware of the frequent discrepancy between the physical beauty of the woman and her moral deformity. Consequently while the machinery of passion, flames, darts, and sighs, is consistently in evidence, the stoic, in part perhaps under the pressure of the epicure's pursuit of physical beauty, tends to take a Christian and truly Stoical turn in exalting goodness above pulchritude. It is commonly less the "beauty" of the woman that inspires virtue than her virtue itself.

Despite the stress, then, upon true love as a marriage of minds or spirit, the stoic does not as a rule conform strictly to the Platonic courtliness of a Bembo. Nor does he exhibit the pure spirituality of Castiglione's philosopher. On the contrary he persistently looks forward to the physical union with his beloved in a state of wedded bliss. By implication at least he reflects thereby the characteristic desire of the Christian humanist from the Renaissance to Milton to find expression for the total man—to combine rather than sunder the desires of body and mind. But in the Jacobean and especially the Caroline comedy of love he is seldom aware of the problems in such a combination. He tends instead to take the combination for granted. The prevailing concern of the dramatist is elsewhere—chiefly upon the epicure as symbol of man's reversion to the beast in his surrender to appetite and sense, his exaltation of the senses above reason, his glorification of pleasure above virtue, and the threat of all this and his sexual promiscuity to the established moral and social order. While the stoic lover of seventeenth-century comedy, then, displays in many respects the trappings, jargon, and predilections of the courtly love tradition, he retains in his terms and emphases a distinctly Christian character. His awareness of "lust" and "sin" helps bequeath to the Restoration libertine his own ironic consciousness of Christian as well as courtly dereliction.

In noting briefly some manifestations of these concerns in the seventeenth-century comedy of love, we may begin at the start of the century with Marston's *The Dutch Courtezan*. Although the play is markedly different in many respects from the later Jacobean and Caroline comedy which we shall want to inspect, the terms in which the two modes of love are contrasted are essentially those which continue through both periods and which prepare in turn for the specific interests of the Restoration. The "full scope of the play," states the "Arguementum," is "the difference betwixt the love of a courtezan and a wife."[2] The statement in a sense might serve to summarize the

2. *The Works of John Marston*, ed. A. H. Bullen (London, 1887), 2, 5. Subsequent references are to this edition.

principal question in the comedy of love from Lyly to Etherege and Vanbrugh. But how fully and startlingly the play reorients and resolves the problems of Lyly and Shakespeare is immediately apparent. As in *Covent Garden,* the problems are introduced by the explicit opposition of attitudes which characterize the epicure and stoic. Although the character of Freevill in the early scenes is in some ways far from clear, at the beginning of the play he has the role of the epicure, and as such is contrasted with his friend, Malheureux. Freevill is betrothed to the "modest Beatrice," but he is nevertheless about to pay a call on the courtesan, Franceschina. To Malheureux' remonstrance he replies that "common houses" are "most necessary buildings," that "Youth and appetite are above the club of Hercules," that if, as Malheureux asserts, "lust is a most deadly sin," it is also "a most lively sin, sure" (1.1.68–80). Malheureux' further arguments against "heat and sensual appetite," against lust as "the strongest argument that speaks against the soul's eternity" (lines 95–8) are equally unavailing. Freevill is determined to go "the way of all flesh" (lines 87–8). And with full consciousness of what he is doing to courtly doctrine, he finds sensual satisfaction in his courtesan's "beauty": "Beauty is woman's virtue, love the life's music, and woman the dainties, or second course of heaven's curious workmanship. Since then beauty, love, and woman are good, how can the love of woman's beauty be bad?" (lines 147–50) His "Dutch tanakin" has "beauty enough for her virtue, virtue enough for a woman, and woman enough for any reasonable man in my knowledge" (lines 158–62).

With the second scene, however, we discover that Freevill has even before the play's opening undergone to some extent that "stoical" conversion which awaits countless unsuspecting Caroline libertines, and which the pens of Brome, Shirley, Nabbes, Marmion, et al., will trace with more dogmatic consistency but in essentially the same terms. Though the "enforcive beauties" of the courtesan compel his "sometimes incontinency" (1.2.202), Freevill has in part at least already seen the light. Combining the gospel of Bembo and St. Paul, he has progressed from sensual to "true" love: "I loved her [Franceschina] with my heart, until my soul showed me the imperfection of my body, and placed my affection on a lawful love, my modest Beatrice." [3] He

3. Lines 197–9. Compare Bembo in *The Courtier,* pp. 342–4: "And bicause in oure soule there be three maner wayes to know, namelye, by sense, reason, and understandinge: of sense, there arriseth appetite or longinge, which is commune to us with brute beaste: of reason arriseth election or choise, which is proper to man: of understanding, by the which man may be partner with Aungelles, arriseth will. . . . Whan the soule then is taken wyth covetynge to enjoye thys beawtie as a good thynge, in case she suffre her selfe to be guyded with the judgement of sense, she falleth into most deepe erroures, and judgeth the bodie in whyche Beawtye is descerned, to be the principall cause thereof."

can, therefore, move from the courtesan in one scene to Beatrice in the next,

> . . . whose chaste eyes, . . .
> Have gaged my soul to her enjoyings;
> Shredding away all those weak under-branches
> Of base affections and unfruitful heats. . . .
> (Enter Beatrice above.)
> Always a virtuous name to my chaste love!   (II.1.3–9)

In the name of virtue and their souls, Freevill and Beatrice pledge their chaste love, and Freevill surrenders sensualism and "beauty": "No beauty shall untwine our arms" and,

> Far, far be all ostent
> Vain boasts of beauties, soft joys, and the rest.
> (lines 30 and 35–6)

But Freevill's complete conversion waits upon the last act and the full revelation of Franceschina's villainy in plotting his death:

> O, thou unreprievable, beyond all
> Measure of grace damn'd irremediably! . . .
> What difference is in women and their life!
> What man, but worthy name of man, would leave
> The modest pleasures of a lawful bed—
> The holy union of two equal hearts . . .
> To twine th' unhealthful loins of common loves. . . .
>   How vile
> To love a creature made of blood and hell.   (V.1.63–80)

Meanwhile, however, the comedy of love has quickened. Malheureux himself has now been captured by the courtesan's beauty, has promptly espoused the naturalistic doctrines used by Freevill against his "stoicism" in the earlier scenes, and has fallen to yearning, like Oldham's Restoration libertines, for the liberty of "the free-born birds," who have

> No polite restraints, no artificial heats,
> No faint dissemblings; no custom makes them blush,
> No shame afflicts their name. O you happy beasts!
> In whom an inborn heat is not held sin,
> How far transcend you wretched, wretched man,
> Whom national custom, tyrannous respects
> Of slavish order, fetters, lames his power,
> Calling that sin in us which in all things else
> Is Nature's highest virtue.

> *O miseri quorum gaudia crimen habent!*
> Sure Nature against virtue cross doth fall,
> Or virtue's self is oft unnatural.[4]

The play, of course, has little sympathy for this concept of Nature or for the naturalist's conviction—now accepted by Malheureux as it previously was by Freevill—that "beauty's for use." [5] Malheureux himself realizes when he has been awakened to the full infamy of the courtesan that such a concept of Nature is merely the prompting of the "beast of man, loose blood," and that "he that lust rules cannot be virtuous" (v.3.66–7). This, we have seen, has been the realization of Freevill also. And it is on this very Christian note that the comedy of love is resolved. The epicure is only the beast in man fallen out of man's proper order of reason and virtue.

For the Jacobean comedy of love, in fact, the beast in man was scarcely less important than for the tragedy. And in the two fields it often emerged in forms interestingly similar. At about the time that Marston was producing *The Dutch Courtezan,* Chapman, in what we consider today one of his minor comedies, was projecting the beast in woman.[6] *The Widow's Tears* seems certainly at a superficial glance well removed from the Restoration comedy of manners. But for the line of development which is our present subject it has considerable interest. Like *The Dutch Courtezan,* it opens with the opposition of attitudes which look to our concern with the epicure and stoic. The widowed Countess, Eudora, had vowed to her husband before he died "to preserve till death the unstained honour of a widows bed." [7] Tharsalio, formerly a page in the Countess' household, undertakes however to win her, believing that such vows are empty and contrary to Nature. He is aware that even when the husbands are alive and happily adoring their wives as saints, the wives are busily "ad-horning" their husbands' "temples" (lines 108–9). How is it to be expected, then, that women should remain chaste when their husbands are dead? "Ere they be fully cold, you join embraces with his groom, or his physician, and perhaps his poisoner" (lines 112–13). It is not within Nature that woman's "eyes and ears should lose their function, her other parts their use, as if Nature had made her all in vain" (lines 129–30).

Countering these charges, Cynthia, wife of Tharsalio's elder brother,

---

4. II.1.73–84. A comparison of this speech with the quotation given above in Ch. 2, p. 12, from Oldham's satire will indicate the continuance of the libertine's "naturalism" throughout the 17th century.

5. I.2.241. Compare again *Comus,* lines 710ff.

6. Marston's play had, of course, a similar interest in Franceschina.

7. I.1.90–1, *The Comedies of George Chapman,* ed. T. M. Parrott, London, Geo. Routledge, 1914.

Lysander, defends the spiritual love and enduring devotion of women. And against Tharsalio's idea of Nature, with its philosophy of pleasure and "use," she poses the more orthodox assumptions of man's virtue (lines 132–9). But to Tharsalio these are only the appearance in man's conventional pretensions. His own convictions are the reality which lie beneath. The "Italian air" has "refined my senses, and made me see with clear eyes, and to judge of objects as they truly are, not as they seem, and through their mask to discern the true face of things." [8]

Out of this opposition the comic action develops. Lysander and Cynthia declare in the opening scene their unquestioning faith, were Lysander to die, in the wife's keeping such a vow as that of the Countess. But under Tharsalio's goading, Lysander decides to test the fidelity of his wife, arranges his own mock death, and is delighted to find that Cynthia, with her waiting woman, Ero, takes up her position of fast and mourning in his presumed tomb. Disguised as a soldier he comes to tempt them first with argument and then with food and drink. Assuming the attitudes of Tharsalio at the opening of the play, he counsels Cynthia to "make use of what you see," to "enjoy the fruits of life" and "live for a better husband" (IV.2.75–90). For the time she holds out; but when he next returns, still disguised and triumphant at the thought of his wife's fidelity, he finds her virtue sadly altered. To his proposition now that "to live freely is to feast our appetites freely, without which humans are stones," Cynthia replies, "I'll pledge you, Sir" (IV.3.66–9). In an instant, too, she pledges her love and body and becomes concerned now only with "If the world should see this" (line 77). Lysander's agonized discovery recalls the earlier Hamlet faced with the similar infidelity of his mother: "Hell be thy home! Huge monsters damn ye, and your whole creation, O ye gods! In the height of her mourning, in a tomb, within sight of so many deaths, her husband's believed body in her eye, he dead a few days before! This mirror of nuptial chastity, this votress of widow-constancy, to change her faith, exchange kisses, embraces, with a stranger, and, but my shame withstood, to give the utmost earnest of her love to an eight penny sentinel; in effect, to prostitute herself on her husband's coffin! Lust, impiety, hell, womanhood itself, add, if you can, one step to this" (v.1.114–23).

8. Lines 140–3. The "Italian air" here reminds us that libertine naturalism came into England and English literature from Italy as well as France. The Italian libertine, Vanini, was conspicuous among those who helped to disseminate the doctrine in all three countries at the beginning of the 17th century. See François T. Perrens, *Les Libertines en France au XVIIe siècle* (Paris, 1896), pp. 62–8.

It is of interest also to remember that the portion of Chapman's play here discussed is based upon the story of the Ephesian matron by Petronius, one of history's more famous Epicureans. The specific opposition of beliefs in which we are concerned, however, is chiefly the work of Chapman.

In the intricate plotting of the play, Cynthia's capacity to "feast her appetites" enlarges to rather gruesome extremes. But the point has long before been adequately made. The epicure has won with a vengeance; and woman's love, as Tharsalio had foretold and as all Etheregean heroes initially assume, is only body and sense.[9] The comedy, however, is not yet complete. With the pattern used for virtually every cuckolded husband in the Restoration comedy of manners, the tables are turned yet again upon Lysander. Finding that the soldier-lover is the husband disguised, Tharsalio informs the wife. When Lysander's trap for exposing her infamy is all but sprung, Cynthia can then pretend that she knew his game from the beginning and can cry her own self-pity as the

> Ill-destin'd wife of a transformed monster,
> Who to assure himself of what he knew,
> Hath lost the shape of man.   (v.3.137–9)

Lysander is thus obliged to view himself as the one transformed into a beast by the force of a baseless jealousy. Accordingly he is only too glad to take back his faultless Cynthia, believing that he has "the only constant wife." [1]

Although the "Italian air" would seem to have made Tharsalio "see with clear eyes," at least so far as woman's love is concerned, his ideas of Nature were not, of course, those of Chapman. If woman in *The Widow's Tears* demonstrates her capacity to play the beast, she is elsewhere in Chapman's work as much the angel. It is this contrast of potential in Nature which is repeatedly expressed by one of the most conspicuous aspects of structure in the pre-Restoration comedy of love. The multiple-plot device in Jacobean and Caroline comedy conveys a wide range of dramatic meanings. But it is probably safe to say that none is more persistent than the opposition of the epicure and stoic. In what is often called the "romantic-realistic" type of comedy this opposition is especially characteristic.[2] Chapman himself repeatedly employs it.[3] And in Fletcher, to whom we may turn next,

9. The widowed Countess also proves unequal to her vows, but in a somewhat less sensational and, for our interests, less significant manner.

1. Line 374. Compare the resolution of the Cockwoods in *She Would If She Could*, Ch. 4, above.

2. The "romantic-realistic" comedy has, like Etherege's *The Comical Revenge*, a "romantic" and usually "tragi-comic" plot or world juxtaposed with a "realistic" and more obviously "comic" one. See the later discussion of Fletcher's *Monsieur Thomas*.

3. See *All Fools, Monsieur D'Olive, Sir Giles Goosecap*. In *All Fools*, for example, Valerio is the courtly lover:

> So Love, fair shining in the inward man,
> Brings forth in him the honourable fruits
> Of valour, wit, virtue, and haughty thoughts,
> Brave resolution, and divine discourse.   (I.1.107–10)

And Dariotto is the epicure who "playest the stallion" and "runn'st through the whole town herd" (III.1.275–7).

the opposition typically constitutes the basis for the two contrasting worlds of the play. In doing so it further defines the issues which prepare for the Restoration comedy of manners.

Unlike Chapman, who consistently views the epicure as man fallen to the level of the beast, Fletcher is content for the most part to let the opposition of epicure and stoic stand as merely two contrasting potentials and sets of attitudes. It is, indeed, probably inaccurate to say that he was interested in the problem of man or of love at all. He was interested chiefly in their sensational possibilities as subjects for his dramas. And in the concern of his age with the epicure and stoic, he found the type of dramatically divergent and flatly oppositional situation which the peculiar dialectic of his art could so well, though from the ideological point of view so inconclusively, exploit.

The Fletcherian rake has been generally accepted as a source of influence for Restoration comedy. Within limits the acceptance is just, though when compared to the studied restraint and ironic self-consciousness of the Restoration comic hero, the typical Fletcherian rake is a little like a rowdy undergraduate.[4] Nevertheless, while largely innocent of distinct ideology, he helps in certain ways to pass on to Restoration comedy a consciousness of its purposes and values.[5] First, he is rather clearly an epicure. His lusty animality declares the pleasure of the senses, and his attitude toward love is purely appetitive. Like Tharsalio, he makes the confident assumption that women, for all their prating of constancy, honor, virtue, and modesty, have in reality much the same attitude. He characteristically sees marriage, therefore, as merely a "custom" at odds with his liberty and indulgence. Second, since the Fletcherian method requires the posing of oppositions at their starkest and most unqualified extremes, the naturalism of the Fletcherian rake, however unlettered, is perhaps the most assertive and vociferous in Jacobean comedy. His vigor, then, if not his bumptiousness, commended him to the Restoration libertine.[6] Third, unlike Freevill and the all but unvarying course of the Caroline epicure in love, his naturalism is not characteristically subjected to the rigors of a stoical conversion.

4. Concerning Fletcher's rakes, at least, Dryden, taken at his own terms, was surely right in believing that "their wit [Dryden is speaking of all "our predecessors"] was not that of gentlemen; there was ever somewhat that was ill-bred and clownish in it" (*Essays, I,* 174-5).

5. The variety of materials and treatment in Fletcher's comedies is likely to render suspect any generalized statement about typical attributes for his characters. Nevertheless the discussion which follows, while it deals in detail with only two of Fletcher's plays, will in outline apply to many.

6. Fletcher's great popularity, together with Jonson's, in the Restoration theaters' repertoires has significance for the lines of development with which this and the following chapter are concerned. For the prominence of the two dramatists on the Restoration stage see the Appendix in John Harold Wilson's *The Influence of Beaumont and Fletcher on Restoration Drama,* Ohio State Univ., 1928.

In this fact lies a point of special interest for the seventeenth-century comedy of love. The Fletcherian rake, like virtually all his Caroline and Restoration successors, customarily ends his course in marriage. But in terms of the problem of love, there is usually little meaning in his doing so. It is merely a way—presumably to Fletcher's audience an agreeable way—of bringing the play to an end after the author has exhausted the sensational situations arising from the naturalistic predilections of the character. There is commonly little or no question of conflict between passion or appetite and reason; there is usually no comic movement from conviction to experience to new awareness; there is seldom the question, as in *The Dutch Courtezan* and the later Caroline plays, of the character's being led from his "beastliness" to a higher love by the virtue and goodness of a woman; nor is there, as a rule, any deliberate ambiguity regarding the implications of the marriage.[7] Nevertheless, the mere lack of reform could make the drama more congenial to the Restoration libertine than the moralistic program of the succeeding period. At the same time the very indecisiveness of the treatment could intensify for the Restoration comic dramatist the problems which Fletcher was not concerned to solve.

In *The Wild-Goose Chase* Mirabel anticipates more fully and explicitly than most Fletcherian rakes the libertine naturalism of the Etheregean hero, though his more than ordinary gusto and obstreperousness serve especially to distinguish him from his Restoration successors. His epicureanism is announced in his first speech.

> Welcome to Paris once more, Gentlemen;
> We have had a merry and a lusty Ordinary,
> And Wine, and good meat, and a bounsing Reckoning;
> And let it go for once; 'Tis a good Physick,
> Only the Wenches are not for my diet,
> They are too lean and thin; their embraces brawn-faln.
> Give me the plump Venetian, fat, and lusty,
> That meets me soft and supple; smiles upon me,
> As if a Cup of full Wine leapt to kiss me;
> These slight things I affect not.[8]

7. There are among Fletcher's comedies some exceptions to these statements which are relevant to our concerns in this chapter. In *Love's Pilgrimage*, for example, Marc-Antonio is converted from his role as epicure in a fashion resembling the prevailing practice in the Caroline comedy of love. On the other hand, Hylas and Dorothea agree to marry at the end of *Monsieur Thomas* with the mutual rights of future infidelity. Neither resolution has much meaning in any "problem" sense. But each of them suggests in its different way the problems faced by the later Restoration plays.

8. *The Works of Francis Beaumont and John Fletcher*, eds. A. Glover and A. R. Waller (Cambridge, 1905-12), Vol. 4, 1.2, pp. 319-20. All subsequent references are to this edition. It is worth noting that Mirabel and his two companions, Pinac and Belleur, have, like Tharsalio in *The Widow's Tears*, just returned from Italy.

Again like all good epicures, and in words reminding us of Wycherley's Horner:

> I hold it as commendable to be wealthy in pleasure,
> As others do in rotten sheep, and pasture.[9]

Like the Etheregean libertine, too, Mirabel and his companions are
in revolt against "stoical" restrictions. They have found Italy a

> . . . brave Country:
> Not pester'd with your stubborn precise Puppies,
> That turn all useful and allow'd contentments
> To scabs and scruples.   (1.2, p. 320)

Concerning love and courtship,

> 'Tis but fleshing,
> But standing one good brunt or two.   (p. 321)

But concerning marriage, they'll none. To satisfy the "senses with
all delicates," with "a plenteous meal," is one thing (II.1, p. 333).
But marriage is another:

> Tug ever like a Rascal at one Oar?
> Give me the Italian liberty.   (1.2, p. 322)

And again,

> I must not lose my liberty, dear Lady,
> And like a wanton slave cry for more shackles.
> What should I marry for? Do I want any thing?
> Am I an inch the farther from my pleasure?
> Why should I be at charge to keep a wife of mine own,
> When other honest married men will ease me?
> And thank me too, and be beholding to me:
> Thou thinkst I am mad for a Maiden-head, thou art cozen'd;
> Or if I were addicted to that diet
> Can you tell me where I should have one?   (II.1, p. 333)

As for courtly vows and protestations:

> . . . I have made a thousand of 'em,
> They are things indifferent, whether kept or broken;
> Meer venial slips, that grow not near the conscience;
> Nothing concerns those tender parts; they are trifles;
> For, as I think, there was never man yet hop'd for

9. II.1, p. 334. Compare the passage quoted from *The Country Wife* in Ch. 2, p. 39,
above.

> Either constancie, or secrecie, from a woman,
> Unless it were an Ass ordain'd for sufferance.   (p. 332)

And again,

> . . . Do'st thou see this book here?
> Look over all these ranks; all these are women,
> Maids, and pretenders to Maiden-heads; these are my conquests,
> All these I swore to marry, as I swore to thee,
> With the same reservation, and most righteously,
> Which I need not have done neither; for alas they made no scruple,
> And I enjoy'd 'em at my will, and left 'em:
> Some of 'em are married since, and were as pure maids again,
> Nay o' my conscience better than they were bred for;
> The rest fine sober women.   (p. 334)

As for women's love, therefore, 'tis but a matter of "crying for a cod-piece" (p. 334).

In all this, despite the bumptiousness of Fletcher's character, there are convictions which are precisely those of the Etheregean hero. But the action of the play has only peripheral importance for the Restoration comedy of manners. Mirabel is pursued throughout by Oriana, who is determined to bring him to the lure of wedlock. Unlike the Etheregean heroines then, she, not the hero, is the prime mover of the action, together with her various allies. In the course of this campaign there are, to be sure, "witty sex duels" (Mirabel's two companions have ladies also with whom they square away in battles of assorted forms and purposes) which sometimes in their tone and naturalistic imagery suggest Etheregean comedy. But the central action of hero and heroine consists largely of a series of tricks and disguises by which Oriana attempts to trap Mirabel into marriage. Finally, when the oppositional nature of the characters' attitudes and situations has been fully exploited, Oriana's trickery succeeds. With total improbability and unprepared abruptness, Mirabel suddenly capitulates at the end:

> Well: I do take thee upon meer Compassion;
> And I do think I shall love thee. As a Testimony,
> I'le burn my book, and turn a new leaf over.   (v.6, p. 389)

"I do take thee upon meer Compassion" at once echoes the surrender of Shakespeare's Benedick and anticipates the tone of capitulation in Etherege's Sir Frederick.[1] Mirabel's turning "a new leaf over" re-

---

1. "Come, I will have thee; but, by this light, I take thee for pity" (*Much Ado*, v.4.92–3).

minds us indeed of Sir Frederick's "reform." And it is even possible
to see in the figure something of the equivocality in the later hero's
"virtuous." But unlike the situations in Shakespeare's and Etherege's
plays, Mirabel's reform and the entire and improbable denouement
have little comic meaning. The play itself has not really been a comedy
of love. There is, in Meredith's famous phrase, no "idea" in it.[2] It has
been, first, a comedy of situation, and second, a comedy of "wit"—
of strikingly oppositional declamations hurled by the characters at
each other, but to no real thematic purpose.[3]

Much the same is true of Fletcher's opposition, within the multiple-
plot structure, of the epicure and stoic. The contrast is seldom resolved
by the play's sanction of one mode or the other. But the Fletcherian
technique of exploiting oppositions consistently brings the two modes
into pointed juxtapositions which propose the problem of love even
while they do not resolve it, and which the Restoration, intent upon
the problem, could therefore utilize. The relevance of Fletcher's method
in this regard will be apparent if we compare one of his "romantic-
realistic" comedies with Etherege's first play, *The Comical Revenge*.

The two worlds of *Monsieur Thomas* are much more closely related
in terms of plot than are the opposing worlds of Etherege's play.
But they divide like the latter and like innumerable Jacobean and
Caroline comedies into a world of serious or "tragi-comic" tone and
treatment on the one hand and a world of obviously comic and semi-
farcical character on the other. In the latter, Thomas, who gives his
name to the title of the play, is a scapegrace whose epicurean propensities do not differ in kind from those of Fletcher's Mirabel. A
little like Marston's Freevill, his attitude toward marriage is not
entirely clear. He has been rejected by his "mistress," Mary, for his
wild ways. And his campaign to regain her "favor" seems to look at
times toward marriage, at times toward seduction. But of his attitude
toward love, his skepticism regarding woman's virtue, and his devotion to the life of sensual indulgence and pleasure there is little doubt.

At the same time Thomas' campaign against his mistress, with its
conniving and trickery, is contrasted, as in Etherege's Sir Frederick,
with the virtuous and honorable proceedings of the serious portion of
the play. There Valentine at the beginning of the play has won, with
the aid of his sister, Alice, the love of his young ward, Cellide. Cellide's
love is of the "mind," engendered by Valentine's "goodness" (1.1, pp.
93–4). Athwart this relationship comes Francisco, a young man whom
Valentine has befriended and whom he has brought home from his

2. George Meredith, *An Essay on Comedy*, ed. Lane Cooper (Cornell Univ. Press,
1956), p. 106.
3. See Eugene Waith, "John Fletcher and the Art of Declamation," *PMLA*, 66
(March 1951), 226–34.

travels to live with him. Francisco falls in love with Cellide after the
approved courtly manner (III.I, pp. 121–6). But his friendship with
Valentine obliges him, in the name of honor, to conceal his passion. He
falls ill of his love. Valentine guesses the cause of his illness and nobly
surrenders his beloved to Francisco. But Francisco, understanding his
friend's sacrifice, cannot accept it. In one of those scenes so characteristic of Fletcher, where one startling contretemps and reversal succeeds
another in swift sequence, Francisco at first believes that Cellide is
offering herself to him (precisely, of course, what Thomas desires of
Mary). He finds her, therefore, a "Woman, perfect Woman" her
"beauty" blemished, with "no share of goodness," her honor "stained,"
her "virtue" gone (III.I, p. 124). But Francisco's virtue and honor
now cause Cellide to love, where before there had been only scorn. The
love, however, is of the "soul" (p. 126). Under the circumstances, honor
and virtue forbid any other. She counsels Francisco to preserve his
"honesty," to guard his senses from the assaults of "the tyrant Beauty,"
to keep his "noble heart"

> Rig'd round about with vertue, that no breaches,
> No subtil [mynes] may meet ye. (pp. 125–6)

Francisco, now in turn, can again love Cellide; but the love, of course,
is spiritual.

> Goodness guide thee: . . . a spell dwells in me,
> A hidden charm, shot from this beauteous Woman,
> That fate can ne'r avoid, nor Physik find,
> And by her counsel strengthen'd: only this
> Is all the help I have, I love fair vertue. (p. 126)

He can, therefore, "kiss that virgin hand" with no "prophane lips now,
nor burnt affections," but with "holy wishes" (p. 126). When all the
dramatic turns of this imbroglio have been exhausted, Fletcher resolves
it by his customary type of *deus ex machina*. Francisco turns out to be
Valentine's long lost son, so that the love of Cellide and Francisco can
become, though with scarcely sufficient comment upon the implications
of the change, something more than "spiritual."

Meanwhile, with a method almost precisely that of Etherege in *The
Comical Revenge* but in many respects looking back to such plays as
Much Ado, Fletcher manipulates into striking juxtapositions this world
of virtue, honor, and spiritual-courtly love with the sensualism of
Thomas' world. The extreme position of the "honor" world in one
scene is immediately followed by the opposite extreme in the next, in
which some parallel of action or circumstance underlines the contrast.
Frequently the contrasting worlds converge upon a single scene. Thus,

immediately after Cellide has cured Francisco's illness with her virtuous love, Thomas arrives to cure it with a bottle of

> Old reverend Sack, which for ought that I can read yet,
> Was that Philosophers Stone the wise King *Ptolomeus*
> Did all his wonders by.   (p. 128)

He then in his turn feigns an illness like Francisco's, caused, he protests, by unrequited love for his mistress, whose "goodness all out-going" has prompted him to repent "too late" of his "so lewd" and "so lamentable" life (p. 132). This, of course, as with Sir Frederick, is only a stratagem by which he hopes to elicit from his mistress an avowal of her love. The stratagem fails, and Thomas goes on to his next trick. But meanwhile the pointed juxtapositions of the two worlds have made their comments upon each. And that presumably is as far as Fletcher wished to take the problem of love, or indeed the larger moral and social problem of the epicure versus the stoic. The extremity of each position qualifies the other. And the effect, however unannounced thematically, suggests an ambiguity, a possible but equivocal solution lying somewhere between the two. At least faintly, then, and by implication, the play in still another way anticipates Etheregean comedy and the Restoration comedy of manners as a whole.

The Caroline Solution—Dubious Grace

But Fletcher's play assuredly does not, in this respect, anticipate the prevailing treatment of love in Caroline comedy. It is not within the scope of this study to discuss the causes lying behind the particular moralistic bent of the Caroline dramatists with whom we shall be concerned. In kind, the generally accepted frame of values was not basically different from that of the Jacobeans. And in final evaluation the epicure fares little better in one period than in the other. But within this similarity are significant distinctions. While the epicure—both in love and in the larger social and moral sense to which we shall presently turn—becomes even more persistent and prominent in Caroline than in Jacobean comedy, we are obliged to take him less seriously. He has lost his convictions, his vitality, and all real "beastliness." Both the soaring sensualism of a Volpone and the unabashed and, on the whole, rather healthy animality of Fletcher's rakes disappear. The earlier probing of divergent potentials is replaced by an unconvincing moralism with courtly-love trimming in which the epicure is little more than a naughty boy, to be lectured briefly and then, by the wave of a good woman's hand, converted into a piece of virtue.[4]

4. This treatment is, in general, characteristic of both the "romantic-realistic" genre, in which the opposition takes the form of two largely distinct worlds (see Broome's *English Moor* and Shirley's *The Gamester* as examples) and the "realistic"

Though so facile a dramatic program offered an easy point of attack to the Restoration, it nevertheless in some important respects moved closer than its Jacobean predecessors to the patterns of Etherege's comedy of love. For the dramatic action of the Caroline epicure centered characteristically about attempted seductions.[5] This development meant not only that the matter of "sex combat" moved onto something like the ground in Etherege's play but that the opposing ideologies were more clearly and more consistently defined than they normally were in the earlier period. Although the Caroline epicure had here several quivers to his bow, including the "Machiavellian" use of courtly protestations, he was likely at some stage in his attempted seduction to bring up the matter of "Nature." This customarily permitted his fair and virtuous adversary to correct his misconceptions in the matter and to bring him by dint of considerable discourse into the order of virtue and reason.

Thus Philautus in *Holland's Leaguer,* having tried the courtly jargon of flames and "divine impulsions," pleads next "the law, / And the command of nature," with its implications of liberty, pleasure, and "use." This provides Faustina, the attempted maiden, with her cue; and the entire stock barrage of spiritual-courtly, Christian humanist refutations is leveled against the heretic.

> Upon these terms, I do deny you love me.
> 'Twas lust that flattered sin, made love a god,
> And, to get freedom for his thefts, they gave
> Madness the title of a deity.
>
> . . . . .
>
> No, true love is pure affection,
> That gives the soul transparent, and not that
> That's conversant in beastly appetites.[6]

Bloody but still fighting, Philautus' naturalism makes a last stand. Scorning her "philosophical love," he counters with

> There's none of you but feel the smart
> Of a libidinous sting; else wherefore are
> Those baits and strong allurements to entice us?

(pp. 59–60)

Not without some sliding away from that issue, Faustina asserts that

---

plays, where, within a single comic milieu, the opposition exists between individual characters (see Marmion's *Fine Companion* and Shirley's *Lady of Pleasure*).

5. Seduction or attempted seduction was, of course, far from uncommon in the Jacobean comedy of love, particularly for the rakes of Fletcher. But it was not, as in the Caroline plays, the fixed and central aspect of the epicure's comic action.

6. Marmion, *Works*, pp. 58–9.

> . . . before my virgin zone
> Shall be untied by any unchaste hand,
> Nature shall suffer dissolution.   (p. 60)

Before the awful power of virginity, Philautus, not unlike the later Comus, trembles: "Now, by this light, I think you'll moralize me" (p. 60). Another barrage against his "vice," and he is defeated. He has come, like Marston's Freevill, to perceive the distinction between "the love of a courtesan and a wife."

PHIL.   I came as to
      A whore, but shall return as from a saint.
FAU. Then leave to prosecute the foggy vapours
      Of a gross pleasure, that involves the soul
      In clouds of infamy. I wonder, one
      So complete in the structure of his body,
      Should have his mind so disproportioned,
      The lineament of virtue quite defaced.
PHIL. I am subdued! she has converted me.
      I see within the mirror of her goodness,
      The foulness of my folly. Sweet, instruct me,
      And I will style thee my Aegeria.
FAU. It is a shame, that man that has the seeds
      Of virtue in him, springing unto glory,
      Should make his soul degenerous with sin,
      And slave to luxury, to drown his spirits
      In lees of sloth, to yield up the weak day
      To wine, to lust, and banquets.
PHIL. Here's a woman!   (pp. 60–1)

To Philautus' courtly-Christian conversion, Faustina now adds the heroic. She sends him off to war with,

> I would have you proceed and seek for fame
> In brave exploits, like those that snatch their honour
> Out of the talents of the Roman Eagle.   (p. 61)

And she ends by contrasting this heroic mode with a portrait of the fashionable fop which is so perfectly a picture of Sir Fopling Flutter that it had best be noticed in the following chapter. The regenerated Philautus with "Henceforth I'll strive to fly the sight of pleasure," prepares at once for "the wars" (p. 62).

    This denouement may be taken as typical of the epicure-stoic conflict in the Caroline comedy of love.[7] It brings into focus most of the op-

7. The reformation of almost any of Shirley's rakes provides further illustration, though not all of them are fully "epicurean" as the term is here employed. Since

posing traditions with which the Restoration comedy of manners was concerned: on one side, Christian humanism, an idealized version of courtly love, the "heroic"; on the other, philosophical and moral libertinism plus at least the faint outlines of the Machiavel. Only the "honest man" is missing. Meanwhile, the "Machiavellianism" of the Caroline rake did not, to be sure, go much beyond the precepts of Ovid and Aretino. But these, of course, were components of the Restoration libertine-Machiavel too. And their use by the Caroline rake pointed in certain directions significant for the Restoration.

With the Caroline libertine's established program of seduction, the virtuous lady who was the object of his designs had greater need than her ancestors in the Jacobean comedy of love and more frequent need than the nymphs of Lyly to be aware, as was Nabbes' Lady Worthy, of the "oyle-tongu'd amorist" who gloried "in diversity of Mistrisses" (*Covent Garden*, 11.6, p. 31). Whether he poured into her ear the honeyed words of courtly protestation or sought, like the "juggler," Comus, to "charm" her "judgment" with the "false rules" of his Nature "pranked in reason's garb" (*Comus*, lines 757–9), he was continuing, if not entirely establishing, a precedent for his Restoration successors. And he was also creating a situation which was something like the context for the sex antagonism of Restoration comedy. But the situation was also very different. Faced with the "oyle-tongu'd amorist," the Restoration heroine could not take easy refuge in the orthodox world of moral order and virtue. Her experience and the aggregate conviction of her society in the plays rendered belief in such a world suspect if not impossible. Yet the double standard of sexual morality obliged her to conform in terms of action to the same restraints of chastity and "virtue" as her Caroline predecessors. In this dilemma she must defend herself, as we have seen, not by denying the validity of the libertine's concept of Nature but by taking full cognizance of its possible reality and of the corresponding failure of her world to fulfill the heroic, courtly, and Christian humanist ideals by which the Caroline dramatists so confidently resolved the comedy of love.

These distinctions relate to others in the Caroline and Restoration libertine. By the nature of his role the Caroline rake is seldom permitted any real conflict between reason and passion. Characteristically he moves through the greater part of the play with such libertine con-

Shirley apparently led the Caroline dramatists' program of reform, Fowler's conversion in a relatively early work (*The Witty Fair One*, 1628) may with interest be compared to that of Philautus. As an example of Brome's participation in this practice, see the concluding reformation of Sir Ferdinand in *The Court Beggar*. Hugh Jerker in Nabbes' *Covent Garden*, discussed earlier in this chapter, presents in his conversion an unusual variation upon the customary pattern, but with the same moralistic aim and meaning (see v.2, p. 61). Additional examples and aspects of the program of reform in the Caroline comedy of love are discussed in the following chapter.

victions as he has undisturbed by his emotional entanglements. His conversion, when it comes, is instantaneous and absolute. What his reason,
therefore, had originally told him about Nature and love is in a moment
converted into an entirely new set of convictions based on "right
reason" and entirely consonant with his new emotions. Nor does the
play invite us to suspect that there may be some degree of validity in
the original attitudes or some question and impermanency in the new.
The rake's original reason, indeed, is customarily projected less as
conviction than as ineffectual and transparent rationalization of temporarily wayward action. Consequently there is not only little of the
comedy of disciplined feeling which characterizes the sex antagonism
in the plays of Lyly, Shakespeare, and the Restoration, but there is
little of the ironic and equivocal opposition of reason and nature, reason
and passion, which is so central a characteristic of these plays. There
is certainly no ambiguous question of the "fall of man." The path of the
regenerated libertine in Caroline drama leads to an unequivocal state of
grace.

8

The Comedy of Manners

Jacobean Satire and Society

I T IS generally recognized that in the satiric social comedy or what
is often called the "realistic" comedy of the Jacobean period, there
were three principal lines of interest—the comedy of manners, the
comedy of humors, and the comedy of intrigue. These interests were
not, of course, mutually exclusive. They were the chief components of
a general practice; and the special emphases of each could be and constantly were adapted to serve the needs of the other. The manners of
social classes and the involvements of intrigue are essential ingredients
in the humors plays of Jonson. Intrigue and the humors method of
portraiture became, in turn, established aspects of the comedy of manners and remained such through the Restoration. At the same time each
of these modes could become distractive for the others. Middleton's
study of social classes is repeatedly rendered "impure" in terms of
manners by the intrusions of humors which are more the reflection of
personal eccentricities than of class values. And Fletcher's habitual
flirtation with the problems of manners in general and the epicure in
particular is as habitually distracted by an involvement in intrigues
which are irrelevant to the social problems proposed.

All this is in a sense merely to state again what is generally understood. The social comedy of the Jacobeans took human follies in society
at large as its field. Consequently the specific lines of practice which
most clearly lead to the Restoration are but parts of a larger preoccupation. Yet within this larger interest the dominant modalities repeatedly
suggest the Restoration. In the plays of Chapman, Jonson, Marston,
Middleton the comedy of intrigue projects a world in which survival is
by wit with as much persistency and candor as does the comedy of
manners in the later period.[1] A multifarious assortment of Jacobean
"humours" supplies the Restoration with stock violations of Nature
and Reason—the jealous or uxorious husband, the tyrannical father,
the credulous astrologer, and above all the social pretender. With the

1. Much of this intrigue shows, of course, the clear influence of Latin and more
immediately of Italian comedy. But particularly when the chief intriguer is the young
"gallant" or "wit," the Jacobean practice prepares for the Restoration, as we shall
presently note in more detail.

last of these, the Jacobean interest in humors merges with the interest in manners. And it is with this latter aspect of its social comedy that we are here primarily concerned.

The Jacobean comedy of manners also kept the total society of its time in view. This means not only that its libertine or "epicure" is part of more inclusive concerns but that its leisure class—in which the epicure is chiefly vested—is only one of several classes. And while this fact bears upon a related diversity in Restoration comedy of manners, it also reminds us of essential differences. The central focus of Restoration comedy is clearly upon the libertine world of its comic heroes. In the Jacobean comedy the focus is upon the entire social structure. To the extent, therefore, that the Jacobean plays propose a comedy of man through the comedy of his manners, they do so by offering a view of him in his several social classes, whereas the Restoration projects the behavior and values of a particularized group as a statement of man's comic nature and aspirations. While we may in one sense, then, say that in the Restoration the materials and views are partial and specialized when compared to the earlier period, we may in a more basic sense say that there is a difference in dramatic method. This distinction prepares in turn for others.

Within the Jacobean range of class, certain groups are especially persistent, well defined, and entirely familiar to the student of seventeenth-century comedy. There is first the "lower class"—the servants, town sharpers and gullers, the "roarers" and bullies; second, the "middle class"—the level of the "citizen" or "cit," with its apprentices, tradesmen, merchants, and their wives and daughters; third, the landed gentry who come to the "town"; and fourth, the upper or leisure classes of town and court in which the epicure is most conspicuous. The characteristic ways in which these classes interact is again entirely familiar. But for our interests here certain aspects of this behavior bear recounting. The "cit" is usually concerned either with marrying his children into the landed gentry and leisure class or with preventing such marriage. The landed gentry, either instead of or in addition to attempting a marriage with the "cit's" daughter and, of course, his money, commonly aspires to the manners of the leisure class and particularly to the life of the epicure. The leisure class, when it is not concerned through impoverishment with marrying the "cit's" daughter, is likely to be involved in seducing her or in cuckolding the father. It is also customarily involved with duping the landed gentry which aspires to its mode of living.

It is apparent that this comedy reflects the breakdown and shift of social classes in late Elizabethan and Jacobean England. The most immediate concern of the comedy, indeed, is with this breakdown and with the force which lies behind it as a social and moral solvent—money.

In still a further sense, then, the primary concerns of the Jacobean comedy of manners become peripheral to the Restoration. A Restoration "wit" may upon occasion attempt to make his "fortune" by marrying a wealthy widow.[2] Or the country knight may, as in Etherege's first two plays, be duped in his attempt to become a town libertine. And his comedy reflects thereby its heritage from the earlier practice. But the principal concerns have been altered. The corrupting power of wealth and the disintegration of a traditional class structure were not the primary interests of the Restoration comic writers.

Yet what did interest them had an essential kinship of meaning with their Jacobean predecessors. The kinship lay in a mutually clear awareness that manners are at once the overt expression of man's nature and aspirations and his capacity to falsify them, of his attempt to realize himself within his society and his misconception of reality. In an essay which has considerable bearing upon our present subject, Trilling has suggested that this is the proper and characteristic awareness of all literature which deals with manners; that the problems which this awareness involves must inevitably concern the question of appearance and reality; and that it is in these terms that the relationship of manners to morals must be defined.[3] Viewed in this way, the several social classes of Jacobean comedy are but variations on a central comic theme. The "cit's" attempt to marry his daughter to a "gentleman," the country squire's attempt to become a town "gallant," and the gallant's "epicurean" pursuit of freedom and pleasure have their special comic functions and implications. But their final and common significance lies in the equally illusory character of their aspirations, in the corruptive capacity of human nature to confound its real and its apparent needs.

While these considerations suggest a continuity of interest between the social comedy of the Jacobeans and the Restoration, they also serve to establish further distinctions. In the comedy of manners no less than in the comedy of love, the Jacobean dramatist's own criteria of reality and value were prevailingly on the side of the established moral law. His view of the disruptive manners and morals which he depicted— whether of the "cit," the landed gentry, or the upper leisure class— tended accordingly to be one directional. This is to say not only that his social comedy was most typically satiric but that its principal service was on the side of reform.[4] In contrast to this view and purpose is the basically ambivalent character of the Restoration comedy of manners— its careful balance of opposing sets of assumptions, its testing of each

2. See Freeman in *The Country Wife*. Young Fashion in *The Relapse* is a comparable case, though the country fortune which he marries does not involve a widow.
3. Lionel Trilling, "Manners, Morals, and the Novel," *The Liberal Imagination* (Viking Press, 1950), pp. 205–22.
4. The senses in which Fletcher represents an exception to this statement have been suggested in the preceding chapter.

by the experience projected in its comic action, but its pervasive equivocality in terms of final convictions and values. It is this distinction
which marks one of the most significant modifications made by the
Restoration in the seventeenth-century comedy of manners tradition.
The nature and extent of this modification can best be understood by a
careful inspection of one of the Jacobean plays which seems most fully
to anticipate the Restoration practice.

Near the beginning of the seventeenth century Jonson's *Epicoene*
(1609) gave to the comedy of manners a dramatic form and expression
which in a remarkable number of ways is prophetic of the Restoration.
It is, of course, indicative of the distinctions between the two periods
that in Restoration terms we must for the most part dismiss what is
for Jonson's play the principal comic action—the duping of Morose.
Once this is done, however, the remaining structure of the play has
many similarities to the works of the later period. First of all, with
Morose dismissed the play divides with more clarity than most Restoration comedy of manners into Palmer's dichotomy of character for the
latter—the people of "true wit and perfect fashion" and those who
only "ape the smartness of the time." [5] At the center of the play, in
other words, stand the three young gallants or "wits," Dauphine, Clerimont, and Truewit. On either side of them, as in *She Would If She
Could,* are the dupes male and female—Daw and La-Foole, who aspire
to the social mode of the wits, and the Ladies Collegiate, who have
similar aspirations. [6] Only the "heroine" is missing here in the Restoration's basic pattern of characters. This alignment in the dramatis personae involves further points of similarity.

That the three gallants of Jonson's play reflect an established "social
mode" is indicated in the opening scene by Truewit's "These be the
things, wherein your fashionable men exercise themselves" (1.1.39–40).
The exercise, we have seen in the preceding chapter, is distinctly
"epicurean." And in this as in other aspects of their role, the three wits
are allegedly in revolt against the orthodox or "stoical" values of their
time. But their differences here from the libertine of the Restoration are
at once apparent. Truewit, for example, can say "O, a woman is, then
[when she is adorned by "art"], like a delicate garden" (1.1.104–5).
No Restoration comic hero is ever guilty even in jest of such roman-
ticism. And the point is symptomatic of more essential distinctions.
The "men of mode" in Jonson's play are not actually very disenchanted.

5. See Ch. 1, p. 6, above.
6. Mistresses Otter and Trusty, in aspiring to join the Ladies Collegiate, are also
"pretenders" at a lower social level. The "humours" character of Captain Otter is,
like Morose, largely outside the scheme with which we are here concerned.

They play the game of life and of love with something of the amused detachment and self-conscious irony of Etherege's "honest men." But they do so through little real conviction of more heroic ideals violated by reality. Consequently though they serve, like the Restoration comic hero, to expose the follies and pretensions in the society about them, the exposure, particularly in the play's action, is more on the side of traditional moral order than against it. Nor does their alleged revolt from conventional morality offer any serious threat to the established social order. The play has no doubt as to the frivolity of their pursuits; and it makes clear that they as well as their several dupes are distorting true values. But the wits know this too. Their pose as epicures is as much a playful "humour" as a "fashion," and they have scarcely more faith in it than does the play. In this fact largely lies their superiority to the dupes and the basis of Jonson's relative indulgence toward them. And while this situation, too, has its similarities to the Restoration comedy of manners, it relates to a further distinction. As epicurean gallants, the three wits have little of the "Machiavel." They preach with fully conscious irony the guiles of Ovidean seduction. But in the play's action they make only the faintest gesture in that direction. In other respects also they postulate and exemplify a world of intrigue where survival is by wit. And in these terms they triumph over the dupes after a fashion having many resemblances to the Restoration comedy of manners. But the intrigue, unlike some of Jonson's other plays, bears little testimony of man's Machiavellian nature. In this respect as in all others the wits do not seriously challenge the traditional moral assumptions against which they are allegedly in revolt.

This fact conditions a further point of similarity to the Restoration. As with the epicure throughout seventeenth-century comedy, Jonson's three gallants embody a central contradiction. While they assert the libertine's freedom of indulgence and at least faintly the "warfare" involved in a state of survival by wit, they also subscribe to values which imply the necessity of restraint, order, and degree. Consequently they propose throughout, as does the hero of Restoration comedy, two opposing concepts of Nature and Art. Their Ovidean art of love and the art of their intrigue posits one set of concepts and values. But in the verbal expression of their wit, in their general restraint and polish of manners, in their attitude toward the dupes who violate Nature's degrees, they epitomize the traditional concepts of Castiglione and the "Renaissance gentleman." In other words they subscribe at once to the values of "civilization" and of "naturalism." But unlike Restoration comedy once more, Jonson's play is not basically concerned with this inconsistency. Though the discussion of art and nature which runs through the play keeps the problem before us, the action of the play does not. The wits' epicurean freedom and pursuit of pleasure have little to do with their intrigues. And this consideration brings us to their dupes.

One branch of the wits' intrigue is an "undertaking" with the Ladies Collegiate which to the student of Restoration comedy has many familiar overtones. Truewit attempts a plot to make all the Ladies in love with Dauphine (IV.1.145–7). As the plot develops, however, its purpose becomes not libertine indulgence but a comic exposure of the dupe's social pretensions. It is in this regard that the undertaking has its chief interest for the Restoration. Though the Ladies Collegiate are less fully developed as female dupes than are Etherege's Lady Cockwood and her successors, they clearly anticipate the later roles. They too are engaged in taking their "freedom" in a society with a double standard of sexual conduct. And they must accordingly play the hypocrite by keeping one eye on their "honor" and the other on their "pleasure." Consequently their protestations and pretensions take many a Restoration turn: "I assure you, Sir Dauphine, it is the price and estimation of your vertue onely, that hath embarqu'd me to this adventure, and I could not but make out to tell you so; nor can I repent me of the act, since it is alwayes an argument of some vertue in our selves, that we love and affect it so in others" (v.2.1–6). The entire comic action, in fact, by which the wits expose both the Ladies' hypocrisies and their general inadequacy for the role they attempt has much the same surface outline as in the Restoration comedy of manners. The resemblance here is especially noteworthy since this precise type of female dupe is not again so clearly or fully projected in pre-Restoration comedy.[7] Yet neither in themselves nor in their relation to the wits do the Ladies Collegiate acquire more than a suggestion of the equivocality of meaning which characterizes the Etheregean dupe. In a general way they contribute like the wits to the comedy of appearance and reality. And to an extent their burlesque espousal of the wits' epicurean values serves to emphasize the falseness in both. But since the wits bring no real conviction to their own values, the dupes' mimicry of them loses much of the comic significance which it has in the Restoration.

The situation is much the same for the male dupes. But of them there is more to be said both historically and dramatically. The indebtedness of Restoration comedy to antecedent practice is in no other respect so extensive and apparent as in the role of the fop. His character had been fully established in nondramatic social satire by the time Jonson, Chapman, and Marston began to write their comic dramas. But with these writers he takes his place as standard material for the social

7. Some of the characters in Caroline comedy who have been viewed as predecessors of Lady Cockwood are noted in subsequent portions of this chapter.

comedy of the seventeenth century. And he displays throughout the works of the pre-Restoration dramatists a set of manners not essentially different from those which he possesses in the Restoration. Prevailingly he aspires in the full sense of the word to be an epicure. Wit, clothes, and sex are, accordingly, the principal objects of his aspirations, as they are for the fashionable "wit" from *Epicoene* to *The Man of Mode*.

But the fop of Jacobean comedy displays a more particularized set of manners which continues into the Restoration. Among the "affected courtiers" in Marston's *The Fawn*, Sir Amoroso Debile-Dosso resorts, like Etherege's Sir Oliver, to aphrodisiacs in order that he may play, or rather pretend to play, the libertine; but like Sir Oliver, he remains too impotent to satisfy either wife or mistress and can only talk of his undertakings. Nymphadoro, like Chapman's Dariotto in *All Fools,* is or attempts to be a "common lover"—a lover, that is, "of all women." Frappatore, like half the fops in both pre-Restoration and Restoration comedy, is one of those "forgers of love-letters, false braggarts of ladies' favours, and vain boasters of counterfeit tokens" (see V.I.302–4). With these characteristics go others which are equally typical of the fop in the seventeenth-century comedy of manners, as the prefatory "character" of Fastidious Brisk in Jonson's *Every Man Out of His Humour* will indicate: "A neat, spruce, affecting Courtier, one that weares clothes well, and in fashion; practiseth by his glasse how to salute; speakes good remnants (notwithstanding the Base-violl and Tabacco:) sweares tersely, and with variety; cares not what Ladies favour he belyes, or great Mans familiarity: a good property to perfume the boot of a coach." Only a moment's reflection is necessary for one to realize how many of these precise characteristics are in Sir Fopling, even down to the detail of practicing "by his glasse how to salute." [8]

The first significance for us in all this is that it makes clear how little the manners of the fop in themselves varied through the course of seventeenth-century social comedy. It suggests also how fully in Jacobean comedy those manners had become the expression not only of "epicurean" values but of an epicurean social ritual. Consequently, though the characters and aspirations of Daw and La-Foole in *Epicoene* are drawn with more than customary fullness, they are not in themselves essentially different from innumerable characters in the comedy of their time. What gives them special interest for our purposes here is their position within the structure of the play. As with the Ladies Collegiate, the relation of Daw and La-Foole to the three gallants of *Epicoene* involves firmer and more nearly Restoration distinctions between the false and the true epicure, the fop and the gentleman, the fool and the wit, the comic dupe and the comic hero than do most Jacobean plays. Balanced by their female counterparts, the two male dupes complete in

8. See *Man of Mode*, p. 260.

action as they do in character a comic pattern which continues to anticipate the structure of the Restoration comedy of manners. These dupes too have their "undertakings" which attempt to imitate the ritual of the epicurean mode, but which in their lack of finesse contrasts with the skill of the three wits. Daw attempts to seduce Epicoene, and both he and La-Foole undertake an "intrigue" with the Ladies Collegiate. For their pretensions they are exposed by the wits much after the Restoration fashion.[9] The parallels continue in other aspects of their attempted role. Daw's absurd affectations, for example, as a writer of witty love poetry contrasts with Clerimont's production of the delightful "Still to be neat, still to be drest" (1.1.91ff.). And in all these respects the dupes of Jonson's play, like those of the Restoration, make clear that it is conformity to and membership in a social mode which is their primary end, rather than the values of freedom and pleasure, nature and art which the terms of the mode itself express.

While aspects of the material and form employed in *Epicoene* are to be found in numerous Jacobean comedies, it seems safe to assert that no other play of the period so fully anticipates the Restoration practice. The "witty sex battles" between comic hero and heroine which Jonson's work lacks will be most conspicuously supplied by the plays of Fletcher, though these, we have seen in the preceding chapter, seldom approach the issues typical of the conflict between the sexes in the Restoration. In Fletcher's plays, too, there is often a stratification of comic hero and dupe which embodies some of the meanings found in *Epicoene*. Occasionally this stratification combines with the relations of hero and heroine to produce a comic structure which shows further advances toward the Restoration plays. In *Wit without Money,* one of Fletcher's nearest approaches to a true comedy of manners, Valentine as hero and his three companions as dupes have many of the characteristics found in the epicurean mode of *Epicoene*. And in addition the hero's encounters with Lady Hartwell as heroine contrast with the dupes' inept attempts to woo her in a fashion which suggests the subsequent comedies of Wycherley and Congreve. But all these relationships are in various ways divergent from the libertine or epicurean point of view. The hero on the topic of "love" will serve to illustrate the divergency: "What do we get by women, but our senses, which is the rankest part about us, satisfied, and when that's done, what are we?" (11.1, p. 158) That this conviction is hardly consistent with other aspects of the comic hero's role is only another indication of the dramatic instability which typifies most of Fletcher's characters. But the instability is itself one of the reasons why the plays of Fletcher have a limited significance for

9. That their exposure is far more protracted than is commonly the case in the Restoration emphasizes the differences between Jonson's program of social satire and the Restoration's interest in the libertine as comic hero.

those lines of seventeenth-century comedy which lead to the Restoration. Beyond this consideration, however, is the fact that in none of his plays is a distinctly epicurean order so conspicuous as it is in *Epicoene*. And in none of them is that order so nearly free from the intrusions of other social modes and manners.

Apart from Jonson and Fletcher, the most significant fact about the epicurean order in Jacobean comedy is that when it occurs in a relatively full form, it is usually the exclusive province of the dupe and fop. This means, of course, that the epicure was commonly treated as an object of satire. But the implications of the treatment have further points of interest. In his "naturalism" the epicure was, we have seen, viewed simply as the beast in man. When he combined with this a concern for the fashions of wit and clothes, he became a fool as well. Despite the historical tradition of the "Renaissance gentleman," the Jacobean comedy of manners as a whole did not, like Jonson's three wits in *Epicoene* and the later Restoration and Augustan writers, view the fashionable concern with dress as a possible means and symbol of ordering Nature. Consequently it was not centrally concerned with the paradox that clothes might be at once a sign and symbol of Nature ordered and Nature disguised. The chief significance of most fops in Jacobean comedy is not that they violate "degree" by attempting to "force Nature." It is rather that they are in Christian terms given over to vanity. They are, that is, concerned with the external and material rather than the inner and spiritual. The value of external dress as a manifestation of internal order or, more precisely, of the two at once as aspects of a total order is more conspicuous in the Caroline comedy of manners than in the Jacobean. And the difference marks a further development toward the preoccupations typical of the Restoration. The history of the fop in seventeenth-century comedy provides one of the many indications of a progression from Christian dualism to neoclassic "monism."

Caroline Manners and Morals

Until relatively recent times, it had been the accepted belief that the social comedy in Caroline drama was much more Jacobean than Restoration.[1] The belief was not without its justifications. The characteristic concerns of Jacobean comedy with humors, manners, and intrigue remain the chief ingredients of Caroline comedy as well. And within these general lines of interest is a vast assortment of more detailed practices which reveal the continuity and in many ways the ex-

1. Lynch's *Social Mode of Restoration Comedy* was one of the first studies to examine in detail the distinctions in Caroline comedy which prepare for the Restoration. See also Harbage, *Cavalier Drama*.

haustion of a tradition—stock characters and "humours," stock situations, stock turns of plot, and even stock speeches. Nevertheless out of
this reworking of traditional materials there emerge certain developments which distinguish the Caroline dramatists from their predecessors. The most fundamental of these developments is an increasing
preoccupation with the comedy of manners. The interest here continues
at least nominally to be with much the same range and variety of social
classes as in the preceding period. But a number of modifying tendencies
create a body of drama which is peculiar to its time yet which prepares
for the subsequent plays of the Restoration.

Under the encouraging eye of Henrietta Maria, in the face of increasing ostracism by the Puritan middle class, and with the greater
prominence of courtier or near-courtier as playwright, Caroline drama
as a whole tended to assume something of the upper-class and aristocratic character which marks the Restoration plays. Consequently, with
the important exception of Brome, the traditional comedy of the citizen
and the lower-class gullers and roarers loses its vitality. It becomes a
hackneyed and lifeless repetition of materials from Jonson, Middleton,
Heywood, and the Jacobean period at large. Such vitality as the plays
have lies largely in their portrayal of an upper leisure class or "polite"
society. At the same time there is a growing tendency to make the
middle class itself "polite"—to free it of some of the "cit" machinery
which characterized the Jacobean comedy, and to move it toward the
polish and wit, such as it was, of the leisure class. One result is a
leveling or uniformity of tone, texture, and concern which prepares at
least in a general way for the Restoration. Further, though the Caroline
writers keep for the most part the Jacobean variety of social groups,
they increasingly accord their "polite" class a predominant position. Its
manners and values become accordingly the central concern around
which the remaining classes take peripheral positions. In this respect,
too, the Caroline comedy of manners moves toward the Restoration.
And it prepares us to find that in a few plays, such as Shirley's *Hyde
Park* and *The Lady of Pleasure,* this predominant class has virtually
become the comic world of the play.

But it is here that the need for further distinctions becomes apparent. A "polite" society is not necessarily an "epicurean" society, nor
need it have much to do with the preoccupations of the Restoration
comedy of manners. Its presence, indeed, need not constitute a true
comedy of manners at all. *Hyde Park,* as probably every authority on
Shirley and the Caroline drama has agreed, is in some sense largely a
comedy of manners. It depicts with careful detail the social behavior of
an educated and articulate upper-middle-class group. Consequently most
members of that group interest us at least in part because they reflect
the manners and values of a social class and because in those terms they

are brought to account by the values of the play. To this extent the work may be called a comedy of manners; and to this extent its char- acteristics are shared by all comedies of manners from Jonson's *Epi- coene* to Clare Booth's *The Women*. But in few other important ways does it suggest Restoration comedy; and even in these broad terms it is itself far from "pure." It is, in fact, of interest to us as a reminder that the Caroline use of "humours" could still become intrusive in a general manners context.

The most prominent comic conflict of the play and the one which has commonly been viewed as of particular significance for the Restoration, concerns the "witty sex battles" of Carol and her wooer, Fairfield. The conflict, however, does not arise primarily from the manners and values of a social class. It stems chiefly, as the play repeatedly makes clear, from Carol's "humour" for contrariety. In this respect her behavior— or what has sometimes been called her "social attitudinizing"—far from conforming to the dictates of her society's "fashionable mode," is viewed by every member of the play, including herself, as eccentric and individual.[2] Her wooer wins her love and thus the sex battle merely by forbidding her to fall in love with him—a common-sense stratagem which has little bearing upon the problem of class manners. The entire situation is distinctly Fletcherian and is, in fact, based upon Beaumont and Fletcher's *The Scornful Lady,* where the lady has a similar "hu- mour" countered by a similar device.

Yet the wit employed in this conflict is not totally divorced from the comedy of manners. Carol, in her humor of contrariety, has some sharp comments upon many of the values and practices which char- acterize her society. She inveighs particularly against "whining" lovers, the "foolish labyrinths" into which love "dost . . . lead us," and the "trouble" of a husband.[3] This sounds pertinent to the Restoration, as indeed it and certain details of the play's general structure are.[4] But the "humorous" impulses lying behind these assertions condition their comic meaning. And in any event they are scarcely an expression of the "fashionable" values in her society. On the contrary, they too are consistently viewed as individual and eccentric—a view shared by her wooer, who explicitly labels them "a new doctrine from women" (1.2, p. 472). Finally, if the play in some respects underwrites Carol's alleged convictions where her society will not, it, no more than the society, underwrites her eccentricity. Those fashionable attitudes and

2. See II.4, p. 490, *The Dramatic Works and Poems of James Shirley,* ed. W. Gifford and A. Dyce, London, 1833, Vol. 2.

3. See especially 1.2, in which these instances of her criticism occur.

4. In a subsidiary portion of *Hyde Park,* Julietta's "sex battles" with Lord Bonvile, her would-be seducer, are more pertinent to the concerns of the Restoration than are those of Carol and Fairfield. But Bonvile's attitudes before his conversion are exceptional in the society of the play.

practices which her humor helps the play to expose are largely surface deviations from an essentially orthodox moral code. Accordingly, Carol's return to the fold is the unequivocal mark of her "dehumouring," not the comic triumph or possible triumph of custom over Nature and Reason.

In the light of these considerations, *The Lady of Pleasure* is of special interest. Unlike *Hyde Park* and most Caroline as well as Jacobean comedy, it is almost purely a comedy of manners. It is probably, in fact, the most nearly pure of any play before the Restoration, if we mean by pure that the attitudes and behavior of all the characters are immediately referable to the manners and values of distinct social groups. Further, the society of the play embodies more fully the epicurean mode than any work since *Epicoene*. Finally, the concern of the play is primarily with the manners and values of that mode. As the result of all this, the work has a particular relevance to the Restoration. Yet in these respects, its essential differences are immediately discernible.

At the center of the play, so far as values are concerned, stand Lord Bornwell—a country nobleman—and the two stewards. They are unequivocally Shirley's spokesmen, which means that they are unequivocally the spokesmen for the orthodox moral and social order. They are, therefore, unequivocally opposed to the epicurean order. On one side of them stands Lady Bornwell, who has come from the country to the town in order to take her "freedom" and "pleasure" in the full epicurean sense. On the other side stands the second "lady of pleasure," Celestina—a young and wealthy town widow who is also engaged in the pursuit of pleasure, but with a difference. Like Alithea in *The Country Wife* and the Lady Townley group in *The Man of Mode*, she desires only to "take the innocent liberty of the town." [5] Like them, her behavior is firmly based upon genuine, not feigned, "honor" and "virtue." And she accordingly stands outside the real epicurean order even while aspects of her social behavior merge to a degree with it. Like the Townley group of Etherege's comedy, therefore, she is criticized by the play for her frivolity of behavior and "manners," not her basic moral values. But like Wycherley's Alithea and unlike the Etherege group, she is never confused or deceived by the epicurean order which buzzes about her. Her express function, on the contrary, is to expose her epicurean wooers and to reform with the firm Caroline moralism already noted in the comedy of love the quasi-courtly lord who also attempts to seduce her.

In all these respects she stands at the opposite pole from the other lady of pleasure, Lady Bornwell. Yet the latter is an epicurean dupe in a very different sense from Lady Cockwood and her successors. She is

5. *William Wycherley*, Mermaid Series, p. 266. Cf. *Lady of Pleasure*, II.2, p. 32.

not primarily portrayed as the "conventional" hypocrite, and she does not misinterpret the epicurean mode while attempting to comply with it. From the play's point of view she understands the values of the mode perfectly well, and she takes her "liberty" accordingly and precisely as she desires. Nor is her "undertaking" in the play centrally concerned with the comic discrepancy between the epicurean order and the double-standard prohibitions of the conventional society in which it must operate. Lady Bornwell is an epicurean dupe only in being an epicure. She has, that is, duped herself in failing to see—as she sees eventually and unequivocally in the terms of the play's own traditional moralism—the hollowness and "sin" of the order to which she had subscribed. Her reform, like the resolution of most pre-Restoration comedy dealing with the epicure, is an unambiguous reaffirmation of the established moral and social order. While in both manners and general structure, then, the play repeatedly suggests the Restoration, it as repeatedly insists upon the essential distinctions.

In this respect it is typical of the prevailing practice. We have previously noted that Caroline comedy, much more than the Jacobean, kept the epicure in view. He became an increasingly conspicuous part of the leisure society to which the comic dramatists gave their best attention. If they did not in any other play so fully project his "order," they dealt at large with its values and with the principal aspects of its comic structure. And in doing so, they continued to modify the practices of the earlier period in ways significant for the Restoration. With the Caroline merger of Fletcher's quarreling lovers and Jonson's social satire, the comedy of love became a more prominent, in fact the most prominent part of the comedy of manners. In this context it remained for the Caroline dramatist as for his predecessors a matter more of public morality and social welfare than of personal experience. But it became, like the comedy of manners in general, less persistently and immediately connected with the breakdown of an established social class structure. It became, in other words, more directly and purely a problem of moral values. And since the epicure was viewed chiefly as an infection in the social organism, his statutory reform became in essence a ritualistic cleansing of the body social. In this respect it looks back to the Jacobeans. But it looks forward also to the Restoration, where "reform" of some kind—whether real or feigned, permanent or temporary —was as much the lot of the epicure as in the preceding periods. It is just here that the Caroline distinctions between epicure as "wit" and the pseudo-epicure as dupe become most significant.

Much more frequently than in the Jacobean comedy, the Caroline dramatists employed this stratification as part of the epicurean order. And characteristically it involved the distinction central to the Restoration plays: The aim of the epicure was freedom; the real aim of the aspiring dupe was ritual and membership in the fashionable mode. But their relationship was also likely to involve distinctions in terms of wit-false wit, fop-gentleman, hero-dupe. To an extent, accordingly, the Caroline epicure was sometimes permitted to be, like the Restoration libertine "honest man," an exposer not only of his dupe but of the conventional pretensions and follies about him. He tended, as a result, to acquire something of the ambivalence which distinguishes the Restoration hero. Since he was himself an epicure, he exposed his dupe not in the Christian terms of vanity but of "degree" and "forcing Nature." The dupe as fop, in turn, began to acquire meaning as a misuser of "refinement," as a disorderer of "Nature" through his false ordering of wit, clothes, and politesse in general. We are introduced to Marmion's Spruce, one of the finest and most nearly Restoration of all the Caroline pseudo-epicures, by his speech, "I met with a disaster coming up. Something has ravisht the tassel of my garter, and discompos'd the whole fabric, 'twill cost me an hour's patience to reform it; I had rather have seen the Commonwealth out of order." [6] He, like numerous compeers, reflects the Caroline dramatist's own increasing concern with "refinement" as a means of ordering Nature—a concern in part conditioned by the interest of Henrietta Maria's court in préciosité.[7] Inevitably in such a context, the "true" epicure began at least to adumbrate the comic inconsistency so central to his Restoration successors—the attempt to assimilate two disparate concepts of Nature.

The sum of all these developments constituted a distinct foreshadowing of the Restoration use of epicure and pseudo-epicure, as Shirley's *The Witty Fair One,* Nabbes' *Covent Garden,* Marmion's *A Fine Companion* and *Holland's Leaguer* make clear.[8] But these relationships were consistently undernourished by the dramatist's program of moral reform—a program which militated also against other conditions essential to Restoration comedy, while at the same time it employed similar lines of dramatic structure. With the comedy of love in the foreground of the comedy of manners, the principal line of action for the pseudo-epicure as well as the epicure became the battle of the sexes. And as in the Restoration, the "undertakings" of the two were con-

6. *A Fine Companion,* 1.5, p. 118.

7. This particular point in the précieuse interests of the Caroline court has not received the attention it deserves. But related aspects of préciosité in the drama of the period have been considerably explored. See especially chs. 3 and 4 of Lynch, *Social Mode.*

8. Characteristically, however, this stratification of characters in terms of the epicure is part of the larger opposition between epicure and stoic. The resultant division of characters points directly to Etherege's *The Comical Revenge.* In *The Witty Fair One,* for example, Aimwell and Violetta are the "courtly" lovers who contrast with Fowler, the epicure, and Sir Nicholas, the "foolish knight" dupe. In *A Fine Companion,* Aurelio and Valeria are the stoical lovers, while Careless is the epicure and Spruce the epicurean fop-dupe.

sistently juxtaposed—either by their pursuit of the same woman (as in *The Comical Revenge*) or by parallel pursuits of different quarry (as in *She Would If She Could*). But since, unlike the Restoration, moral purification was the certain and overriding destiny of both, the favored Caroline arm of destiny for one as for the other was the transforming virtue of their quarry.[9] This meant not only that the position and meaning of battle was fundamentally different from that in the Restoration—a point sufficiently stressed in the preceding chapter—but that the transformation of epicure and pseudo-epicure alike tended to level, indeed to lay waste all previous distinctions. In light of the courtly-Christian grace which descended upon each, "degree" became impertinent. If the most conspicuous task of the Caroline comedy of manners was a ritualistic purging of the body social, it was also an unequivocal, however convincing, assertion of the ultimate goodness of man.

Athwart the line of moral reform which we have sketched in Caroline comedy, there developed to some extent what might be called a countermovement. A few plays by dramatists such as Killigrew, Davenant, and Newcastle clearly do not conform to the moral program which we have noted. And it has been the custom of most previous investigations to make much of these plays as significant antecedents of Restoration comedy. It is, of course, a pertinent fact that these dramatists are the ones who most conspicuously continued their work into the Restoration. Consequently the temptation is great to stress their importance for both the Caroline and later period. But apart from their relative smallness in number, several considerations—particularly in the terms of this study—tend to minimize their importance. In the first place, the specific point of departure for most of these works was the *précieuse* and so-called "Platonic love" practices and assumptions of the Caroline court. While this development involved questions of both love and manners which were by no means irrelevant to the Restoration, the points of central satire upon the "Platonic" were. The question of "fruition" versus "nonfruition," for example, with which Killigrew and Davenant, among others, made merry was clearly not the issue in the Restoration. And if the "Platonic" was in certain obvious ways a "stoic," his spe-

9. There were, to be sure, numerous variations upon this practice. Kickshaw in *The Lady of Pleasure* is converted from his epicureanism by Lady Bornwell after she herself has reformed. And Spruce in *A Fine Companion,* who in addition to being an epicurean fop is something of a "Machiavellian villain," is reformed in both respects when he is led to believe that a lady whose "honor" he has slandered has as a consequence gone mad.

The Caroline reform of both epicure and epicurean fop-dupe frequently reveals by the nature of its contrivance a lineal descendency from the "dehumoring" techniques of Jonson's plays. But the heavyhanded moralism involved distinguishes the process from the firmly comic and satiric methods of Jonson.

cialized excesses in this as in other directions made him an object of satire for the moralistic dramatist as for the others.

Apart from the specialized interest in the "Platonic," there are in terms of Restoration antecedents other significant limitations in these plays. None of them is so nearly pure a comedy of manners as *The Lady of Pleasure,* and none of them focuses so clearly upon the specific problems of the epicurean order. It is probably true that the general social milieu of *The Parson's Wedding* and even of *The Country Captain* suggests more clearly the Restoration in broad terms of "atmosphere" and tone than do many of the moralistic plays which we have considered. But they are less specifically concerned with the problems of the Restoration comedy of manners and their lines of structure are less clearly anticipatory. In *The Parson's Wedding,* the two young rakes who square away with the two "witty" ladies are not really "epicures" at all in any precise sense. They are merely an unusually bawdy type of Fletcherian wencher whose lineage is through Brome rather than Shirley. The basis of their "battles" with the young ladies has little to do with epicurean values or assumptions; and the single purpose of their "intrigue" is to trick the ladies into marrying them. The ladies in their turn are far from epicurean in their convictions; and while they countenance the bawdry of their wooers without the moral preachment of Shirley's or Marmion's virtuous maidens, there is scarcely anything else to identify them with the Restoration heroine. As for the lecherous and hypocritical "Platonic," Lady Love-all, her combination of appetite and hypocrisy certainly does in a generic sense suggest Lady Cockwood. But she is even here more remote than the Ladies Collegiate, and she is quite divorced in meaning and action from the affairs of the two rakes and their ladies. The play, indeed, has no "theme" or centralized comic concern at all. It is what Etherege's first play has often been called—a hodgepodge of entirely traditional materials. It nowhere displays the specific interests in the epicurean order which characterize the plays of the moralists.

Much the same is true of *The Country Captain.* The alleged point of interest for the Restoration is here in Lady Huntlove and her repeated attempts to cuckold her husband. But this part of the play, like all the rest, is almost entirely free of distinctly epicurean ideology and implication. Lady Huntlove is frustrated in her attempt merely by a long series of farcical contretemps in incident. And she reforms at the end like Lady Bornwell, but with little of that lady's significance for the Restoration. The "lowering of moral tone" in the language of this play, as of *The Parson's Wedding,* certainly does set it apart from Shirley, Nabbes, Marmion, and even most of Brome. But to assume that this in itself is significant for the Restoration is to ignore all that is most distinctive in the later comedy. The sheer and abandoned lubricity of language in Killigrew's play is farther from the studied irony of wit in the Restoration than are the morally righteous but ideologically relevant preachments of Marmion's Faustina. What all this really means is that despite the bawdy language and general lowering of moral tone, the comic concerns and ideas—when any—of these plays leave the bulwark of orthodox moral assumptions as essentially undisturbed as do the comedies of Fletcher. The most pertinent lines of development for the Restoration remain in the hands of the moral reformers.

Sensibilities Old and New

Our examination of pre-Restoration English comedy has, it is hoped, made clear that the materials, interests, and form of the Restoration comedy of manners had in most basic respects become an established part of seventeenth-century dramatic practice by 1642. We have inspected the growth of this practice primarily in terms of the opposing lines of thought and behavior discussed in the second chapter of this study. One purpose of the study has been accordingly to inspect on grounds different from those previously investigated the continuity of dramatic traditions from Jonson and Fletcher—and in part from Lyly and Shakespeare—to Etherege and the Restoration. At the same time our purpose has been to define the ways in which the Restoration modified those traditions so as to produce a distinctive kind of comic drama. We have viewed that modification chiefly in terms of a shift in attitude toward the opposing values and beliefs with which the preceding drama dealt. The study as a whole, however, has informally suggested additional though related points of distinction between the plays of the Restoration and their native antecedents. It is not the intent here to examine these distinctions precisely or at length. But as conclusion to the interests of this chapter and of the study as a whole, some of them deserve at least a brief and final comment.

In the sense in which we have used the term, neither the writers of pre-Restoration comedy nor the characters of their plays were "honest men." The term is not meant here to indicate the general "social mode" of the comic hero in the Restoration plays, but rather the characteristic temper, tone, and language which distinguish that mode and the historical social class which it reflects. More specifically it refers to those general qualities of studied restraint, ironic self-awareness, and lack of enthusiasm which by simple, empirical test so clearly separate the Restoration comedy of manners from its native precursors. Whatever increase in "refinement" may distinguish the Caroline dramatists from the Jacobeans, it moves very little in the direction of the Restoration "honest man." Killigrew's *The Parson's Wedding* has often, we have seen, been thought to approach in tone and substance the later comedy of manners. We may, therefore, note one of the play's "wits," Careless, in the act of being witty about one of the play's "fools," Sadd:

> Hark, if he be not fallen into a fit of his Cozen; these names of places he has stollen out of her Receipt-book; amongst all whose diseases, find me any so dangerous, troublesome or incurable, as a fool, a lean, pale, sighing, coughing fool, that's rich and poor both; being born to an estate, without a mind or heart capable to use it; of a nature so miserable, he grudges himself meat; nay, they say, he eats his meals twice; a fellow whose breath smells of yesterday's dinner, and stinks as if he had eat all our Suppers over again.[1]

Or we may turn to Shirley and one of his witty ladies who has been almost universally considered an important forerunner of the Restoration heroine. Celestina, of *The Lady of Pleasure,* is here also being witty at the expense of fops and fools:

> Yet I will talk a little to the pilchards.—
> You two, that have not 'twixt you both the hundred
> Part of a soul, coarse woollen-witted fellows,
> Without a nap, with bodies made for burdens!
> You, that are only stuffings for apparel,
> As you were made but engines for your tailors
> To frame their clothes upon, and get them custom,
> Until men see you move; yet, then you dare not,
> Out of your guilt of being the ignobler beast,
> But give a horse the wall, whom you excel
> Only in dancing of the brawls, because
> The horse was not taught the French way.   (III.2, p. 61)

Or we may for a moment return to an earlier wit, Fletcher's Mirabel, who is here expressing in substance a thing which every Etheregean hero knew or thought he knew:

> For look ye, father, they are just like melons,
> Musk-melons are the emblems of these maids;
> Now they are ripe, now cut 'em, they taste pleasantly,
> And are a dainty fruit, digested easily:
> Neglect this present time, and come to morrow,
> They are so ripe they are rotten gone, their sweetness
> Run into humour, and their taste to surfeit.
> (*Wild-Goose Chase,* I.3, p. 326)

Or, finally, we may return to the master himself, Ben Jonson, and listen to the wit, Clerimont, discoursing on the female dupe, Lady Haughty:

---

1. *Restoration Comedies,* ed. Montague Summers (London, Cape, 1921), p. 130.

"A poxe of her autumnall face, her peec'd beautie: there's no man can bee admitted till shee be ready, now adaies, till shee has painted, and perfum'd, and wash'd, and scour'd, but the boy here; and him shee wipes her oil'd lips upon, like a sponge" (*Epicoene*, 1.1.85–9). It is scarcely necessary for our purposes here to set beside these passages a quotation from Etherege's plays or from the plays of Wycherley, Congreve, or Vanbrugh. One looks in vain in pre-Etheregean comedy for the many-sided awareness, involuted irony, indirection, and complexity of view which is the peculiar badge of comic expression in Etherege's plays and which in a generic way serves to distinguish the Restoration comedy of manners.

These, however, are loose and general terms of distinction; and they are but symptomatic of more profound differences. In the preceding chapters of this study we have tried to characterize certain central aspects of comic expression in Etherege's plays. We have suggested that the comic awareness which informs the plays operates prevailingly at a highly intellectualized and abstract level of classes and values in which the sensuous, the concrete and particular surfaces of experience are only tangentially relevant. The quotations which we have just reviewed from pre-Etheregean comedy will serve in this respect to mark an easy distinction. The comedy of the Jacobean and Caroline periods is always, whatever else it may be, the comedy of life at the level of concrete and particular surfaces. Indeed, the comedy of manners in those periods is, after the general fashion of its master, specifically the process of accumulating and ordering the immediate, concrete, and sensuous data of experience. The natures of the various types, classes, and values with which that comedy deals are largely mediate and inhere in the shape and contour of the accumulated physical data which constitute their reality. The comic incongruity of character lies in the discordant clash of that physical data, as does the wit: "A poxe of her autumnall face"; "coarse, woollen-witted fellows, without a nap"; or even Killigrew's lame and puffing efforts, "a lean, pale, sighing, coughing fool." It is the particular contribution of Congreve to the comedy of manners that, while keeping both the abstract and intellectualized language and the complexity of awareness which distinguish Etherege's plays, he returned to that comedy something of the concrete and bustling world of sensuous experience which Etherege had so extensively removed. But it is the particular contribution of Etherege that he made the comedy of manners the expression of man's mind and wit ambiguously groping among the abstractions by which he had thought to order his world.

Index